Praise for
Restoring the Kinship Worldview

"Humans have a particular ecological niche, a role as the custodial species of this earth. We must return our species to this niche within the next decade, or perish. This book is a perfect place to start—the foundation is good relations, making kin both human and nonhuman—and here we have story from a gathering of some of the finest Indigenous thinkers on the planet. Four Arrows and Darcia Narvaez have a particular way of bringing the right people together for such purposes."

> —**TYSON YUNKAPORTA,** author of *Sand Talk,* senior research fellow at Deacon University, woodcarver, and poet

"This collection of ideas and clarity fills my heart! Feeling Spirit in the worldview of Native peoples and hearing the mutual emergence of two friends in dialogue is quite something! Tears well up thinking of our future, our children scrambling over stones and climbing trees and learning of the sentient nature of all things. To love again in this way! Mahalo Four Arrows and Darcia Narvaez for this collection, this eloquence and grace through time so we can recognize and honor the common sense and purpose of continuity. *All of it is needed now.* We are all meant to wake up together."

> —**MANULANI ALULI MEYER,** director of Indigenous education, University of Hawaiʻi–West Oʻahu

"A richly creative approach to teaching Indigenous wisdom. Lending their ears to a diverse array of mostly contemporary Native voices, Four Arrows and Darcia Narvaez take each brief quote as the seed for a conversation regarding one or another element of the *kincentric* worldview—a vision of our earth not as a collection of objects and objective, mechanical processes, but as an interactive community of sensitive and sentient powers: a communion of subjects."

> —**DAVID ABRAM,** author of *Becoming Animal* and *The Spell of the Sensuous*

"A glorious prism of voices calling out to us to imagine a more inclusive and sustainable way of being. I ache for the kind of world that is invoked within these pages."

"This book is like brilliant sunlight from the past that reaches us now and illuminates our way forward. It's Indigenous wisdom and more. For we also keep company with Four Arrows and Darcia Narvaez in conversation on how to change the world's trajectory from one of domination over people and nature to relation, kinship, love, and bounty. To Life itself."

"This sourcebook is unique in its presentation of a shared worldview that sees humans as part of a living fabric of earth and sea, flora and fauna, rather than its occupiers and owners. These voices speak from ancestral traditions ranging from northern Arctic shores to Central America, with a notable contribution from Australia. As it becomes starkly obvious that our future, and life on and of the earth, are in peril, ancestral Indigenous voices are speaking the only words that can save us. The Kogi Mamas teach that everything is a manifestation of thought and that to listen is to think. Understanding ancestral eloquence is our last and best chance, and these pages can only help."

"*Restoring the Kinship Worldview* provides a much-needed and well-stocked medicine cabinet to begin healing how we think and talk about the suffering of our planet and its struggling inhabitants. Open your mind and heart to its multi-Indigenous balms that are administered through the psalms of elders and a dialogue that leaves us ready to begin anew."

"I have long known Four Arrows (Don Jacobs) to be at the forefront of understanding and articulating the culture, legacy, and (in)justice issues of First Nations. His latest thinking and compilation of spiritual, cultural, and political insight pairs him perfectly with fellow scholar and ideal coauthor Darcia Narvaez. Whether one is a long-time champion of Indigenous rights and social justice, a lover of the deep wisdom and aesthetics of natural cultures, or a neophyte seeking just the right orientation to this field and to our hosts on this continent, this is just the right book for you."

—TOM COOPER, PhD, professor of ethics and visual and media arts at Emerson College and author of *A Time Before Deception*

"I can think of myself, bound by my skin, as a separate being that uses all around me to survive and thrive, or I can think of myself as an integral part of all around me, doing my bit to help it all survive and thrive. Objectively, both ways of thinking are equally true. But if we think the first way, we destroy all around us, including one another. If we think the second way, harmony rises, and loneliness and fear decline. Four Arrows and Darcia Narvaez are wonderful guides, using the wisdom of Indigenous thinkers to teach us how to think the second way (which historically is really the first way)."

—PETER GRAY, PhD, research professor of psychology and neuroscience at Boston College and author of *Free to Learn*

"A dialogue between psychological science and wisdom tradition of the Indigenous populations is long overdue. This book marks an important step in this direction, which will open up a new horizon for research on Indigenous psychology."

—LOUISE SUNDARARAJAN, PhD, founder and chair of Indigenous Psychology Task Force

"Four Arrows and Darcia Narvaez draw from and integrate essential insights from diverse traditions and disciplines to help us see and feel ourselves and our human place in creation in ways from which most of us have been too long excluded. A very special and important book for our time."

—DAVID KORTEN, author of *The Great Turning* and *Change the Story, Change the Future*

"If we are to thrive—or even survive—as a species, we must shift soon from the life-destroying, domination-based worldview of industrialized societies to a life-affirming, relational, and animistic worldview as embraced by intact Indigenous cultures. Darcia Narvaez and Four Arrows have gathered an inspiring pastiche of wise Native American voices woven together by their own insightful and heartfelt dialogues to gift us with an invaluable bundle of tenets and templates for the urgent project of decolonizing and rewilding our minds and communities."

—**BILL PLOTKIN, PhD,** author of *Soulcraft, Wild Mind,* and *The Journey of Soul Initiation*

"I read this book every night. The cited quotes express so clearly how we can live in the world more lovingly. The reflective dialogue between Darcia and Four Arrows is thought-provoking. This book must be read again and again. There's so much to remember. It gives a perspective that most people have never considered. The authors deserve an eagle feather for this one!"

—**HARRIET HANTAYWEE GREENE,** sculptor, artist, and author of *Crossing the Boundary*

"*Restoring the Kinship Worldview* will make you think, laugh, cry, and perhaps do more ceremony. And, if you take heed of the wisdom of the precepts it gathers from Indigenous leaders, it may enable you to achieve a good life. Four Arrows and Darcia Narvaez's reflections on these quotations are wise and profoundly important for this era in which we must rebalance the world."

—**GRAHAM HARVEY,** professor of religious studies at Open University and author of *Animism*

"This book satisfies an urgent need of Euro-American and other seekers to receive the Indigenous worldview in a way we can understand and that can allow us to activate our own heritage of sanity, still present in the model of the gift economy of maternal care of infants. Perhaps this will allow us to relinquish the worldview of patriarchal capitalism that is presently perpetrating the matricide of Mother Earth."

—**GENEVIEVE VAUGHAN,** independent researcher and author of *The Maternal Roots of the Gift Economy*

"Science is but one way of knowing, but far too often scientism offers detached perspectives because it is supposed to be 'objective' and 'removed' from what is really happening on the ground. In *Restoring the Kinship Worldview*, we learn that *experiencing* and *being* are essential parts of knowing—because we are *a part of* nature, not *apart from* nature. A most important message in this landmark book is that, as we move forward and try to restore balance to an imbalanced world, we must pay close attention to this fact. The so-called anthropocene, often called 'the age of humanity,' is in reality 'the rage of inhumanity' and is leading us on a path of global annihilation. To change course for future generations so as not to steal their futures, we need to decolonize our minds, and more importantly, our hearts. There is no other way forward."

—**MARC BEKOFF, PhD,** professor emeritus of ecology and evolutionary biology at University of Colorado, Boulder and author of *Rewilding Our Hearts*

"*Restoring the Kinship Worldview* is a rich source of Indigenous lore and wisdom. The quotations and stories reveal holistic worldviews that challenge dominant Western precepts and that have the potential to make a seminal contribution to addressing the deep social and environmental problems that currently confront us globally. Their significance is amplified by the perceptive ongoing commentary and discussion provided by Four Arrows and Darcia Narvaez that encourages a more nuanced and accurate reading of Indigenous views than has often been the case hitherto. This is a most timely and thought-provoking book."

—**MICHAEL BONNETT,** author of *Environmental Consciousness, Nature and the Philosophy of Education*

"The history of America is one of a major, or dominant, voice, with its emphasis on hustling, consumerism, and exploitation, and a minor one, the values of which are craft and community, friendship and reciprocity, and the life of the spirit. The political events of 2016 and beyond have made it abundantly clear where the dominant mode leads: to self-destruction. America failed because it persistently ignored or repressed the minor voice, from the late sixteenth century right down to Lewis Mumford, Jimmy Carter, and Native American writers in our own time. If we have any future at all, it lies in 'the road not taken,' and the essays in this book are an attempt, once more, to get that alternative voice heard. The crucial question thus remains: Is anyone listening?"

—**MORRIS BERMAN,** former professor and award-winning author of books including *The Heart of the Matter*

"'As long as there remained the least understanding between Adam and the stars, rivers and horses with whom he had once known complete intimacy... there was still a hope that the effects of the poison would wear off, that the exile from Paradise was only a bad dream, that the Fall had not occurred in fact.' W. H. Auden wrote these lines. The Fall was the fall out of one worldview into another. Indigenous eloquence is about that original consciousness. It's still here. It can never be annihilated, for the simple reason that 'the Original Instructions are not ideas. They are reality. They are actually Natural Law, The Way Things Are—the operational manual for a working Creation,' writes Manitonquat (Wampanoag) in these pages. If you have the least understanding with the stars, rivers, and horses, rejoice with me in the arrival of this book."

> —CALVIN LUTHER MARTIN, PhD, author of *The Way of the Human Being*

"As our civilization hurtles toward a precipice of ecological devastation and climate breakdown, the need for a fundamentally different worldview has never been greater. This expansive, deep, and thoroughly researched work offers a rich exploration of Native American Indigenous knowledge that could help reorient our dominant culture toward a regenerative way of living on the earth. Covering an unusually broad range of topics—from gender roles to restorative justice, and from sacred competition to mutual dependence— it provides insights into the practices that have enabled Indigenous communities to live in harmony with each other and the nonhuman world for millennia. It is an important contribution to the deep cultural transformation that represents our society's best hope for a flourishing future."

> —JEREMY LENT, author of *The Patterning Instinct* and *The Web of Meaning*

"Worldviews create worlds. A thriving, healed world—in alignment with the life-affirming contexts long-abandoned by our disconnected Western worldview and its resulting fragmented, unsustainable world—is made possible with the collected wisdom in this welcome, nourishing work."

> —LISA REAGAN, editor of Kindred Media

Restoring *the* Kinship Worldview

Indigenous Voices Introduce 28 Precepts *for* Rebalancing Life *on* Planet Earth

Wahinkpe Topa (Four Arrows)
AND Darcia Narvaez, PhD

North Atlantic Books
Huichin, unceded Ohlone land
aka Berkeley, California

Published by
North Atlantic Books   Cover art © gettyimages.com/saemilee
Huichin, unceded Ohlone land   Cover design by Jess Morphew
aka Berkeley, California   Book design by Happenstance Type-O-Rama

Printed in Canada

Restoring the Kinship Worldview: Indigenous Voices Introduce 28 Precepts for Rebalancing Life on Planet Earth is sponsored and published by North Atlantic Books, an educational nonprofit based in the unceded Ohlone land Huichin (*aka* Berkeley, CA) that collaborates with partners to develop cross-cultural perspectives, nurture holistic views of art, science, the humanities, and healing, and seed personal and global transformation by publishing work on the relationship of body, spirit, and nature.

North Atlantic Books' publications are distributed to the US trade and internationally by Penguin Random House Publisher Services. For further information, visit our website at www.northatlanticbooks.com.

All royalties from book sales will be donated to Indigenous Peoples.

A note from the authors about the excerpts from primary Indigenous sources that open each chapter:

For some of these quotations of Indigenous voices, we have combined various sources to create their oration and transcribed them with slightly modified wording to enhance flow and focus with regard to the targeted worldview precept. We have done so without changing the intentions or meanings of the original presentation(s).

Library of Congress Cataloging-in-Publication Data

Names: Jacobs, Donald Trent, 1946- author. | Narvaez, Darcia, 1952- author.
Title: Restoring the kinship worldview : indigenous voices introduce 28 precepts for rebalancing life on planet Earth / Wahinkpe Topa (Four Arrows) and Darcia Narvaez.
Description: Berkeley, California : North Atlantic Books, [2022] | Includes bibliographical references and index. | Summary: "A collection of 28 excerpted passages from Indigenous leaders that reflect the wisdom of Indigenous worldview precepts, accompanied by analysis"— Provided by publisher.
Identifiers: LCCN 2021052804 (print) | LCCN 2021052805 (ebook) | ISBN 9781623176426 (trade paperback) | ISBN 9781623176433 (ebook)
Subjects: LCSH: Indian philosophy. | Indians of North America—Quotations. | Wisdom. | Kinship.
Classification: LCC E98.P5 J33 2022 (print) | LCC E98.P5 (ebook) | DDC 970.004/97—dc23/eng/20211129
LC record available at https://lccn.loc.gov/2021052804
LC ebook record available at https://lccn.loc.gov/2021052805

3 4 5 6 7 8 9 MQ 27 26 25 24 23

This book includes recycled material and material from well-managed forests. North Atlantic Books is committed to the protection of our environment. We print on recycled paper whenever possible and partner with printers who strive to use environmentally responsible practices.

For the future of the earth
and all our relations

Epigraph

According to the United Nations 2019 *Global Assessment Report on Biodiversity and Ecosystem Services:* "The findings of this Assessment . . . are based on an unprecedented collection of evidence, integrating natural and social science perspectives, a range of knowledge systems and multiple dimensions of value. This is the first global-level assessment to systematically consider evidence about the contributions of Indigenous and local knowledge and practices to the enhancement and maintenance of wild and domesticated biodiversity and landscapes."[1]

"The report shows that 75% of the land-based environment and about 66% of the marine environment have been significantly altered by human actions. On average, these trends have been less severe—or avoided—in areas held or managed by Indigenous peoples."[2]

"The notion of a good life that most Indigenous peoples share is deeply relational: the relation to the land with all its interconnected human and nonhuman inhabitants constitutes their collective self-understanding as community. Livelihoods sovereignty is an essential condition to keep this bond. These contributions of nature to notions of a good life may be under threat as access to nature—or key components of nature—are lost."[3]

"Consumption patterns are a fundamental driver of material extraction, production, and flows, but they too are driven—by worldviews and notions of good quality of life."[4]

"The loss of Indigenous languages is potentially a major problem for value diversity and authenticity. In many regions, community values that support sustainable trajectories using Indigenous knowledge are at risk of extinction, which results in the loss of biodiversity. The value of the knowledge-practice-belief complex of Indigenous peoples relating to conservation of biodiversity are central to the sustainable management of ecosystems and biodiversity."[5]

"Sociocultural framings, norms, worldviews, and relational values influence the outcomes of sociotechnological innovations enormously. Nevertheless, these factors remain largely overlooked in studies on sustainable sociotechnological transformations."[6]

The more uncertain I have felt about myself, the more there has grown up in me a feeling of kinship with all things.

—CARL JUNG, *Memories, Dreams, Reflections*

Contents

Acknowledgments

We wish to acknowledge not only the Indigenous individuals quoted throughout this book, but the many past and present persons who continue to stand, against all odds, for the kincentricity necessary for rebalancing life systems on Mother Earth.

We also acknowledge the sculptor Harriet Greene Goldman. Moved deeply by the eloquence and wisdom of seven American Indian leaders, she spent fifteen years carving their images and speeches into large marble slabs. Her commitment and artistry inspired Four Arrows to write his recent monograph, *Sitting Bull's Words: For a World in Crisis,* as well as this text. The story of her remarkable project can be viewed in Marty Goldman's documentary, *Native American Oratory of Seven Great Chiefs,* at www.youtube.com/watch?v=RHBtCbJxjVY.

Finally, we want to express our appreciation for the editorial efforts from the editors at North Atlantic Books and their partners at Penguin Random House, with a special callout to NAB's Brent and Janelle for their fine-tooth combing of our words and citations, which make the flow so much better for the reader.

Introduction

*When we grasp fully that the best expressions of our humanity were
not invented by civilization but by cultures that preceded it, that
the natural world is not only a set of constraints but of contexts
within which we can more fully realize our dreams, we will be on
the way to a long overdue reconciliation between opposites which
are of our own making.*

—PAUL SHEPARD (1998)[1]

This book is about worldview and the consciousness it creates
and reflects. It is a topic of utmost importance for the continuation of humanity. "Worldview is a concept 'whose time has come,'
and its increasing appearance in the contemporary climate change
and global sustainability debates can be understood as both response
to, and reflection of, the challenges of our time and the solutions they
demand."[2] Everyone acts according to their worldview, an implicit set
of assumptions that guide behavior.

Among scholars, the term *Weltanschauung* was first used, and only
once, by German philosopher Immanuel Kant (1724–1804) to refer to
sense perception of the world.[3] The term spread through German scholarship, with Heidegger interpreting it as "a world-intuition in the sense
of contemplation of the world given to the senses."[4] It evolved to mean

an intellectual and intuitive concept of the universe. Mark E. Koltko-Rivera's seminal integrative work on the psychology of worldviews referred to the concept as vital for cognition and behavior and noted how it has been underused.[5] He described the Indigenous worldview of cultures around the world as seeing "subjectivity inherent in the natural world itself" with all that is, and he contrasted it with the Western world, which sees in a segmented way. He wrote: "In summary, the scholarly study of mysticism defines at least three dimensions of worldview: beliefs regarding the underlying unity of reality, the existence of a conscious nature, and the possibility of a truly ego-transcendent consciousness. Implicit in the mystical approach to the world is the notion that it makes a difference as to whether one sees the world in materialist terms or in terms that allow for an ontologically real spiritual dimension to reality."[6]

We go further than Koltko-Rivera to assert that the worldview that considers Nature as intelligent and living and the worldview that perceives Nature otherwise are the only two essential worldviews. As we discuss below, it is difficult to find a third category. This may be illustrated by the mystical experience of Edgar Mitchell, one of the Apollo 14 astronauts and the sixth man to walk on the moon. He founded the Institute of Noetic Sciences to explore the relationship between worldview and the suffering that civilization has caused on the earth. Looking back at planet Earth from outer space made him realize that the "great frontier wasn't the exploration of outer space, but a deep and systematic inquiry into the nature of our inner awareness."[7] After witnessing the research of his institute, he would later write that "only a handful of visionaries have recognized that Indigenous wisdom can aid the transition to a sustainable world."[8]

We two authors have searched for a better word to describe the proverbial invisible waters in which we swim that are the foundation for our assumptions and actions. The Indigenous worldview as we describe it is not a matter of perception or conception alone, but of *experiencing* and *being*. It is more of a "world-sense"[9] because it involves dozens of senses and a coordinated way of moving through the world.[10] Indigenous peoples have a broad integrative understanding of body, mind, and Spirit that allows for a more holistic orientation than the narrow perspective that has led us toward extinction. Robert Wolff called it "original wisdom."[11] Because of its wide, cross-sensory scope, Indigenous worldview in its fullest sense is more of an *existencescape,* Steve Langdon's term for describing the Tlingit people's way of being.[12] Langdon explains that reciprocal sensations, not "seeing," are how Tlingit understand humanity's place in the universe. Indeed, tribal knowledge worldwide stems from language birthed in its speakers' wilderness environment, cultivated through interactions with local spiritual entities, and passed on through thousands of sacred stories and ceremonies grounded in resident relationships. Existencescape prioritizes this *place-based* knowledge, knowledge that varies according to the interaction between a particular landscape and the people who live there. In this book, however, we wish to emphasize the *common* precepts shared by Indigenous peoples across the global landscape. As vital as place-based knowledge is, this book is designed to help those with a Eurocentric mindset to begin the journey toward a kincentric relationship with the earth, starting with the larger worldview that diverse Indigenous cultures share. Dennis Martinez, who identifies as O'odham, Chicano, and Anglo, coined *kincentric* as a way to include all aspects of "harmony between people and other people, and between communities and people and the natural world."[13] Kincentrism is the first step toward returning to an earth-based consciousness, a starting place for relocalizing or restoring place-based knowledge.

With all this in mind, we have selected speeches and writings from Indigenous leaders that reflect Indigenous worldview precepts that are rooted in the ancestral human nature and collective unconscious we share. The precepts represent different dimensions of life. Some precepts are principles put into practice on a daily basis. Some are assumptions about how the world works based on generations of observation. All are guidelines for behavior and living a good life. We consider the precepts to be an essential starting place for bringing balance back into the world.

The twenty-eight Indigenous worldview precepts we address in this book stem mostly from a chart published in Four Arrows's 2020 book *The Red Road: Linking Diversity and Inclusion Initiatives to Indigenous Worldview.* The chart contrasts forty dominant worldview precepts with forty Indigenous worldview precepts. There are likely other contrasting Indigenous worldview precepts beyond these forty to be found in the literature. For example, Wade Davis, a celebrated anthropologist who has written about Indigenous cultures from around the world and about the tragedy of their loss, said in a published interview that "the fluidity of our memory, our capacity to forget, is the most haunting trait of our species. It accounts for why we're able to adapt to almost any degree of environmental or moral degradation."[14] Upon reading this quote, Four Arrows contacted Davis and asked if he'd really meant to refer to "our species," as opposed to the relatively recent *dominant worldview* of our species. Davis responded with an apology, agreeing fully that this was what he should have said. Wade's mistake is all too common. More and more people seem to be attributing to human nature traits that have only emerged in the past 1 percent of human history. This is why understanding our original, Indigenous worldview precepts is so important. Thus, another Indigenous worldview precept might include "the capacity to remember."

This chart is not intended as a rigid binary, but a true dichotomy best viewed as a continuum. It is meant to encourage seeking complementarity and dialogue. Absolutism is discouraged with the realization we are all participating in dominant worldview precepts to some degree. The chart assumes that all diverse cultures, religions, and philosophies can be grouped under one of the two worldviews. "Indigenous worldview" does not belong to a race or group of people, but Indigenous cultures who still hold on to their traditional place-based knowledge are the wisdom keepers of this original Nature-based worldview. All people are indigenous to Earth and have the right and the responsibility to practice and teach the Indigenous worldview precepts. All have the responsibility to support Indigenous sovereignty, dignity and use of traditional lands. For non-Indians who are concerned about misappropriation, see the peer-reviewed article, "The Indigenization Controversy: For Whom By Whom," https://ices.library.ubc.ca/index.php/criticaled/article/view/186438.

COMMON DOMINANT WORLDVIEW MANIFESTATIONS[15]	COMMON INDIGENOUS WORLDVIEW MANIFESTATIONS
1. Rigid hierarchy	Nonhierarchical
2. Fear-based thoughts and behaviors	Courage and fearless trust in the universe
3. Living without strong social purpose	Socially purposeful life
4. Focus on self and personal gain	Emphasis on community welfare
5. Rigid and discriminatory gender stereotypes	Respect for various gender roles and fluidity
6. Materialistic	Nonmaterialistic
7. Earth as an an unloving "it"	Earth and all systems as living and loving
8. More head than heart	Emphasis on heart over head
9. Competition to feel superior	Competition to develop positive potential
10. Minimal empathy, humility, and gratitude	Strong emphasis on empathy, humility, and gratitude
11. Anthropocentric	Animistic and biocentric
12. Words used to deceive self or others	Words as sacred, truthfulness as essential
13. Truth claims as absolute	Truth seen as multifaceted; accepting the mysterious
14. Rigid boundaries and fragmented systems	Flexible boundaries and interconnected systems

COMMON DOMINANT WORLDVIEW MANIFESTATIONS[15]	COMMON INDIGENOUS WORLDVIEW MANIFESTATIONS
15. Unfamiliarity with alternative consciousness	Regular use of alternative consciousness
16. Disbelief in spiritual energies	Recognition of spiritual energies
17. Disregard for holistic interconnectedness	Emphasis on holistic interconnectedness
18. Minimal contact with others	High interpersonal engagement, touching
19. Emphasis on theory and rhetoric	Inseparability of knowledge and action
20. Acceptance of authoritarianism	Resistance to authoritarianism
21. Time as linear	Time as cyclical
22. Dualistic thinking	Seeking complementary duality
23. Acceptance of injustice	Intolerance of injustice
24. Emphasis on rights	Emphasis on responsibility
25. Aggression as highest expression of courage	Generosity as highest expression of courage
26. Ceremony as rote formality	Ceremony as life-sustaining
27. Learning as didactic	Learning as experiential and collaborative
28. Trance as dangerous or stemming from evil	Trance-based learning as helpful and natural
29. Human nature as corrupt or evil	Human nature as good but malleable
30. Humor used infrequently for coping	Humor as essential tool for coping
31. Conflict resolution with revenge, punishment	Conflict resolution as return to community
32. Learning is fragmented and theoretical	Learning is holistic and place based
33. Minimal emphasis on personal vitality	Personal vitality is essential
34. Social laws of society are primary	Laws of Nature are primary
35. Self-knowledge not highest priority	Holistic self-knowledge is most important

COMMON DOMINANT WORLDVIEW MANIFESTATIONS[15]	COMMON INDIGENOUS WORLDVIEW MANIFESTATIONS
36. Autonomy sought in behalf of self	Autonomy sought to better serve others
37. Nature as dangerous or utilitarian only	Nature as benevolent and relational
38. Other-than-human beings are not sentient	All life-forms are sentient
39. Low respect for women	High respect for women
40. Ignorance of importance of diversity	Aware of vital importance of diversity

In this book, we use our unique scholarship specialties to ana-lyze and explain our perspectives on the Indigenous quotes via brief dialogues. Darcia's work encompasses evolutionary moral develop-mental psychology. She studies how humans develop best within our evolved continuum of child raising, patterning the individual's psyche, and relationships to humans and beings other than human, including the world of Spirit. Four Arrows has been a proponent of the origi-nal Indigenous worldview and its incorporation into education. The result of our collaboration is a deeper understanding of what it means to be a human being, a member of the earth community, in ways that contrast with the dominant anthropocentric/materialistic worldview. Throughout the book the two of us bring forth insights from our expe-riences and scholarship in an effort to help readers learn and apply the precepts to their own lives.

Our combined years of research and experience have brought us together for this serious task. We believe that the original Indigenous understanding of the world offers the most crucial way to rebalance life systems. This is not a romanticized notion. It is ancestral wisdom. The 2019 global assessment report of the Intergovernmental Science-Policy Platform on Biodiversity and Ecosystem Services provides con-crete evidence of this wisdom.[16] This report, which was based on data contributed by hundreds of scientists from fifty countries, is the larg-est ecological analysis ever undertaken. Although we believe it may be too late to stop many of the impending extinctions of life on earth, this is all the more reason to heed the words spoken by our selected guests. They show us how to live with the fullness of appreciating the wonder of the gift of life on Mother Earth, no matter how great the challenges. For those who want to transform what lies ahead, our book provides an opportunity to reembrace our original Indigenous worldview. We hope it will strengthen you in your personal journey while you do what you can for future generations, both in your current life and in whatever existence follows it.

When reading the quotes and our dialogue about the worldview precept they represent, understand that worldview is not interchangeable with concepts such as ideology, paradigm, religion, or discourse, although such concepts do emerge from a worldview, the source of our beliefs and behaviors. Worldview goes deeper than culture, religion, or philosophy, all of which are fueled by the underlying assumptions we have.

We adopt the idea that there are only two observable, essential forms of assumptions—worldviews—to choose from today. One has us as creatures that are intrinsically part of Nature, physically and spiritually. The other has us separated from Nature, also physically and spiritually. Dualistic either/or thinking, which does not seek complementarity between apparent opposites, is not part of the Indigenous worldview. Making comparisons between the two worldviews may therefore seem to be a contradiction. We maintain, however, that although there may be some mysterious symbiosis at play, we are at a point where either/or decisions must be made regarding which way of understanding our place in the world will best serve life systems. For us and many other scholars, the choice is clear because the Indigenous worldview has proven itself over thousands if not tens or hundreds of thousands of years.

We are not alone in our identifying only two worldviews. Robert Redfield, considered to be the "father of social anthropology," introduced this hypothesis while at the University of Chicago in the

1950s.[17] Redfield considered the replacement of the Indigenous worldview by the dominant worldview as one of the great tragedies of human history, substituting the moral order of precivilized societies with the technical order of modern civilization. Based on his fieldwork and academic research, he asserted that the "primitive" cultures he studied seemed to have an automatic or natural morality that emphasized empathy and compassion for all. From this perspective, "industrialized humans have become unvirtuous and holistically destructive in comparison to 99% of human genus existence. . . . The pillars of original virtue include relational attunement, communal imagination, and respectful partnership with the natural world."[18] We think you will see such morality in the words we offer in the following chapters.

To shift from the dominant worldview to the original Indigenous worldview takes some decolonizing of the mind. Our minds have been suckled on the milk of civilization's domination and coercion of life, with industrialization and capitalism increasing disconnection and alienation from earth consciousness. This book plants the seeds for decolonizing your mind. Please take further steps in this direction by investigating the speakers and resources we cite.

One concern or question that often comes up with our recommendation to decolonize and Indigenize our minds and institutions relates to the right of "non-Indian" people to attempt to re-Indigenize themselves and their systems such as education. Indeed, many Indigenous people believe that non-Indigenous teachers have no right to try to "teach" the Indigenous worldview. They call it a cultural appropriation. Such a concern is well grounded and must be respected in light of the massive mistreatment of Indigenous peoples in the last half millennium.

However, many Indigenous elders believe otherwise. They know about misappropriation, but they also know that with sincerity, respect, and support for Indigenous rights, allies are necessary. An increasing number of leaders are sharing Indigenous wisdom in order to restore harmony and balance.[19] And as others note too, "the aim is not to return to the details of Native ways, but to apply Indigenous values appropriately for our time and with an eye to the future."[20] The Indigenous worldview reflects the original instructions for how to approach living well on the earth. As Manitonquat (a.k.a. Medicine Story; Wampanoag) noted: "The Original Instructions are not ideas. They are reality. They are actually Natural Law, The Way Things Are— the operational manual for a working Creation."[21]

One of the most respected of the Oglala Lakota spiritual leaders was Frank Fools Crow. When he passed away at age ninety-nine in 1989, many considered him the most revered holy person of the twentieth century. He spoke about certain good spirits as a gift to the whole of humankind. He talked about how he helped individuals with vision quests and the sweat lodge so they might better understand themselves and find peace. Then he added, "and these ceremonies do not belong to Indians alone. They can be done by all who have the right attitude, and who are honest and sincere about their belief in Grandfather and in following his rules. . . . Grandfather's spirits serve others as well as the Indian."[22] Fools Crow knew that survival of the world depends upon our working together and sharing what we have. He continued: "The ones who complain and talk the most about giving away medicine secrets are always those who know the least. If we don't share our wisdom, the whole world will die. First the planet, and next the people."

With careful effort to make connections to the Indigenous way of understanding our place in the world, we write this book to share such wisdom. We ask you, dear reader, to keep Fools Crow's wisdom in mind. At the same time, we remind all that without the place-based Indigenous languages and memory of local traditions that the remaining Indigenous wisdom keepers are holding onto against overwhelming odds, our ability to reclaim the Indigenous worldview is severely compromised. If these speeches and our dialogues about them move you to rethink your place in the world, please make it a point to do what you can whenever you can to support the sovereignty of First Nations as well. First Nations people remain on the front lines in defending what biodiversity remains on Mother Earth, and they need our prayers and supportive actions.

GERONIMO

GO KHLA YEH
1829 1909

BEDONKOHE
APACHE

THERE IS ONE
GOD
LOOKING DOWN ON
US ALL WE ARE ALL
CHILDREN OF THE ONE
GOD.

GOD IS LISTENING TO ME
THE SUN, THE DARKNESS, THE WINDS,
ARE ALL LISTENING TO WHAT WE NOW SAY.

Geronimo
marble linocut

Harriet Greene
Taos, N.M.

1

Recognition of Spiritual Energies in Nature

Mourning Dove (Okanagan and Sinixt) (1884–1936)

*I*ndians had a staunch belief that the Creator made the world according to a divine plan that gave power from the animal world to our
ancestors and now to us. . . . Children, at the early age of six or seven,
were continually sent out each night to hunt for a guardian spirit. Both
boys and girls were obliged to undertake this search. As children grew
older, they were sent a little farther away each night until they graduated
from short to long distances, when the teacher or parents gave them something special to take along on these night journeys. The article might be a
small piece of fur from the medicine bag of a shaman or a bone from some
animal. The hope was that the child would receive a vision of the animal
spirit associated with the entrusted skin or bone.

The child was always instructed never to run away from any animal
form or apparition that chose to speak to him or her while on these expedi-
tions hunting for knowledge. A child might find these supernatural powers
almost anyplace: water, cliffs, forest, mountains, remains of lightning-
struck trees, animal carcasses, old campfires or a sacred sweat lodge. The
spirits were supposed to appear when they were impressed by the dedication and purity of the persistent seeker. The spirit's appearance came to a
child in a vision, in the form of an animal or an object that spoke about
how the spirit would help with future life, especially when needed during
times of distress. It sang its spiritual song for the child to memorize and use

when calling upon the spirit guardian as an adult. Such a vision did not always come to a child while awake. Sometimes it came while the child was asleep beside the token he or she had been given.

It was thus a natural necessity that parents should send their children out into the night to hunt for this secret knowledge to make themselves great and powerful. This training, for all its hardships, continued until puberty, when particularly strenuous work was added to the regime to give the child energy and stamina for a long life.

There were many things that we practiced that the priests had no knowledge of. People still believed in the old ways and no one was criticized for sending their children out alone; instead they were honored for doing so. During my childhood, people were just beginning to think that we were foolish. Later, Jesuit and white teachings won out.

Source

Mourning Dove. *Mourning Dove: A Salishan Autobiography.* Edited by Jay Miller. American Indian Lives. Lincoln: University of Nebraska Press, 2014.

Contextualized Biosketch

Hum-ishu-ma (Mourning Dove) published under her spiritual name but generally used her Christian name, Christine Quintasket, owing to the discrimination of the times in which she lived. Her autobiography was also rare in that it featured a woman protagonist. She grew up on the Colville Reservation, located in northeastern Washington state; however, she considered herself a member of the Nicola band of the Okanagan tribe of British Columbia. Salish was her first language, which she was punished for speaking at the Goodwin Catholic Mission near Kettle Falls between 1897 and 1899. Throughout her life her goals were to shatter white stereotypes of the American Indian. Her 1927 book, *Cogewea, the Half-Blood: A Depiction of the Great Montana Cattle Range,* is the first novel written by an American Indian woman.

Indigenous Worldview Precept Dialogue

Four Arrows: In the Indigenous way of being in the world, spirits entwine with Nature. Spirituality is at the core of being Indigenous to our planet. Everything on Earth has a spiritual purpose and function, from herbs to human beings. All things in the world live and share this mysterious web of interconnected energy. In such an animistic universe, nothing is an "it." Everything is animistic and equal in stature to us. The many who have been on Earth longer than our species are our teachers. In addition to spirits of visible entities, invisible spiritual forces also exist. All spiritual energies inform or respond to intentionality, and we must treat them with reverence. The languages and ceremonies of traditional Indigenous cultures reflect ways to manifest appropriate understanding and respect. Visions, dreams, and stories also help us engage with the spirit world and remember our interconnectedness.

Indigenous spirituality is grounded in and on Mother Earth. Each traditional culture lives according to the spiritual and physical interconnectedness of all life-forms. This means a holistic knowledge about plant medicine, star knowledge, waterways, and lessons about how to live from local creatures of every kind. Landscape is sacred because it lives and because it holds the spiritual energy of ancestors. Being in tune with all this spiritual energy and entering into dialogue with it through praying, singing, vision questing, ceremony, and daily life is vital. This is why the children in Mourning Dove's quote are encouraged to find spirits that can help guide them through this invisible part of our world in ways that maintain harmony. Spirit guides help children grow into adults who give sacred significance to all that exists. Different people and different clans or groups hold on to different specializations relating to Spirit knowledge so that the Whole can remain healthy.

Darcia: What really strikes me is Mourning Dove's emphasis on how children shape their identity by finding spiritual powers in the natural landscape. This represents a deep faith in the living world to guide human lives. Perception of a living world was universal among humanity before the rise of the Western worldview, beginning with the Sumer civilization, which led over millennia to an emphasis on univocity (one right perspective) and materialism, along with a decreased ability to perceive the permeability of living beings, or to welcome the presence of ancestral spirits.[1] Perceiving the world to be full of sentient beings was labeled by Enlightenment Western scholars as "animism" and treated as primitive or childish. These dismissive attitudes are changing as other scholars point to the Indigenous worldview's universality and its wisdom for living sustainably—durably—with all life.[2]

It is so important to trust both children's inner compass and external nature for spiritual guidance. With good nesting, children are aware of energies around them and if encouraged will maintain and build that awareness, rather than suppress and forget it, as many industrialized children are forced to do. Those who live according to an Indigenous worldview allow one another a great deal of freedom, in part because they provide for the basic needs of their children, which, over the course of development, leads to a virtuous character. There is a general sense of trust among individuals, extended outside the group to the natural world. The Indigenous worldview allows for a large sense of community, a belonging to the overall Commonself, a deep sense of kinship with All.

Four Arrows: With both you and Mourning Dove emphasizing the connection between spiritual energies in nature and children's early identity formation, I took a moment to search for something I had come across about how Australian Aboriginals make this connection. Here it is: "Aboriginal selfhood springs from and is bound up with 'Country' (sentient landscape), and hence with ancestor and totemic figures who left their trace in the landscape during the 'Dreaming' or creation period that continues to ramify in the present. One result is that each person is not a conscious isolate affirmed through identitarian thought. An Aboriginal equivalent of Descartes's 'I think therefore I am' might be 'I am emplaced, therefore I am.'"[3]

I have to admit I had to look up "identitarian" again and remembered doing so last time. The term describes, for readers who also have not come across it, the kind of white supremacy racist perspective we see in the growing anti-Muslim, anti-Black, and anti-Indigenous movement. I think it is worth mentioning here because it supports the idea that the Indigenous affiliation with Nature's spiritual energies is being expressed as a counter to this problematic.

I want to add that creation of one's personhood can happen at most any age, whether it is exclusive, as with identitariansim, or inclusive, as with Indigeneity's alignment with Nature spirits. It happened to me on the Rio Urique, a river running through Mexico's Copper Canyon. I was attempting, with a friend, to be the first to kayak down it from El Divisadero all the way to where it empties into the ocean. While we were kayaking, flooding waters, giant boulders, and an error in judgment caused me to drop into what I thought was an eddy. Instead, it was water waiting its turn to disappear into an underground hole. When my inflatable kayak hit the hole, I fell out and went down the drain. Before being shot out at the end of a long tunnel, I felt an indescribable peacefulness, saw the beautiful golden-white light, heard an unusual but calming sound, and was greeted by many almost glowing people. Previous to this experience, I had never really thought about transformational spiritual energies in Nature, yet I felt a spiritual energy that transformed me in ways that reflect what Mourning Dove means when she talks about going out into the night to gain "secret knowledge to make themselves great and powerful."

Darcia: Your story is so moving each time I have heard you discuss it. Thanks for showing us that a spiritual nature connection can happen at any age. Ideally, it is encouraged by one's community all life long, but if not, there are ways to move your awareness into that animist, living earth consciousness. I've been trying to help my college students get in the habit of moving into this awareness with various practices that Jon Young and his group suggest,[4] like finding a "sit spot," outside where plants and animals live, that you regularly visit. While there, let yourself get into a daydreaming, relaxed state and expand your senses. My lab also did an experiment to help college students over three weeks to build their kinship consciousness with all of life, and it worked (at least according to the post-test).[5] The public can do something similar over twenty-eight days with the Eco Attachment Dance we set up online.[6] These are some initial steps one can take toward awakening the deeper spiritual connection common to our ancestors and Native peoples.

The other thing you point out in your experience is the importance of working through fear with courage and moving into a fearless trust in outcomes and accepting what comes. Some years ago I was visiting my father's homeland, Puerto Rico, standing in the waves on a beach wearing a dress and straw hat. All of a sudden, a large wave pulled me in and under and rolled me over, soaking me and my hat. Instead of feeling afraid, I felt loved. But this is not the usual response of Westernized people. Western culture creates fearful people, for all sorts of reasons, who then have a hard time trusting themselves and others, opening up to others and to the natural world. I think overprotection of children owing to fear is an important idea that Mourning Dove addresses when she says "people still believed in the old ways and no one was criticized for sending their children out alone." This speaks to an important principle I discuss in connection with my evolved nest work about noninterference, a topic we cover later.

2

Nonhierarchical Society

Wenona Victor Hall (Stó:lō)

*H*ierarchies within Indigenous communities are commonly based upon levels of respect as opposed to the ability to oppress and control. To yield power, within many Indigenous worldviews can mean either internal personal power and/or can be tied to personal and collective spiritual power, which in turn respects the autonomy of others and contributes to the collectivity. Power and hierarchies, therefore, are often very different concepts within Aboriginal communities. They are based upon relations with others, a holistic view that respects difference in each individual's ability to contribute to the whole. For example, relationship between women and men can be represented by the eagle's two wings. An eagle soars to unbelievable heights and has tremendous power on two equal wings—one female, one male—carrying the body of life between them. Women and men are balanced parts of the whole, yet they are very different from each other and are not "equal" if equality is defined as being the same. A woman's self-determination manifests when this balance is honored.

Yet it becomes extremely complex when its recognition is denied under a colonial regime. While self determination nurtures human dignity, human responsibility, self and collective actualization and continuity, a colonial regime thrives on its ability to oppress, to maintain hierarchical orderings of power and importance, authority, ignorance and a concept of time that is both linear and extremely short. If time has taught us anything *it is that there are no winners under a colonial regime. To oppress human diversity and assert authority without consent is to deny human capability both in terms of individualization and collectivities. Colonial ideologies such as eurocentrism, racism, oppression and hegemonic control are used to promote and sustain a colonial regime that denies equally the colonized and the colonizers of their full human potential.*

Sources

Wenona Victor Hall. *Alternative Dispute Resolution (ADR) in Aboriginal Contexts: A Critical Review* (Ottawa, ON: Canadian Human Rights Commission, April 2007), 13–14.

Wenona Victor Hall. *Indigenous Justice: Clearing Space and Place for Indigenous Epistemologies.* Vancouver, BC: Centre for First Nations Governance, 2007. https://fngovernance.org/wp-content/uploads/2020/09/wenona_victor.pdf.

Contextualized Biosketch

In the 1990s, Wenona Victor Hall served six years as manager of the Stó:lō Nation while working on her master's degree. She lived most of her life in tribal territory with the Skowkale First Nation community located in Chilliwack, British Columbia. Her 2013 doctoral dissertation was titled "XeXa:Is and the Power of Transformation: The Stó:lō, Good Governance and Self-Determination." As the first Indigenous studies faculty member hired at the University of the Fraser Valley, she teaches Indigenous content courses for criminology, history, teacher education, and social work as well as Indigenous peoples knowledge courses. She is a dedicated advocate for processes of decolonization and Indigenous governance and resurgence.

The context for the quotes given above may best be understood in light of another excerpt from *Indigenous Justice: Clearing Space and Place for Indigenous Epistemologies:*

I was confused about my identity and traumatized from my removal.
My confusion and trauma meant I couldn't always see things clearly.
But being home allowed me to begin my healing journey. Looking

back I am sure I cried for a decade straight. And if I wasn't crying I was angry. As I came to realize the extent and purposive nature of the colonizing process I became very angry indeed. I pray for understanding. It is slowly coming. By keeping my ears (and heart) open I find many teachers along my path that bring me hope and understanding. . . . When I began working for my Nation with my criminology and psychology degree in hand, there were several colonial phenomena I was ill-prepared to deal with. My university training did not equip me with the skills and knowledge to address oppression, eurocentrism, colonial relationships and internal racism. My university training as an undergrad did very little, if anything to challenge my own colonial thoughts and opinions. So here are a few of the colonial phenomena that I wish I had a better understanding of when I began working for my Nation. For the Stó:lo, I can honestly say that revitalizing our own ways of resolving conflict was the easy part. What I was not prepared for was the negative response it would receive from some of the Eurocanadian criminal justice personnel and even more surprising was the negative response it would receive from some of the Stó:lo people. I now know why, but at the time I was completely unprepared for Stó:lo people who may want anything to do with Stó:lo ways and culture. And I was completely at a loss to understand why criminal justice personnel would resist and even have the gall to tell us we had no right to resolve our conflicts with our own ways! Colonial mentality and eurocentrism were obstacles I was ill equipped to answer back to.

But that was then. I have since achieved a better understanding of colonial ideologies that pervade Canadian society and adversely influence interactions and relations not only between Indigenous and non-Indigenous peoples, but often between Indigenous peoples themselves. I have come to see that the application of an Indigenous worldview to the area of justice has much to offer all Canadians. There are many obstacles in the way of such a realization. It requires a decolonizing process take place, it requires a complete paradigm shift, and most importantly it requires a partnership based upon acceptance and respect for human diversity.[1]

Indigenous Worldview Precept Dialogue

Four Arrows: Wenona Victor Hall reframes power-based hierarchy to varying levels of respect for different individuals based on different traits but with complementarity always in mind. I appreciate how she connects self-determination with Indigenous collectivistic, egalitarian principles. Too often people feel that Indigenous collectivistic cultures sacrifice individual autonomy, self-sufficiency, uniqueness, and independence, as may be seen in collectivistic societies operating under a dominant worldview. However, quite the opposite is true, according to my experiences living with and knowing individuals from significantly traditional Indigenous communities. Just after writing this assertion, I thought I would see if anyone had studied this question. The first publication I came upon was a 2012 piece about whether Indigenous motivational profiles actually reflect collectivism. The authors analyzed similarities and differences between groups classified coming from individualist or collectivist cultures. The authors concluded that on most dimensions the Indigenous students were similar with those from the individualist group, except with lower competitiveness. "Another interesting result was that the Indigenous collectivist group (comprised of Aboriginal Australians and Native Americans) was significantly higher on personal effort, disconfirming our hypothesis," they wrote.[2]

This conclusion would not have been surprising if the nonhierarchical precept of Indigenous worldview was understood. Under it, and when attached to other Indigenous beliefs about interconnectedness, such "individualist" traits as autonomy, independence, uniqueness, and self-sufficiency are necessary for ensuring the well-being of the group. The problem with hierarchy is, as Wenona says, about how colonized hierarchical perspectives assert authority without consent. Such authoritarianism is being witnessed more and more in political regimes during our COVID-19 pandemic. People are experiencing increasing fear and stress. This in turn creates in people "desire for order and hierarchy and a fear of outsiders."[3]

Darcia: A number of scholars have suggested that *static* hierarchical societies are a recent phenomenon.[4] Even some large civilizations of the past were characterized by egalitarianism. Moreover, humans historically have shown the flexibility to move between egalitarian and hierarchical structures based on the season. So according to an evolutionary science perspective, *static* dominance hierarchy represents less than 1 percent of human existence (and only among some humans) and is a U-shaped shift back to our *primate* ancestry of domination.[5] However, our human instincts still are to be egalitarian when we are well-nurtured and have experiences of playful egalitarianism—but modern society raises children to be easily stressed and stresses them as adults so much that many can't think or feel properly and so learn to prefer authoritarianism.[6]

In my analysis, following Alice Miller,[7] instinctive submission to authority comes from an early life experience of trauma or neglect that creates a brain that is threat reactive and easily submits to a powerful authority figure. The Nazis knew to mistreat young children to create submissive conformists. The brain learns, from early life stress, to shut down when distress becomes too great, going into a type of survival mode related to shutting down thinking and feeling—an immobility—in order to stay alive. After rehearsing this routinely without mitigation, the child automatically enters this dissociation habit when afraid. When you have a society, like the USA, that undermines parenting, even making it a competition between parent and child or parent and parent, such damage is pervasive.

As implied above, noncivilized communities—small-band hunter-gatherers—are fiercely egalitarian. They do not harbor coercion or big egos.[8] They report that an inflated ego is dangerous to everyone else.[9] Egoism and hierarchy often go together in today's world, showing the brittle inflexibility arising from early life undercare (i.e., when our species' evolved nest is not provided). Anthropologist Tim Ingold[10] has summarized the sociality of hunter-gatherers around the world (who demonstrate the Indigenous worldview). They are highly individualistic in that they do what they want to at any given moment—no one coerces anyone else, no matter their age or gender. For example, an individual can stay back in the settlement when a group goes off to hunt or gather, or take a walkabout when they like.

Small-band hunter-gatherer individuals are also highly communal in that they enjoy being with others most of the time (to the consternation of anthropologists who are trying to organize their notes in private), interacting with cheerful cooperation and implicit empathic concern. Cultural anthropologist E. Richard Sorenson, who started the field of film anthropology, learned that when he studied the footage he shot while living with different "preconquest" peoples around the world, only then could he notice what he did not perceive while living with them. He described each group's "heart-felt rapprochement based on integrated trust [which] provides remarkable efficiency in securing needs and responding to nature's challenges while dispensing ongoing delight with people and surroundings . . . in a ceaseless, spirited, individualistic input into a unified at-oneness."[11] There was no need for rules or authority because of this sense of automatic individuality-in-communion.

I see unified at-oneness as the baseline for human nature, a capacity honed by early life experience, when worldview is shaped.[12] Sorenson noted that the rapprochement he perceived was fostered by a "socio-sensual type of infant and child nurture [where] babies were simply not put down, not deprived of constant, ever-ready, interactive body contact."[13] Eliciting delight from a baby was a desired social norm, and the baby soon learned how to please and extend delight. I think egalitarianism and respect are expected by children, who also expect equal say and participation in the community, as observed in these societies. Unfortunately, in "postconquest" or civilized societies, babies are undercared for (and even punished, traumatized, or neglected), undermining at-oneness. In my work, I link this to the dominator mindset that many in the Western world have.[14] They have not learned partnership because they lacked that early practice.

Four Arrows: Darcia, you say that people's tendency to submit to authority, as seems to be happening around the world more and more, comes from early life experiences that create a sort of programming for such submission. Suppose such a change in brain functioning can occur from early childhood trauma in one's lifetime. Would you agree with the theories being proposed in the relatively new field of epigenetics that claim traumatic events can be passed down to subsequent generations by altering the way genes are expressed? It seems reasonable that a baby would use early experience to prepare for what lies ahead in the short term. Surviving authoritarianism with functional adaption may help explain why some children I know who had non-authoritarian parents tend still to be submissive to tyranny, and some children with abusive, authoritarian parents grow up fighting against authority. Perhaps the dominant worldview maintains the unhealthy adaption not only through ideological behavior choices, but also by reinforcing epigenetic influence via media, education, religion, and culture. I think Wenona's final sentence supports this idea. She refers to our "colonial ideologies such as eurocentrism, racism, oppression and hegemonic control" as ways "to promote and sustain a colonial regime that denies the colonized and the colonizers of their full human potential equally."

My reference to an epigenetic phenomenon creating hierarchical tendencies assumes that we are evolutionarily prone to egalitarianism. I agree with this and so does Darwin, in spite of the neo-Darwinian emphasis on survival of the fittest with reference to nonhuman animals. Since Indigenous worldview is not only sourced in our biology but also in place-based understandings and teachings from other-than-human life, I think it useful to look at the animal kingdom.

First, many other-than-human cultures are organized according to hierarchy or "pecking orders." However, this is done to minimize conflict, not to cause it or do anything other than create symbiotic relationships for the greater good. Gender does not seem to be the main factor; rather, individuals who assume leadership, whether male or female, often have the entire group's welfare in mind. Some species have primarily female leadership, including ants, hyenas, lions, whales, elephants, and bonobos. Most other species tend to have larger, male patrilineal systems. However, even in male-led animal societies, groups of females often form coalitions to counterbalance any diversion from greater-good priorities.[15] In small human hunter-gatherer groups, a balance of male-female power is generally organized according to individual talents and dispositions. Thus, leadership in the nonhuman world is not usually about dominance (competitive authoritarianism).

This said, however, when novel situations occur—such as loss of territory, serious injury, psychological disorder, or even greed—all of the animals can become authoritarian. Moreover, the animals that share 94 to 99 percent of their genome in common with humans sometimes have cultures that are severely dominant and even cruel.[16] At least in one case, once the dominant males die, more peaceable males take over with less aggressive behaviors, including lots of grooming. It is interesting to note that chimpanzees are usually led by males, but bonobos, who are studied much less and share a similar genetic relationship with us, are female led. That bonobos are known for not having such authoritarian dominance seems to indicate that they have epigenetic or cultural markers that are much more egalitarian.[17] So I conclude from this that the Indigenous worldview we are promoting is not only based on our animal biology, but is also based on intimate knowledge and relationships with other-than-human beings who are, in effect, role models or teachers. I contend that our recent hierarchy is not so much a new invention in the world, but rather a loss of wisdom that humans practiced for most of our history. "The animal world taught man how to live close to the earth, and the connection that has been established between the animal world and that of man has instilled a respect for all life in those who follow the traditional Aboriginal way."[18]

Darcia: Thanks for bringing up our ape relatives. It is true that through the tree of life prior to *Homo sapiens,* the human genus appears to have lived more like other apes with a hierarchical structure.[19] There is a division among anthropologists about who we resemble more, the aggressive, male-dominated chimpanzees or the sex-loving, female-dominated bonobos who are the only other animals that French kiss like humans. Primatologist and ethologist Frans de Waal wondered which theory would have dominated if the bonobos instead of the chimpanzees had been discovered first.[20] More recently, anthropologists are pointing out that accompanying the evolution of a larger brain in our species (which is three times as large as that of chimpanzees), we developed several characteristics socially and individually not found in other apes.[21] Socially, female communal child raising was necessary along with enlisting the hunting capacities and commitment of males (through female coalitionary playful deception) to help nourish children's big brains.[22] Individually, mutual mind reading, egalitarianism, and cumulative culture accompanied these group characteristics.

You are right that all animals go into survival mode when threat is perceived: flight-fight-freeze-faint. Social mammals, like humans, developed a social calming mechanism too. Let's imagine a loud explosion just occurred. For humans who are well raised or who have not been traumatized (neurobiological structures working well; layers of social skills fostered by social embeddedness), the first impulse is to reach out to another person to calm down. If this is not possible, the flight-fight-freeze mechanisms (sympathetic autonomic system) activate, and if this doesn't restore a feeling of safety, then the dissociate-faint option (parasympathetic autonomic system) activate to stay alive. If young children are left in distress during critical periods, routinely or for long durations, they will be conditioned to automatically shift into these modes. Corporal punishment in the early years, as the German Nazis knew, shapes the child-as-adult to use the survival modes of response under threat, making them nicely compliant to authoritarian leadership.[23] Young children are highly malleable, in part because of plasticity from immaturity but also epigenetic factors.

Regarding epigenetics, there are two kinds. Epigenetics is what happens to your own genes based on your experience—they get "turned on" or "turned off." So it is not enough to have particular genes; they have to be expressed to have any effect on your life. Lots of animal studies show that nurturing mothers affect genes of all sorts, for example, to control anxiety during sensitive periods. If you don't have nurturing care during a sensitive period, you never turn on those genes, and so for the rest of your life you will have trouble with anxiety (unless you take drugs).[24] What you are referring to is called epigenetic *inheritance*. In this case, if your parents or grandparents experienced trauma, you can inherit such things as anxiety or, physiologically, a "survival phenotype" where your body organs are shaped to be ready for physical hardship.[25] If you are born into an environment where food is widely available without much effort, you can develop obesity and other health problems associated with the Western-pattern diet.[26]

So I think you are right about the shadows of ancestral history affecting a person's behavior. The important thing is to know how to honor children, paying attention to how you are treating them, because you are affecting not only their lifelong well-being but that of future generations. That's why I study and remind people of humanity's evolved nest for optimizing normal development.[27] It fosters long-term well-being and resilience. The evolved nest is our promise and responsibility to forthcoming generations, as well as to the rest of the natural world, because an unnested—poorly regulated and developed—human being can do a lot of damage, not only to humans but to the more than human. We see that happening in the world today. I write about all these things in my book *Neurobiology and the Development of Human Morality: Evolution, Culture, and Wisdom.*

It should also be said that individuals can find ways to revamp themselves and self-heal from early life toxic stress, at least to some degree, with the help of others, human and other-than-human. Other precepts will touch on this.

Four Arrows: We close by giving one example of how Indigenous cultures chose nonhierarchical structures by learning about "leadership" from the other creatures who are part of our earth family. This one was included in a paper about how to resolve a dispute about leadership and authority *(naat'aanii baa sah has liligi hane)* that was presented to the Navajo Nation Supreme Court in 2010.[28] The Navajo Nation president and vice-president were petitioners-appellees, and the Navajo Nation Council and its speaker were the respondent-appellees. It opens with reference to a Navajo original story describing how animals were involved in deciding who would have authority:

A group of the People nominated the wolf Ma'iitsoh and they talked about his qualities, that he would protect the People so that we would come to no harm, and he had powerful words and connection to the Holy People. Another group nominated the bluebird Dolii, that he was compassionate and had qualities of nurturing, which the People need because that's the way people grow. Yet another group nominated the mountain lion Nashdoitsoh because he was a hunter, so the People would never go hungry, so it was about survival. Finally, the last group nominated the hummingbird Dah yiitihi, who was swift and would go from plant to plant bringing back pollen, and the pollen represents spirituality and reverence which the People need to have honor for one another. The People couldn't agree to choose one leader among those nominated, they each wanted the one each nominated. Finally, they resolved to send the wolf towards the East and bring back something for the People that will sustain life. The bluebird was sent to the South, the mountain lion was sent to the West, and hummingbird to the North.

The People waited and waited and no one came back. They kept looking into the four directions for their leader until one day, the People looked into the North and there was something white that was moving, and it was the dawn moving towards them. They saw it was the wolf, who had brought back the dawn Hayoolkaai as his coat, which is thought Nitsahakees, white shell which is used in mineral offerings, the white corn for food, and songs Sin doo Tsodizin. At midday, the People looked into the South and there was something blue that was moving, and it was the blue sky moving towards them. They saw it was the bluebird, who had brought back the blue sky

Yadihil Nihodeet l'iizh as his coat, which is planning Nahat'a, tur-
quoise which is used in mineral offerings, the blue corn for food,
and wise words Yodi doo Niitl'iz Saad. When the sun set, the People
looked into the sunset and there was something gold that was
moving, and it was the mountain lion moving towards them, who
had brought back the gold of the sunset Nihotsooi as his coat, which
is Iina life, abalone shell which is used in mineral offerings, yellow
corn for food, and birth and development Oochiil doo anoohseel.
Finally, after dark, the People looked into the North and saw all kinds
of different colors moving into each other, and it was the hummingbird moving towards them, who had brought back the night Chahal-
heel as his coat, which is Sihasin hope, jet [lignite] which is used in
mineral offerings, squash for food, and reverence Hodilzin.

The People were awed as each of these was brought out. In spite
of what each group had previously assumed was vital to sustain life,
the People felt that Ma'iitsoh, Dolii, Nashdojtsoh and Dah yiitihi,
each brought back a crucial element for life, therefore all would be
leaders and must work together to sustain life. The People decided
to make all of them leaders. We re-tell this story to emphasize that,
since beyond recorded time, the People have understood the separation of functions of leaders, and that in order to survive as a People,
there must be collaboration and coming together both in the community and in the leadership chosen by the People to pool skills,
resources and characteristics. There is no supremacy of any one
portion of the day over another, therefore there is no greater skill,
resource, characteristic, or leader over the others. The People choose
and challenge their leaders to give something useful and valuable to
the People in equal parts, and the leaders provide. With this episode,
Fundamental Law was established that there should not be concentrated power.

This is but one of thousands of stories that show how the Indigenous worldview is inherently rooted in its origin mythology. Dan
Longboat says it this way: "Human beings are sacred teachers meant

to impart and remember and are duty bound to the spiritual because we were the last beings created. The other creatures chose, as part of their responsibilities, the duty of caring for us and also exercised their spiritual and intellectual capabilities by instilling in us and sharing among us their knowledge of how to live, their stories, songs, and identities."[29]

THERE WAS A TIME WHEN OUR PEOPLE COVERED THE LAND AS THE WAVES OF A WIND-RUFFLED SEA COVER ITS SHELL PAVED FLOOR, BUT THAT TIME LONG SINCE PASSED AWAY WITH THE GREATNESS OF TRIBES THAT ARE NOW BUT A MOURNFUL MEMORY. THE WHITE MAN'S GOD CANNOT LOVE OUR PEOPLE OR HE WOULD PROTECT THEM. THEY SEEM TO BE ORPHANS WHO CAN LOOK NOWHERE FOR HELP. HOW THEN CAN WE BE BROTHERS?

DAY AND NIGHT CANNOT DWELL TOGETHER. THE RED MAN HAS EVER FLED THE APPROACH OF THE WHITE MAN, AS THE MORNING MIST FLEES BEFORE THE MORNING SUN.

IT MATTERS LITTLE WHERE WE PASS THE REMNANT OF OUR DAYS. THEY WILL NOT BE MANY. BUT WHY SHOULD I MOURN AT THE UNTIMELY FATE OF MY PEOPLE? TRIBE FOLLOWS TRIBE AND NATION FOLLOWS NATION LIKE THE WAVES OF THE SEA. IT IS THE ORDER OF NATURE AND REGRET IS USELESS. YOUR TIME OF DECAY MAY BE DISTANT BUT IT WILL SURELY COME, FOR EVEN THE WHITE MAN WHOSE GOD WALKED AND TALKED WITH HIM AS FRIEND WITH FRIEND CANNOT BE EXEMPT FROM THE COMMON DESTINY. WE MAY BE BROTHERS AFTER ALL. WE WILL SEE. AND WHEN THE LAST RED MAN SHALL HAVE PERISHED AND THE MEMORY OF MY TRIBE SHALL HAVE BECOME A MYTH AMONG THE WHITE MEN, THESE SHORES WILL SWARM WITH THE INVISIBLE DEAD OF MY TRIBE. AT NIGHT WHEN THE STREETS OF YOUR CITIES AND VILLAGES ARE SILENT AND YOU THINK THEM DESERTED THEY WILL THRONG WITH THE RETURNING HOSTS THAT ONCE FILLED THEM AND STILL LOVE THIS BEAUTIFUL LAND. THE WHITE MAN WILL NEVER BE ALONE. LET HIM BE JUST AND DEAL KINDLY WITH MY PEOPLE FOR THE DEAD ARE NOT POWERLESS. DEAD DID I SAY? THERE IS NO DEATH ONLY A CHANGE OF WORLDS.

SEATTLE
SUQUAMISH
1786 1866

Seattle
marble stonecut

Harriet Greene
Taos, N.M.

3

Courage and Fearless Trust in the Universe

Berta Cáceres (Lenca; 1973–2016)
and her daughter, Bertha Zúñiga Cáceres (Lenca)

*B*erta Cáceres (mother): *The Lenca are an ancient people that inhabited the regions of Mesoamerica in central Honduras. We are a people strongly dedicated to the earth. We are beings who come from the earth, from the water and from the corn. Our worldview is centered on the earth and the balance that we maintain with all living things. What is happening to us is happening to all people suffering from colonialism. For those who want justice and freedom we must be fearless in defending our communities and the earth. We are the ancestral guardians of the rivers, in turn protected by the spirits of young girls who teach us that giving our lives in various ways for the protection of the rivers is giving our lives for the wellbeing of humanity and of this planet. Let us wake up, humankind! We're out of time. We must make our conscience free of the rapacious capitalism, racism, and patriarchy that will only assure our own self destruction. . . . They are afraid of us because we are not afraid of them. . . . Let us come together and remain hopeful as we defend and care for the blood of this Earth and of its spirits. I dedicate this award to all the rebels out there, to my mother, to the Lenca people, to Río Blanco and to the martyrs who gave their lives in the struggle to defend our natural resources.*

Bertha Zúñiga Cáceres (daughter): *My mother taught me how important it is to get involved in communities, to stand up to those who* *wield political and economic power, and to learn from the struggle itself. It was part of my personal and political education. My people—the Lenca people—taught me from a very young age that you can't remain indifferent to the unjust situation in our communities and the country as a whole. You always have to think about the interconnectedness of these struggles: you can't separate one issue—such as land—from the others, because it's a struggle against the whole system. For example, when you're campaigning for access to school, you're also fighting for health and healthy food. We need to build movements that are consistent with our values, and what goes on inside our movements needs to reflect that. The need for justice means we have to struggle, because we can't live like this. We have fought for our rights for centuries—against the Spanish colonial powers to begin with, and now today against other types of colonialism. We draw strength from our ancestors, who liberated the country and defended our identity as Indigenous people. It's part of our worldview: our ancestors are still walking with us, accompanying us. My mother was never silent in the face of injustice; she was steadfastly committed to the fight against impunity and injustice, and she taught us that we have to face up to the elites who are undermining our future.*

Sources

Beverly Bell. "They Fear Us Because We Are Fearless: The Life and Legacy of Berta Cáceres." *Counterpunch,* March 11, 2016. www.counterpunch.org/2016/03/11 /they-fear-us-because-we-are-fearless-the-life-and-legacy-of-berta-caceres/.

Bertha Isabel Cáceres. "Drawing Strength from Our Ancestors." *New Internationalist,* January 22, 2018. https://newint.org/features/web-exclusive/2018/01/22 /strength-from-our-ancestors.

Skylight. "Berta Cáceres: In Her Own Words." September 22, 2016. Video, 3:15. www.youtube.com/watch?v=KjM81tYBew4.

Contexualized Biosketches

In 1993, Berta Cáceres—a Lenca Native—cofounded the Civic Council of Popular and Indigenous Organizations of Honduras (COPINH). At that time in the country, there was little pride and even less power in being Indigenous. Berta co-created COPINH and served as its general coordinator to build the political strength of Lencas, campesinos, and other grassroots sectors to transform one of the most corrupt, anti-democratic, and unequal societies in the hemisphere. Berta loved to say, "They fear us because we're fearless." That fearlessness paid off over the years. COPINH has successfully reclaimed ancestral lands, winning unheard-of communal land titles. They have stalled or stopped dams, logging operations, and mining exploration—not to mention free-trade agreements. They have prevented many precious and sacred places from being plundered and destroyed. On March 2, 2016, one year after Berta won the prestigious Goldman Environmental Prize— sometimes called the Green Nobel—and one day before her forty-fifth birthday, gunmen pushed into her home and shot her to death.

Bertha Zúñiga Cáceres is the general coordinator of COPINH and the daughter of Berta Cáceres. She faces the same dangers her murdered mother faced in her environmental and human rights work. The murderers of Berta and other COPINH members remain unpunished. At least 124 environmental and land activists have been murdered in Honduras since 2009. On Friday, June 30, 2017, Bertita barely escaped an assassination attempt, right after she supported a bill to stop the provision of US military aid and weapons to Honduras until the country can take action on the many assassinations of activists. As she wrote in a column published in Spain, "Don't worry: your fight lives on in me, in my brothers and sisters, and in our community."

Indigenous Worldview Precept Dialogue

Four Arrows: In a *Democracy Now* interview on July 7, 2017, Amy Goodman asked a twenty-six-year-old Bertha, "What makes you so brave?" She replies: "I was born of people with great dignity and of great strength, and my mother, Berta Cáceres, instilled upon me at a very young age that the struggle is rooted in dignity and that we must continue forward defending the rights of our people."[1] This

response—coupled with her and her mother's beliefs about being dedicated to the earth; having emerged from the earth, water, and corn;
being ancestral guardians protected by spirits; and having a worldview centered on balance with all living things—describes our idea of
having a "fearless trust in the universe." It is a trust grounded in the
Indigenous worldview expressed by such beliefs. R. Michael Fisher
refers to such fearless courage as "defense intelligence" (DI). I bring
this up because it seems to fit with the defense of Mother Earth and
human beings involved here.

Dr. Fisher says such bravery is the most primal DI there is. "It spontaneously undercuts the circuitry of panic patterns at the core" that
come from being "disconnected from the primal wisdom and primal
brave-circuitry, to tap into what Indigenous peoples have known for
99% of human history."[2] In other words, trusting the flowing balance of
life's interconnectedness is key. It is the basis for full engagement when
defending the gift of life, or even when simply participating in the gift
so you know it must be protected. With such perspectives in mind, we
can move from fear to courage and then once committed to action, to
fearless trust in whatever outcomes occur.

Darcia: Yes, yes! The ability to sense the interconnectedness of
life is related to the functioning of the right-brain hemisphere, which
develops most rapidly in early life but also throughout childhood—
building the practical wisdom that will be accessed later in life.[3] Spending childhood in the great outdoors with wild animals and plants,
and multi-aged playmates, fosters receptive attention and ecological
intelligence.[4] When industrialized civilized people minimize their care
of young children—e.g., separating them from the community but
also from spending most time outside with multiple playmates—the
result is impaired right brain development.[5] Also, civilized schooling
traditionally emphasizes left-brain hemisphere functioning (reading,
linear thinking, intellectualism), often way too early, while belittling
right-brain orientations (social imagination, relational attunement,
etc.). Growing up walled away from wild nature makes it easy to be
fearful of the natural world and incur "nature deficit disorder."[6]

The other aspect of civilized child raising (meaning outside our evolved nest) is the undermining of a confident core self.[7] It is easy to scare babies—when you leave them in distress alone—into distrust of the world, relationships, and themselves. They experience soul molestation, throwing off normal healthy development.[8] Then they carry around a deep, subconscious sense of insecurity throughout life that takes a lot of work to overcome.

But even in noncivilized communities, there are stages of child development to help children overcome fear and grow into courage. I'm thinking of vision quests. Maybe you want to discuss those.

Four Arrows: I'm happy you asked me to talk about vision quests and their connection to courage and fearless trust in the universe. Indeed, there is a strong connection between this worldview precept of interconnectedness, human development, and what we call in Lakota an *hanbleciya,* which translates to "crying for a vision." Certainly these connections are most important in the early years. We know from Mourning Dove's quote in our chapter on "Recognition of Spiritual Energies in Nature" that her people sent young children out into the woods as young as six years old to find the guardian spirit. This was a way to develop courage and fearless trust when committing to overcoming fear when a choice is made to do so. Initiation rites occur in traditional communities also at the end of early childhood; puberty; early, middle, and late adulthood; and old age, and vision quests are done at any time for many reasons. Although I've never thought about it before you brought it up here, I would say that overcoming fear is a common theme for them. *Vision quests are a way to go outside ourselves to find ourselves when we are lost in some way. From them we find courage to live as co-creators with and in the world, and discover from the vision that which we needed to acquire a new level of personal power to face difficulties.* I will share an example of this from my own experience. I doubt I have ever put it in writing before, as it is a sacred story. But then, we are writing what I consider to be a sacred book.

My wife, Bea, and I had left Pine Ridge and were living in Fairfield, Idaho. I was preparing to go back to finish my fourth Wiwanke

Wachipi (Sun Dance). About a week before my trip back to Porcu-
pine, South Dakota, I heard a weather report for the week of the event
saying to expect temperatures well above 105. For my previous dances,
I was living in such heat and acclimated to it by the time of the four
days of fasting, without water, and dancing from sunup until sundown
while praying and sacrificing intensely for the world. I suddenly felt
a fear building in my gut. Would I be able to manage going without
water in such heat? I decided to do an *hanbleciya*. I made my tobacco
ties, grabbed my *chanupa*, and headed up to the top of a foothill in the
wilderness at the base of the Sawtooth Mountains. When I was not
yet settled into my spiritual mindset, having just sat down in the circle
of my ties facing west, a rodent stepped out of the woods and starting eating the tobacco out of one of the red cloth bundles. Instantly, I
kicked my leg out and chased it away.

Yes, I chased it away. I knew that animals are very often the messenger spirits sent to us on vision quests, but I reacted inappropri-
ately anyway. I realized my mistake immediately and starting praying.
Within a minute, it came back. I watched it joyfully. It ate some more
tobacco, then moved inside the circle and took a break. It was sitting
there with its back to me like a pet dog. It had long back legs and a
long tail, and I craved to know what its appearance meant. After all,
I was not a native of Idaho and had no knowledge about the creature
nor anyone to ask about its meaning. I continued to pray throughout
the night, occasionally thinking about getting to a computer to learn
what kind of a rat it was and what it had to help me overcome my fear
of going without water.

When I came down the mountain and went home, I started a fire
for the *inipi* (purification lodge, more commonly known as a sweat
lodge) ceremony outside and burned the clothes I was wearing. Then
I ran naked into my house and turned on the computer. I googled
images of "rodents of Idaho" and there it was—a kangaroo rat. When
I googled kangaroo rat, the first thing that popped up was: "The only
mammal in North America that can survive without ever drinking any
water, getting needed moisture from their seed diet." Needless to say,

my fearless trust in whatever conditions were to occur in South Dakota returned.

I told this story because you were suggesting that people learn to overcome fear and develop courage, and you mentioned vision quests as a way Indigenous people do this. Certainly they can be used to overcome fear, as I used mine. However, the usual goal is to seek guidance from Nature and Spirit, to find answers, and to connect to a purpose. Courage may be required to do a vision quest. I know a number of young and old Lakota braves have fear when they "go up on the hill" to sit alone in the wilderness and engage the Spirit world. So surviving it might indeed develop courage to do another vision quest sometime. However, I do not think of the sacred event as a courage-building exercise. In the dominant worldview, becoming courageous to do something does involve skill building, as when learning to parachute or walk on a high wire. However, the fearlessness that Bertha and Berta represent is different. Acting to save a river or one's people, never knowing when an assassin is around the corner, requires a more intrinsic source of courage. In fact, as I read their quotes again it came to me that their words reveal how their courage stems from their oneness with nature identity. Their references to being "strongly dedicated to the earth," being centered on an identity that is of the earth, and being strengthened by their ancestors whose bones dwell in it, seem to support my idea that an *hanbleciya* ultimately serves fearlessness by enhancing the human/nature bond.

Interestingly, I had a doctoral student whose dissertation used, in part, fMRI brain scans to show that even a simple connection to nature via a short film could physically enhance left and right hemisphere balance in contrast to watching a film about the destruction of environments.[9] This may offer another insight into Indigenous courage and fearlessness. It is not so much about resisting those who are destroying life systems as it is about loving the systems.

Darcia: I love the stories of your experiences. Certainly, nature experience can generate feelings of calm (e.g., lowering cortisol levels). But while sitting around the fire in the dark can calm you, it doesn't necessarily simultaneously make you fearless to leave the fireside and wander into the darkness. You need some place-based knowledge.

I think courage is more skill based. A person's immersion would have to be combined with learning skills to feel like they can cope with whatever they encounter. I think of the ex-marine who jumped down onto subway tracks in New York to save a woman who had fallen into the path of an oncoming train. Clearly, he had a lot of skills that came into play in the situation, along with a sense of relational connection and self-efficacy (confidence plus skills and a history of successful effort). In another example of fearless connection, those who risked their lives to rescue Jews during World War II also had self-efficacy and a trust in the universe.[10] When asked why they had intervened, they said things like, "What else could I do? There was a human being in need." Interestingly, when nonrescuers were interviewed, they also said "What else could I do?" They were lacking the self-efficacy that comes from practice and were less likely to have strong attachments to others. We build expertise from relational connection and modeled/coached practice in a particular domain.

In our work with classroom teachers on building moral character,[11] we identified four levels of expertise development (to simplify it for teachers working with our model): (1) immersion in examples and opportunities; (2) attention to facts and skills; (3) practice procedures; (4) integrate knowledge and procedures across contexts. This is natural, Indigenous pedagogy. Let's imagine what a World War II rescuer would have had to experience to build a fearless moral self-efficacy. (1) They would have been immersed in narratives of inclusion (oneness with all of humanity) and seen their parents and family members acting compassionately toward outsiders; (2) their attention would have been drawn to ways to help others, and they would have contributed in small ways, then (3) in larger ways, and (4) in different contexts. With all this practice, their responses to others in need then become almost automatic. Thus, courage in a particular domain, the golden mean between being foolhardy or reckless, which a novice might exhibit, takes experience. In other words, for courage in wilderness and trust in the natural world, extensive practice of surviving there—as in vision quests—may be needed to build up courage. However, taking "nature baths" *can* build a greater sense of connection to and responsibility for the other-than-human, as we found in an experiment we did to increase ecological empathy and mindfulness (related to ecological attachment).[12] Ecological attachment may increase motivation to learn survival skills and take on a vision quest, thereby increasing fearless trust in the universe.

4

Understanding/Embracing Death and Dying

Coyote Marie Hunter-Ripper (Cherokee, Choctaw)

I am often called to help people in their last days, hours or minutes of life. Sometimes they just want reassuring. Many are frightened. Some say they feel unprepared. Others are lonely because of how our dominant culture tends to dismiss elders and people are uncomfortable with death, including the death of their relatives.

I have also spent time with a few individuals who still managed to hold on to their Indigenous worldview. They show a serenity that is hard to describe. Humor even shows itself sometimes. Those who were fluent in their Native language and participated in ceremonies throughout their lives usually had some kin who would help them with their transition with a particular ancient way for the spirit to leave the body. Traditions vary of course between First Nations, as do expectations for where the person's soul goes. Each has both individual and cultural diversity as relates to ceremonies, burial, mourning rituals, etc. For example, some Cherokee believe our spirit or soul lives on as a spirit, sometimes unseen and sometimes in a new physical human, animal or plant. Some believe we return to certain heavenly bodies. All who have acquired immunity to the Eurocentric feelings about death have a sense of where we came from and where we are going, accepting our experience and destiny on our beautiful Mother Earth. She nourished our physical forms in life and reclaims them in death.

In my work, I cannot remember a person who did not have spirits come to their consciousness in their last days, once we evoke them. At first, some deny them or fear them, but those who have not been taught such things, embrace them. Traditional Indigenous people with their worldview still strong often smile at them. They know the cyclical way life and death operate and see little difference between living a good life and dying a good death. They are not attached to materialistic things and it is easier to let go the body as well. I believe there would be a lot less angry families that fight over material items if people were open to connecting with spirits. In fact, it is a beautiful, even magical experience to be with someone who is going through that stage when he or she recognizes and embraces the spirits.

Even those without Indigenous worldview who come to me seem to leave the world without the pain that brought them to me. I believe this is the work of the Spirits. The departing person is in a state of inner wisdom and they know they are going to a place that they want to go to. Unfortunately, many Indigenous and non-Indigenous people have learned to deny the truth about dying. Individuals begin fearing death early on and usually this fear leads to a similar emotion toward life. When death comes, too many die alone and sad. Even when family comes, they are often in a hurry to be done with this event called death. However, if they can be with someone who can remind them of the truth, they seem to remember it. Once people begin the transition and into the ascension, it is a blissful, beautiful, honorable place to be with someone who is going through that stage. All the people that I have worked with in that aspect, I have seen that they are leaving with no pain. They are really in a state of inner wisdom, whatever their connection to that might be. Their consciousness, as well as their nine energy fields, are going to a place that they want to go to.

Of course, in our Western culture, this wisdom has eroded. I want to share that I have recognized I sometimes have fear about my own death. Part of it is a mother's concern about the well-being of the children left behind, but part of it comes from too much exposure to the Western culture's approach to dying that I have witnessed all my life. I have learned that I am not the only Indigenous healer who has admitted this. It is a legacy of colonization. It is a legacy of pandemics like when families learned to stay away from relatives dying of smallpox. I share this to say all of us must begin to learn how to re-embrace all of our Indigenous ways of being in the world in life, so we will be comfortable with them in death. We must remember that we are all one and that our essence continues on. I know when it is my time, that my deeper understandings will guide me to realize I am just continuing my journey. Ultimately, we live so we know how to die and we die to live again.

Sources

Coyote Marie Hunter-Ripper. Personal interview with Four Arrows. April 12, 2020.
Coyote Marie Hunter-Ripper. Personal Interview with Four Arrows. May 24, 2020.
Amanda Provenzano. "We Live So We Know How to Die, and Die to Live: Community and Indigenous Cultures." Ernest Becker Foundation. http://ernestbecker.org/this-mortal-life/Indigenous-culture/coyote-marie-hunter-ripper/.

Contexualized Biosketch

Coyote Marie Hunter-Ripper is a traditional Cherokee healer. She is also an ordained interfaith minister, a member of the Committee of Native American Ministries, and director of All Nations Education and Wellness. She has long served as an international volunteer for human rights and social/civil justice, with an emphasis on empowering women. She has done ceremonial work throughout the world and is known for her humorous resolve and compassionate dedication to helping others. Her work is based on being an intermediary between the natural and supernatural worlds.

Indigenous Worldview Precept Dialogue

Four Arrows: My friend Dianne M. Longboat, a traditional Mohawk teacher and healer, captures what Coyote Marie shares with her opening to her paper "Indigenous Perspectives on Death and Dying":

We understand who we are—
We know where we came from—
We accept and understand our destiny here on Mother Earth—
We are spirit having a human experience[1]

Each Indigenous nation has its own complex origin story and details about what happens when we die. The great diversity of beliefs, and relevant funeral rites, are largely based on place-oriented factors. These factors include local flora and fauna, food, weather, latitude (and area of sky that can be viewed), etc. What they have in common is a holistic view of body, mind, and Spirit as operating in a life cycle of which death is a natural part and oneness with all is a given. They also share a sense of continuation, with most either referring to a return to the Milky Way or a return to Earth in another form, or both. Such Indigenous beliefs about death, oneness, and immortality can partially explain why concern for the "seventh generation" of life prevails as part of Indigenous consciousness. This is very different from the idea of having only one life, which can lead to the kind of selfishness that contributes to destruction of Earth's life systems. If we assume that we have souls that are interconnected with all, now and in the future, we tend to behave without such selfish attitudes.

Dr. Larry Dossey, who wrote the foreword for Sherri Mitchell's book on Indigenous worldview, *Sacred Instructions,* defines soul as "the nonlocal aspect" of who we are."[2] Consciousness is a phenomenon that is both within us and all around us. He further supports the idea of endless consciousness with references to the reincarnation studies of Ian Stevenson and to the large number of documented near-death experience narratives. Traditional Indigenous narratives have embraced such views since long before quantum physics or reincarnation research.

As I mentioned previously in chapter 2, I also have personal experience via a near-death experience that supports Dossey's ideas about nonlocal consciousness, souls, and their immortality. The experience, for me, was transformational in many ways that I write about in *Primal Awareness: A True Story of Survival, Transformation and Awakening with the Rarámuri Shamans of Mexico* and that I narrate with photos on YouTube ("Four Arrows and the Shaman's Message Journey"). I agree with Gregory Shushan's conclusion that "near-death experiences provide perfectly rational grounds for beliefs that the soul can leave the body, and that it can survive death and join spirits of the dead in another world."[3]

Darcia: Your and Hunter-Ripper's experiences are deeply moving. A lot of Western religious culture is about coming to grips with death. The mystical traditions accomplish this through self-calming activities like prayer or meditation and contemplation. Most churchgoers, though, are typically admonished to follow the rules of their church and maintain correct beliefs so they end up in heaven. I grew up in a fundamentalist church and remember the sermons emphasizing how evil humans were and how we had to stay in the fold if we did not want to burn in hell. Women were second-class citizens. In my twenties I felt "called" to be a minister, which was not allowed in our denomination. It was a dilemma. I actually decided that even if I ended up in hell, I had to leave my denomination and join another to attend seminary. It was like stepping off a cliff. I was ready to die in order to follow my heart of hearts. Ironically, although I enjoyed my years in seminary, which propelled me to graduate school studies later, I found that I did not believe the doctrine I was being taught and could not preach on it, so although I graduated I never agreed to be ordained.

In discussing ancient matriarchal perceptions of the divine as Goddess represented in the trinity of Virgin-Mother-Crone, Barbara Walker suggested that the premise of Christianity to reject death required rejecting the Mother manifested in women generally.[4] Life given by Mother is cyclic, not eternal, as desired by ego-dominated men who replaced the Goddess. Fear of death represented fear of the Crone stage of the Goddess, where decisions about life and death were made. As Iain McGilchrist has documented extensively,[5] Western civilization shaped culture to primarily value the conscious, thinking mind—left-brain-hemisphere dominance, oriented to categorizing and controlling static things while detached from relational attunement—the kind of thinking that noncivilized peoples often refuse to do,[6] and the aspect of human functioning that has been characterized by mystical traditions worldwide as dangerous if relied on too much.[7] Valuing emotionally and relationally detached ways of thinking and its accoutrements has come about at the expense of the right hemisphere's emotional, relational, and transpersonal awareness. The inability to tune into transcendent reality, reliant on right-brain-hemisphere functioning that is undermined in civilization's child raising, will make death seem like "the end" rather than a transition to a new beginning. This contrasts with the integrative nature of mystical and spiritual intuition, which, Christian DeQuincey points out, "includes, while transcending, both reason and somatic feeling," something sorely lacking in dominant views.[8] When we have a fully developed and integrated brain (right and left hemisphere together) we understand what Hunter-Ripper describes: *that we are all one and that our essence continues on.*

5

Emphasis on Community Welfare

Doña Enriqueta Contreras (Zapotecan)

I believe each and every one of us has within our hearts a hidden feeling
and that this feeling is moving us to find a channel of energy, light, and
hope. A hope that someday will touch us deeply in our hearts so that we
may see life from another perspective.

I am Zapotecan from the Northern Sierra of the state of Oaxaca. I
speak my own native language. There is a law, considered sacred, that
has been handed down to us from our ancestors. Zapotecan culture in
the Sierra Juárez is based on four life principles: first, everything has life;
second, reverence for Mother Nature; third, reverence for our ancestors;
fourth, the relationship between human beings and Mother Nature. These
four principles have been the foundation of our laws in our communities
for thousands and thousands of years.

Despite the invasion of the Spaniards, and their intention to destroy
our culture and kill off our curanderos (healers), we have survived and
are still here today. This has unified our communities. There is equality
between our communities and between men and women. Beginning from
the nucleus of the family, our grandparents, our ancestors, taught us a
value called "respect." The mutual respect that is found at the heart of the
family has made our communities "united" communities. As the Sierra
Juárez is located to the north, at quite a distance from Oaxaca, we sometimes refer to ourselves as living in the "corner of the forgotten." But our
hearts live and continue to shine because we have preserved and continue
to conserve our culture. And we have preserved all our traditions, despite

our poverty. . . . We are all one: mentally, physically, and spiritually. Let us connect ourselves to the Mother Earth and open our hearts and remember that within us, there is a great and powerful divinity. Because nobody is going to fix this world; it is the women of the world who are going to have to do it. Women must take back their authority.

Source

Doña Enriqueta Contreras. "Matriarchal Values among the Sierra Juárez Zapotecs of Oaxaca." In *Societies of Peace: Matriarchies Past, Present and Future,* edited by Heide Goettner-Abendroth, translated by Mary Margaret Návar, 76–78. Toronto: Ianna Publications and Education, 2009.

Contextualized Biosketch

Doña Enriqueta Contreras (Doña Queta) was born into a family of *curanderos* (healers) but was orphaned as a child. Her adopting parents were neglectful alcoholics, often not providing food for days. This led her to seek food in the landscape, where she learned from experience about the healing powers of plants. She first learned midwifery with goats and became a midwife for human beings at age seventeen. She trained in first aid and became a health worker, traveling great distance on foot or by animal to serve multiple communities in Mexico. She has served as a healer and teacher for over fifty years, applying the wisdom of *curanderismo* (folk healing) of her culture. She teaches her students outdoors on mountain paths, showing them how to recognize the local plants and learn their use.[1]

Indigenous Worldview Precept Dialogue

Darcia: Doña Queta's life gives us some insight into how so much Indigenous knowledge is still "out there," still being taught and experienced. The Europeans did not exterminate American Natives nor their knowledge. Much of the knowledge may be buried deeply. According to Native elders, most of our knowledge comes from the landscape, when we honor, observe, and listen to the other-than-human. My hope is that this land-based knowledge can be a source once again for the rebuilding of our divided communities. We are, despite our living in cities, still on and of the earth.

Attention to community welfare is critical for human survival. Whether we realize it or not, we depend on one another. Attention to the common good is a truly conserving/conservative orientation, as C. A. Bowers noted,[2] but it is not associated with American conservatism. Bowers pointed out that what has been called "conservative" in the USA actually orients to a liberal consumption of everything, a market liberalism ("free markets," little regulation to protect consumers, unfettered corporate power). Bowers suggested a rethinking of what "conservatism" means in light of the current context of ecological crises, suggesting that we should ask ourselves: *What is it we want to conserve?* True conservatism means concern for the well-being of the local ecology—comprising animals, native plants, waterways, forests, and more. This undergirds original, Indigenous wisdom and the practices of First Nation peoples the world over who have lived sustainably but uniquely in their local landscapes for millennia. Before capitalistic pressures, First Nation communities around the world respected the ecologies of their local landscape, or perished.[3]

As an example of Native knowledge, the Kogi of South America had been living out of contact for centuries until 1990, when they contacted a BBC journalist to convey a message to the modern world (the "younger brother"). This message is captured in the film *From the Heart of the World: The Elder Brother's Warning.*[4] Their priests (mamas), raised from babyhood to be deeply attuned to Mother Earth (Aluna), were sensing the weakening of the earth and warned of ecological disasters. "The Great Mother taught us right and wrong. Now they are digging up the Mother's heart, and her eyes and ears. Stop digging and digging. Do not cut down trees—they hurt, like cutting off your own leg. . . . If crops aren't properly blessed, they dry up. . . . That's how it is."[5] A decade or so later after finding their earlier message

unheeded, they created their own film, *Aluna*.[6] In one scene they show
how damming up a river affects the climate up the mountain, something that ecological scientists were just beginning to document. The
science of ecology started at the end of the nineteenth century, but
Native peoples have been practicing it for thousands of years. The Kogi
show us the deep connection to community welfare, not only locally
but globally; ancestral understanding of how earth entities interrelate;
and the know-how to keep the earth flourishing—all characteristics of
First Nation peoples.

Four Arrows: This famous call to the world by the Kogi and how
it was ignored was a tragic moment in time for me.[7] Sometime after-
ward I was in communication with Alan Ereira, the director of the first
documentary, and I could imagine how he felt. I think it is great that
you brought this up as an example of how the Indigenous worldview
truly is all about community welfare. The Kogis' ecological values are a
model for reembedding non-Indigenous communities in Earth-based
kincentricism.

It also reveals how Indigenous peoples, who represent all of our
ancestors, knew how to listen to others. There are many ways that
come to mind from my time with traditional cultures or groups within
cultures that have lost the old ways. Of course, open-mindedness and
courage to hear what one may not want to hear are obvious listening
skills most people know about. Silent praying, however, is one people
rarely consider. Respectful listening often involves pausing after a
strong declaration to just sit quietly, not only reflecting on what was
said, but also seeking a spiritual perspective. I've seen elders even walk
to a place outside when the conversation was indoors to find a sacred
place on the earth or gaze at a star, as if to get help in understanding
what is being communicated.

An example of this more spiritual approach to true listening comes
to mind. Once, when I was in Puerto Rico for a North and South American Indigenous elders conference, a bitter conflict arose between several individuals about which First Nation's names would be at the top
of an important document that was to be sent to the UN or some other

important agency (I don't remember which one now). Each of us was invited because of our stature as leaders, but here we were displaying our worst. A number of us spoke in an effort to bring things back into harmony, but we had let anger bring us into the very Western frame of mind we had long opposed. Things just got worse. I recall seeing the teenage children and grandchildren that were accompanying their parents and grandparents to the week-long conference whispering to one another and getting up respectfully and leaving the room while we continued arguing. The women elder leaders had not participated in the arguing, and I noticed that they had stepped away from the group and formed their own. Then, just about when it looked like the events for the night—which included a healing ceremony at the top of a mountain—were going to be cancelled (and the rest of the week did not look promising either), two spokesmen for the group of teens quietly walked up to the person holding the microphone and asked if they could talk.

I don't remember their words, but I do remember the feeling I got from hearing them. After just a few powerful sentences from each, they asked if we would join them outside. I felt embarrassed and ashamed, as did my colleagues. We quietly followed. The women spiritual leaders did not join us and were sitting with the men's wives, some Indigenous and some not, who had remained sitting in the stadium chairs. I now don't know if it was because they took authority or if, as Doña suggests in her last sentence as being a problem, they relinquished their authority. I do remembering wondering, however, if the wives, not the official members of the negotiating elder group, somehow organized the children or inspired them to take action. Doña's sentence about how women must be the ones that bring back an emphasis on community welfare reminds me of this possibility.

When we arrived at the place they took us to, the rest of the children, not just the teens, were in a line. Each one took a short turn to tell us something that was in one way or the other relevant. I spontaneously started to listen in the old Indigenous ways, with telepathy, compassion, understanding, historical context, fearlessness, with the seventh-generation considerations blossoming in our minds and hearts. I felt this blossoming and confirmed later that this happened to all the others. Then the line of children walked past each of us with their international array of smudging herbs. I remember crying.

Of course, the story has a happy ending. The point is the children, who were to a non-Indian observer unbelievably quiet and respectful during the two previous days of the conference, surprised us with their courageous, insightful actions. Actions that the elders had taught them! And it was all about true listening—listening that keeps us (1) remembering the ultimate, longer-term importance of our decisions and actions; (2) never forgetting our interconnectedness with all; (3) appreciating the nature of feelings and how they often relate to forgetting to accept the unknown; (4) holding on to authentic humility; and (5) remembering who we really are, with great appreciation for those who came before us who did similar work or who have made our work somewhat easier or clearer.

Darcia: Ah, this is so inspirational. The young will lead us, when well-tended. There are so many wonderful messages to take in. I love how you describe the "old Indigenous ways of listening... with telepathy, compassion, understanding, historical context, fearlessness, with the seventh-generation considerations blossoming in our minds and hearts." That is true practical wisdom. I am reminded of the characteristics that Jon Young ascribes to a healthy person,[8] which Young and colleagues have learned from collaborating with First Nation peoples around the world:

- A quiet mind—emotionally present and creative
- Inner (childlike) happiness
- Vitality—an abundance of energy
- Unconditional listening
- Empathically connected to the world
- Humble

- Generous

- Authentically helpful—uses gifts to "pay it forward"

- Fully alive—aware of the sacredness of all

- Loving—compassionate and forgiving

I wish our leaders today demonstrated these characteristics. But in too many civilized cultures, we have undermined the development of wisdom with the mistreatment of babies, including punishing them for their "original sin," distorting development with underground feelings of deep insecurity, anger, and fear. Consequently, without opportunities for healing, the person is not going to be very oriented to community welfare, human or other-than-human. As James Clark Moloney wrote: "A baby frustrated too often during his state of preverbal helplessness is well on the way toward developing enduring and crippling feelings of ugliness, inferiority, and futility."[9] It is hard to care for the community of life if you do not feel cared for.

Four Arrows: I just reread Doña Queta's opening quote and our dialogue to see how I could best conclude this chapter. Three things popped up that seemed interconnected somehow. The first is Doña Queta's sentence, "Let us connect ourselves to the Mother Earth and open our hearts." The second is Jon Young's descriptor of typical traditional Indigenous adults around the world having an "inner childlike happiness," something I have been observing for several decades. The third is how you, as the world's foremost developmental psychologist and scholar of how early life experience influences the ultimate well-being and morality of adults and cultures, have come to make connections between traditional Indigenous approaches to care for children and the existence of such a childlike inner happiness, even in challenging environments. Then my mind jumped to Augustine Ramos, the 102-year-old Rarámuri shaman, for whom an inner childlike joyfulness was a most prominent feature, not to mention vitality and fitness sufficient to walk twenty miles of difficult terrain to help a child recover from a fever.

I pondered on what my mind's foci on these four things meant in terms of what to say, and it came to me that it had to do with the *vibrational frequency* one feels when one is genuinely part of a healthy, happy community *that is connected to the land and its creatures.* Then it hit me that where Augustine lived and where Doña Queta grew up, Sierra Juárez, are both in the Sierra Madre, not far from one another. Both places are inhabited by traditional Indigenous cultures who against all odds hold on to their old ways and are intrinsically part of their surroundings. When in such places, one literally *feels* interconnected. I think it is a main part of Doña Queta's message. As she might say, community health requires a sacred relationship to Mother Earth.

There is something in our electromagnetic field that is disruptive to harmony. I feel it sitting here in front of the computer for hours writing, in contrast to stepping outside and smelling the ocean breeze or standing next to the cactus. There does seem to be a vibration, a rhythm that influences how social relationships change in relationship to nature-culture dynamics. I wonder if anyone has studied how communities surrounded by trees and birds fare in contrast to those surrounded by concrete and glass. Of course, Pino Gordo, where I lived with Augustine and the Rarámuri, as I describe in *Primal Awareness,* is an extreme example of maximum nature-culture interaction. To get there it is at least sixty miles from Agua Azúl by foot across some of the most difficult mountainous terrain imaginable.[10] There the Rarámuri *gentiles* who had rejected Christianity and maintained their original animist beliefs were safe from *narcotraficantes* who in many other areas have invaded villages and forced the Natives to grow opium poppies instead of beans and corn, killing those who resist.

Claire Revol does a great job of explaining Henri Lefebvre's challenging writings on "rhythmanalysis" as they relate to rhythm differences between traditional societies and modern ones. She explains how "cyclic rhythms compose the temporalities of agrarian and traditional societies, in which repetitions of periods in social life are ritualized to become part of symbolic exchanges between life and death, of the cosmic relationship of the community to the earth."[11] She describes how Lefbvre shows that these rhythms correspond to natural and vital ones that are predominant in Indigenous communities. "Natural and vital rhythms are predominant in archaic societies, linked to ancient symbols that ritualize social practices, introducing rhythms in order to include individuals in a community," she writes. However, in modern civilization, which is full of linear repetition, rhythms bring about tiredness and alienation. She writes that Lefebvre sees modernity as a process of abstraction, "as it introduces linear temporalities marked by the advent of machines, and above all clocks, representing a time that is fictitiously homogeneous and fragmentable."

All this tells us that a worldview that promotes feminine leadership, sees children as sacred beings, and connects us to the natural world is the path to healthy communities!

6

High Respect for the Sacred Feminine

Paula Gunn Allen (Laguna Pueblo; 1939–2008)

If American society judiciously modeled the traditions of the various Native Nations, the place of women in society would become central, the distribution of goods and power would be egalitarian, the elderly would be respected, honored, and protected as a primary social and cultural resource, the ideals of physical beauty would be considerably enlarged. Additionally, the destruction of the biota, the life sphere, and the natural resources of the planet would be curtailed, and the spiritual nature of human and nonhuman life would become a primary organizing principle of human society. And if the traditional tribal systems that are emulated included pacifist ones, war would cease to be a major method of human problem solving.

The belief that rejection of tradition and of history is a useful response to life is reflected in America's amazing loss of memory concerning its origins in the matrix and context of Native America. . . . America is ignorant of the genesis of its culture and that ignorance helps to perpetuate the long-standing European and Middle Eastern monotheistic, hierarchical, patriarchal cultures' oppression of women, gays, lesbians, people of color, working class, unemployed people, and the elderly. . . .

Even though Indians are officially and informally ignored as intellectual movers and shapers in the United States, Britain and Europe, they are peoples with ancient tenure on this soil. During the ages when tribal societies existed in the Americas largely untouched by patriarchal

oppression, they developed elaborate systems of thought that included sci-
ence, philosophy, and government based on a belief in the central impor-
tance of female energies, autonomy of individuals, cooperation, human
dignity, human freedom and egalitarian distribution of status, goods, and
services. Respect for others, reverence for life, and, as a by-product, paci-
fism as a way of life; importance of kinship ties in the customary ordering
of social interaction; a sense of the sacredness and mystery of existence;
balance and harmony in relationships both sacred and secular were all
features of life among the tribal confederacies and nations. And in those
that lived by the largest number of these principles, gynarchy was the norm
rather than the exception. Those systems are as yet unmatched in any con-
temporary industrial, agrarian, or postindustrial society on earth.

Source

Paula Gunn Allen. *The Sacred Hoop: Recovering the Feminine in American Indian Tra-*
ditions. Boston: Beacon Press Books, 1992, 210–11.

Contextualized Biosketch

Paula Gunn Allen's father was Lebanese, and her mother was Laguna
Pueblo-Métis. She received her PhD in American studies from the
University of New Mexico and was a professor of Native American and
ethnic studies at the University of California, Berkeley. Her book *Poca-*
hontas: Medicine Woman, Spy, Entrepreneur, Diplomat (2004, Harper-
Collins), received a Pulitzer Prize nomination. *The Sacred Hoop:*
Recovering the Feminine in American Indian Traditions (1986, Beacon),
a collection of critical essays, is a cornerstone in the study of American
Indian culture and gender.

Indigenous Worldview Precept Dialogue

Four Arrows: Reading Paula Gunn Allen's opening words should give
all men pause. It is men who have pulled the triggers in most police

shootings of people of color. The mass shootings and most daily murders are done by men. If we studied war, we would find a similar problem from the top administration to the man in the trenches. Men and the corporations mostly led by men are also responsible for the pollution of Mother Nature. I believe there is a better than 60 percent chance that if non-Indigenous women had had more sway during the past hundred years, we would have had fewer wars. We might not be facing climate change nor in the midst of a pandemic. I would guess if traditional Indigenous women had had sway, even over other women leaders, the 60 percent would reach 95 percent.

So much for my imaginings. We do know that the majority of pre-contact societies meet the criteria for being peaceful and living in unpolluted environments.[1] We know even today that extinction rates are significantly less or absent where traditional Indigenous people have control of the land, according to a May 2019 biodiversity report issued by the UN.[2] And we know that most Native cultures were matri-archal. Even in the patriarchal ones, the woman's voice was strong. It might also explain why Indigenous origin stories about how humans should live in the world are so filled with female characters, such as Hard Beings Woman (Hopi), Sky Woman (Iroquois/Seneca), She Who Thinks (Keres), Thought Woman (Acoma Pueblo), White Buffalo Calf Woman (Lakota), Spider Woman (Navajo), Corn Woman (Cherokee), Deer Woman (Ojibwe), and many more.

And yet, in spite of Mother Earth traditions and the feminine principle being woven into all aspects of our original worldview, Western hegemony has managed to remove the significance of female power in almost every domain, including conservation, farming, economics, peaceful societies, child-rearing, science, and politics. In the anthology *Unlearning the Language of Conquest,* Seneca scholar Barbara Alice Mann closes her chapter—titled "Where Are Your Women? Missing in Action"—with a call for correcting this problem that is more urgent today than when she wrote it: "In the twenty-first century, it is incumbent upon scholars (especially Native American!) to rectify the Western obliteration of women from the record, surely the most unconscionable of the many misrepresentations that have been foisted upon Native America by Euro-America."[3]

Darcia: Allen's statement and your comments are beautiful renderings of what we have lost and how far we have fallen away from longstanding sustainable societies that were matriarchal. Goettner-Abendroth points out that while the term "patriarchy" is associated with domination by males,[4] the etymology of *arche* in "matriarchy," because of women's ability to grow life, better refers to "from the beginning" or the "original pattern from which models are made," the meaning related to *arche* in "archetype."[5] She writes: "Lacking a clear scientific definition of 'matriarchy,' the term has been misunderstood as 'rule by women,' provoking a lasting, ideologically distorted prejudice against it. The field of modern matriarchal studies reorients the field with more precise definitions."[6] Matriarchal societies are centralized around the feminine principle that sources the beginning of every human's life. So matriarchy does not refer to "ruling over" but to egalitarianism and freedom for both genders through complementary functions. Goettner-Abendroth identified the characteristics of matriarchies around the world: economic mutuality and a gift economy; matrilineal, nondomination kinship; egalitarian consensus; and sacred cultures of the feminine divine.[7] All these characteristics seem to match up with the Indigenous worldview we are discussing.

Historian Marvin Bram described how Western civilizations largely reshaped culture and the Western mind.[8] Prior to the Sumer civilization and subsequent civilizations, human societies shifted between polysemy, a multisensory participation in a living, permeable world, and univocity, linear logical thought used to solve a specific problem with conscious cause-and-effect analysis. Polysemic mentalization does not make differentiations between self and others, including particular animals, plants, or natural entities (e.g., rivers), whereas univocity is all about differentiation, categorizing, and creating hierarchies. Western history, as Bram tells it, is a story about the suppression of polysemy and dominance of univocity, which parallels the suppression of the feminine principle of cycling through birth, life, death, and rebirth. In contrast, patriarchy focuses on linear progress and conquering nature/death, robbing the fullness of the "now" to worry about controlling the future.

Even with the rise of patriarchy and the diminishment of women's status over millennia, according to historian Carolyn Merchant some European cultural groups still considered the earth to be alive and sacred until the sixteenth century, when a mechanistic view took over and "the female earth and virgin earth spirit were subdued by the machine."[9] The view of a sacred earth continued to erode with commercial and technological expansion. This is an illustration of how actions shape attitudes. I am reminded of how this was documented among a forest people by David Naveh and Nurit Bird-David, who studied the Nayaka of India.[10] When first visited, the Nayaka were forest dwellers who treated the local animals as persons. After years of pressure from government and nongovernment officials, the Nayaka were convinced to raise animals to sell. When the anthropologists returned, they observed that those animals were no longer treated as persons. Nayaka attitudes changed based on their behavior. In a way, their shift may also display the paradox of power. Research shows that when humans have more power than others, they lose empathy for the less powerful and treat them as inferiors.[11] This may be why small-band hunter-gatherers were fiercely egalitarian and would not tolerate anyone puffing themselves up—they knew it was dangerous to themselves and the biocommunity.[12] Dominant humans today, through political, corporate, religious, and legal structures, have often violated this principle, valuing men more than women, valuing masculine over feminine values.

Four Arrows: I love your short explanation of Bram's description about the loss of "polysemic mentalization," a term I had never come across before. The timeline fits with what I say in *Point of Departure,* a book for which you wrote the foreword. Things started going south early, and by 3000 BC Europe was fully engaged in the dominant worldview, at least functionally, giving credit to some holdout farmers who may still have prayed for the lost wildlife. In the middle Bronze

Age, most of Europe was exploited, cultivated, and overpopulated, and hoarding was rampant.[13] Jump forward to pre-Christian and early Christian Europe, and one quickly realizes it was not a golden age for women. Then in 1492, when men saw how well women were treated by the American Indians, well, I won't go there.

This is why it is difficult for me to accept the Merchant reference about Europe still seeing the earth as "alive and sacred" until the sixteenth century. I remember Merchant's wonderful, inspiring book and how it was full of stories, but I remember even when I first read it in the late 1990s, I felt it possessed too much, I don't know, positive thinking or too much subjective creativity. So I looked just now at the page you quote from it because it still gives me pause. Europe seeing sacredness in Mother Earth and/or in women has too many leaks in it. I won't go so far as to say it "won't hold water," but not enough to bring home. Nonetheless, your main point is that when some humans feel they have more power than others, "they lose empathy for the less powerful and treat them as inferiors." This, of course, is why anthropocentrism is so dangerous to the world, because humans at large feel superior to an ant, which allows less empathy for any creature that is not human.

Since all Indigenous worldview precepts are inseparably interconnected, it is difficult to avoid talking about a given precept in chapters about other precepts. However, I want to suggest a hypothesis put forth by Howard Teich (which we'll discuss in a later chapter) that the very words we use for "men" and "women" in European languages prevent us from achieving a more natural understanding of their relationship.[14] For example, in Dakota and Lakota thought, the word for woman is *winyan,* which represents the concept of woman as "First Spirit," implying a sacred creation foundation of all people. The word for man, *wicasa,* conveys "protector." When used together they represent a sacred complementarity such as the natural world's ultimate partnership between the sun and the moon. This offers a deeper way of understanding what Paula Allen is saying.

Darcia: I love the Lakota and Dakota terms. I'm reminded of Charlotte Black Elk's description of the Lakota creation story.[15] After creating the growing and moving, the winged and the four-legged, Earth Mother created her special child two-legged child Mato, the bear, to whom she gave wisdom. After that she created one who could make choices and who is complete *(winyan)*, the woman. After that she created the one who is a step from completion, the man *(wicasa)*. That's a different take on creation from the usual understanding, eh?!

I think the focus on property, the focus of herding and agricultural societies, played a large role in removing balance from gender relations. Did you know that when men are around young children, they have lower testosterone (and higher empathy)?[16] Our longstanding heritage is to live in multi-gender, multi-age groups. But with herding and hierarchy, men get isolated from children, so their testosterone will rise, just like a tribal raiding party will separate itself for a few days from the community to build up their "energy" for the raid. In high-income nations, the mostly male leaders spend lots of time with other adult men, increasing rivalry, lowering empathy. Maybe we should recommend babies in every workplace!

On the other side, mothers are more attentive to their children's needs when they feel the support of the community.[17] Among First Nation peoples traditionally, the village raised the children, not just mothers or parents. Mothering is initially a unilateral gift-giving to the child, a nurturing orientation that comes naturally to mothers and everyone in gift economies.[18] In monocultural agricultural civilizations, when mothers started to work in fields (and later, factories) instead of going gathering with community members and their children as was done in hunter-gatherer communities, they did less mothering. All children are affected, but boys in particular are affected by the quality of nurturing because they have less built-in resilience and mature more slowly.[19] So they need *more* of humanity's evolved nest, which includes years of breastfeeding, carrying, and co-sleeping— aspects of parenting linked to societal peaceableness.[20]

In patriarchal societies and especially industrialized societies, all children are offered much less of the evolved nest. Mothering, and nurturing generally, is crippled. Saint Augustine is credited for advancing the notion of original sin and attributing it to the nature of babies,[21] a notion that was taken up and used to encourage denial and punishment of children by Protestant denominations in particular, and that took hold especially in the United States.[22] Distressing a baby intensely or routinely seeds physical and/or psychological illness, including less self-regulation and less socioemotional intelligence and more of a dominance-submission orientation to relationships.[23] Punishing children has long-term negative outcomes.[24] In industrialized societies today, everyone is suffering from not enough mothering, degraded over millennia because women's power to mother was taken away—by ideology, work, culture. Despite increasing neurobiological evidence for its importance, quality mothering has been increasingly dismissed by a technological, mechanistic, capitalistic, patriarchal worldview.

Instead of accepting the cyclical nature of life, men invented a progressive linear religion, associated with hierarchy and control of underlings through promises of a heavenly reward for obedient behavior. Rosemary Ruether writes, "Male eschatology is built on negation of the mother. . . . The escape from sex and birth is ultimately an attempt to escape from death for which women as Eve and mother are made responsible. Male eschatology combines male womb envy with womb negation."[25] Philosopher Christian DeQuincey writes that parents and children "have been seduced by a system of education that trains all of us to neglect and deny our deepest instincts toward ourselves and toward our children . . . [a] severe shock of amputation from the natural relationship between mother and child. The price we pay is high: stunted emotional and spiritual growth of our children—and as adults, we carry the scars."[26]

The earth, too, carries the scars. To restore the feminine sacred means honoring all the stages of life—birth, life, death, and transformation into new life—in earth communities generally and among humans specifically.

How the Indigenous worldview uses such earth communities to honor women is embedded in the Indigenous languages. This story told by Alex White Plume, one of the remaining speakers and teachers of Lakota and former president of the Oglala Lakota, explains this in his interview with Amy Goodman on *Democracy Now:*[27]

> And I'll share a story about how I asked to marry her. I was sitting at the house. And her grandfather's name was Mark Big Road. And we spoke Lakota. So, we were sitting in the living room and just enjoying a discussion, and she was sitting at the table. So, in Lakota, I ask Uncle Mark, "How do you ask a woman to marry you in Lakota?" And he just laughed and laughed. And she kind of looked up at me with one eye. And he said, "You know, you can't take a woman and own her. You can't declare her your wife. Our Lakota women are matriarchs, and they have power that you can't control. And so I recommend to you that you sing a beautiful song. And if she likes the song, maybe she'll marry you." So, at the table, she was sitting there. I looked at her, and I sang a song that I knew. And here, she looked at me. She says, "OK, White Plume, I'll take you for my man."
>
> And so, what Uncle Mark described was the description of marriage. It's called *tawicuton. Tawicuton—ta* means "his"; *wi* is the sun; *cu,* you take part of the sun to create life. That is our definition of married people, two people living together. And that's so important. It's so different from the word "married." You say "my wife" like you own a woman. That's just contrary to Lakota belief. So, therefore, the Lakota language is real important. It's a natural language that evolved over millions of years, with many different other species that were existing at the time.

7

Respect for Gender Role Fluidity

Laura Hall (Haudenosaunee)

*The violence enacted against Indigenous women and Two-Spirit/
LGBTQ people evokes deep questions about the intent and impact
of colonization in a Canadian settler and state context. The horrors of
colonial violence—bodies were violated and abandoned at the sides of
highways, in ditches, in rivers—tell stories of the vital importance of Indigenous women's leadership, their warriorhood, their gifts and their medicines, and also of the centrality of gendered freedom and fluid belonging
in Indigenous cultures. It is a system of colonization that seeks to erase
and subsume these realities and to replace Indigenous truth with illusions
of our weakness. We are at a pivotal moment now as state and settler
voices seek to understand what is needed, and it is a pivotal moment best
informed by threads of anarchist and feminist thought woven within
Indigenous worldviews. Vital intersections are made between gender and
Indigeneity because the conversation is always in danger of being rerouted
by policing and state voices, as well as settler voices. The work that Indigenous women and Two-Spirit/LGBTQ people do on the ground—to renew
our connections to culture, to renew the innovations and economies of our
nations—needs more support in every way, from allies across intellectual
lines. . . . Indigenous worldview presents an alternative vision that ensures
environmental sustainability, gendered equity and fluidity. . . . Addressing
the nature of heterosexism and misogyny, or "heteropatriarchy" remains
central to decolonization efforts. This work continues to be rooted in the
whole cultural and environmental context of Indigenous knowledge.*

Source

Laura Hall. "Indigenist Intersectionality: Decolonizing an Indigenous Eco-Queer Feminism and Anarchism." Institute for Anarchist Studies, February 15, 2017. https://anarchiststudies.org/indigenist-intersectionality-decolonizing-an -Indigenous-eco-queer-feminism-and-anarchism-by-laura-hall/.

Contextualized Biosketch

Laura Hall identifies as having Haudenosaunee (Kanienkehaka) and British roots. She grew up and learned on Anishinaabe territory in Northern Ontario. A champion of promoting Indigenous worldview, she holds a PhD in environmental studies, with an emphasis on Haudenosaunee community planning. Her work utilizes a decolonizing intersectional lens that necessarily prioritizes and centers the concerns of Indigenous peoples, inclusive of the return of their lands and full cultural autonomy. For many years she has directed a nonprofit relating to land-based education for Indigenous people, with an emphasis on safe spaces for Indigenous youth, LGBTQ+ individuals, and women. As an assistant professor at Laurentian University, she has conducted research on Indigenous environmental theory and practice, social justice, and health and well-being through Indigenous cultural interventions.

Indigenous Worldview Precept Dialogue

Four Arrows: There is so much to unpack in this section from Hall's article about how the Indigenous worldview's emphasis on the sacred feminine, diversity, and interconnectedness relates to regard for personal gender identity. For me, one thing that stands out is how yet another problem of colonization relates to how dominant-worldview-oriented civilization has oppressed women and nonbinary-identifying individuals. It is especially tragic to me because it is more widespread, not just violent oppression by white males. The forced colonization of Indigenous communities has caused many Indigenous men, even traditionally minded ones, to follow suit. My goal in this section is to argue that the traditional Indigenous worldview, despite controversial interpretations of diverse First Nations' origin stories, if followed, would not allow for such oppression and violence. Because I have some personal experience with Navajos around this topic, I want to support my contention by briefly referring to a document that discussed this issue comprehensively with regard to the Navajo nation.

Between 2014 and 2016, the Navajo Nation Human Rights Commission did a study on Navajo women and gender violence.[1] Many people testified before the commission. Most spoke about respect of women in a matrilineal society, where the feminine plays a powerful role in origin stories. Dismay over crimes against women was unequivocal. Similar attitudes regarding violence against LGBTQ+ Navajo individuals prevailed as well, of course. However, support for recognition and/ or acceptance of nonbinary-identifying individuals was mixed. Some traditionalists did not support allowing anyone but heterosexual men and women to be married, according to Navajo traditional marriage, saying the ancient laws were clearly about procreation.

However, in many oral origin stories of Indigenous peoples around the world, sacred beings sometimes were hermaphrodites. Some of the beings changed back and forth between sexes. Other traditionalists at the hearing used such stories to support respect and inclusion of nonbinary individuals in the Navajo Nation.

One medicine man stated that LGBTQ+ people should not draw upon the *nádleehí* traditional stories as a way to affirm their presence and roles "because they have not been exposed to Navajo traditional thought." (The *nádleehí* were historical mythological figures who had fluidity between genders, whether gay or lesbian, using today's terms.) However, there was agreement that "there is evidence for claims that pre-contact Indigenous societies included gender non-conforming people who may or may not have conformed to the definitions of who LGBTQI are today," the commission's report states. Indeed, the report cited numerous studies about how this is true for many Indigenous cultures. As for nonbinary sexual activity, not much was discussed before the commission, but because sexual freedom is a high value in matriarchal societies, in traditional times it would not have been problematic.

Another medicine person who spoke was Marie Salt. She affirmed that Navajo sacred stories, ceremonies, chants, prayers, and songs are fundamental teachings that secure the survival of Navajo people. She said the teachings show that it is the woman's responsibility to "orchestrate a nurturing holistic environment that maximizes the opportunity for the success of her children, her government and her people" by always weighing thought and action to ensure that they lead to balance. She concluded that discussions about violence against women and gender would not be happening if this role of women was still respected and employed. Medicine woman Rita Gilmore referred to the twin children of First Man and First Woman, saying: "The twins were clothed in both male and female clothes as their gender identity was unclear. The twins were male and found to transform themselves and thus were referred to as 'nadleeli' (transformers). . . . The twins would never be able to father a child or give birth, as they were formed in a spiritual manner."[2]

Throughout the report it is made clear that domestic violence against women in Indian country, abuse of Indigenous women by white men, and violence against LGBTQ+ individuals by both whites and Navajos are products of European colonization. "This includes colonization and how European and Christian influences changed the view of sexuality," the report says.[3] What is especially disturbing to me is how even Navajo traditionalists, people striving to bring back respect for ceremony and language, can interpret the origin stories, such as those handed down to them from their grandfathers, in ways that are hostile to LGBTQ+ people. They believe LGBTQ+ people violate the goal of balance between men and women on behalf of procreation. I am convinced that this represents the colonization—a legacy from Christian boarding schools to contemporary schooling and the dominant culture—that has made its way into the language itself, and continues to do so.

Darcia: This makes me very sad. To squelch life is to commit a sin against creation. I'm afraid the poison of colonization, in all its crimes, has pushed some Indigenous elders to take up the mistaken notions purveyed by the colonizers. The history of child neglect and abuse gets passed on neurobiologically. When neurobiology is misdeveloped, you move toward self-protectionist mindsets and attitudes. Your vision, perception, and affordances (action possibilities) narrow. In order to feel safe, you have to follow scripts you've learned, something that worked in the past. These are governed by reactive survival systems, which are enhanced when young children are miscared for.[4]

Physicist David Bohm expressed what Indigenous wisdom understands.[5] The world is one of dynamic unity; everything is connected and interacting, with no separable or static objects. Barry Commoner noted this to be the first law of ecology.[6] Bohm demonstrated that the universe consists of interwoven vibratory energies of different kinds—the implicate order. Whatever is manifested in the explicate order is already enfolded in the energy of the implicate order. The implicate order is consciousness (a notion that directly corresponds with Indigenous thought) and has far greater power than any explicit manifestation. The whole physical universe, emerging from complex mathematical frequencies in the implicate order, is a mere ripple in consciousness, for the implicate order has vastly more powerful energies within it.

According to Bohm, there are two kinds of thought. There are thoughts generated by one's own brain, and then there is insight-intelligence, generated and given to us by a "deeper mind." At the core of the implicate order is "insight-intelligence"—a *state,* not a place—and the source of creativity, which he calls "holomovement." This kind of intelligence requires letting go of narrow, egoistic attention so we can become open to communications from outside the self. This idea corresponds to what wisdom traditions say is necessary to reach a state of wisdom.[7] Bohm pointed out how we get trapped in our schemas or conceptual structures of thought that arose in early life but subsequently shape our perceptions, attitudes, thinking, and approach to the world. As Joseph Chilton Pearce explains, humanity's typical problem is a "closed circuit, tape-looped effect of the brain, wherein the brain feeds on its own output, so to speak, rather than on insight-intelligence," thus losing "its connection with consciousness and insight."[8] Thought isolated from the implicate order seeks prediction and control, leading to chaos and confusion. "Only thought which results from alignment with the holonomic movement can itself be orderly, and creative. (Order is creation.)"[9]

Colonizers use explicate-order concepts that do not fit dynamic reality. Thus, the way most of us are raised and socialized encourages us to get caught in an enclosed feedback loop of cultural distortion. The idea of a static world full of separated objects has caused endless problems as experts isolate fragments of reality and take actions that do not account for their impact on the whole. And then they try to fix the symptom instead of the cause of the problem, creating more problems. If we don't step back from our own ego involvement in an opinion or action, we can actually perpetuate misinformation and error, factors that underlie all the human problems we face. Sociocultural beliefs are part of the distortion.

It's not part of our species' hominid heritage to shun difference. In our ancestral context—small-band hunter-gatherers—individuals have high autonomy and high communalism.[10] Coercion is grounds for breaking relationship, and if too harmful, the perpetrator would be banished or killed for the good of the community. "Freedom to be" is a fundamental principle.

Four Arrows: We could teach an entire term based on only what you have so powerfully expressed in these six paragraphs, starting with talking about colonization's influence narrowing "affordances," which I understand is how humans alter environments to suit them better. As you explain with your wonderful references, when we lived in recognition of our deep interconnectedness with all surrounding life, changing landscapes via fire or mulching had mutual benefits for all. With the artificiality, hierarchy, and violence of colonization, our fear-based egos seek protection from distorted scripts. Going back to reacquaint myself with James Gibson's work, the psychologist who coined the idea of affordances, I came upon this definition from Don Norman, which I feel dovetails with your points. He says, "An affordance is a relationship between the properties of an object and the capabilities of the agent that determine just how the object could possibly be used."[11] The colonized mind sees natural diversity as property or objects to be used rather than sentient living beings, based on explicate-order concepts that do not fit reality.

It is incredibly sad when traditionalists use or interpret Indigenous languages in ways that reflect historical trauma, cultural and educational hegemony, media, and Western religion to hold on to the left-brain's "narrow, egoistic attention," to quote you again. Of course, it is understandable in light of the continuing pressures that stand against the more holistic, Indigenous approach to life. Last night I watched an old movie on Geronimo that was far more accurate than I expected it to be. As an old man, he speaks to a "civilized" nephew who says he would rather have died in battle than live like a white man. Geronimo tells him to continue the struggle because "it is easy to die in a world we understand, but more difficult to live in a world we do not." He advises his nephew to keep the Apache worldview alive by learning both worlds.

I think this sentiment is what Laura Hall is talking about when she says, "It is a system of colonization that seeks to erase and subsume these realities and to replace Indigenous truth with illusions of our weakness." Such illusions are at play when an Indigenous person, despite wanting to practice traditional beliefs, nonetheless misinterprets or modifies them owing to external colonizing hegemonic education that divides and conquers and replaces respect for diversity with mandates for "the one right way."

Darcia: Oh, yes. It's not weakness we find in diversity, but strength. Darwin, from his observations leading to a theory of evolution, pointed out that evolution turned on greater and greater diversity, "endless forms most beautiful."[12] Acclaimed poet and author Barry Lopez wrote that diversity is *necessary* for life, for survival, as protection against extinction.[13] It is civilization's capitalism, industrialism, and authoritarianism that desire sameness, which makes things easier to predict and control—the goal of univocity and de-differentiation of life's dynamic diversity.[14] Stiff-mindedness is promoted in such systems. If you fall outside the cherished categories, you will be ignored or abused. Feeling superior to others is one of the dangerous ideas that seeds conflict and abuse.[15] I am reminded of the HIV/AIDS crisis in the 1980s, which was dismissed contemptuously as a gay disease and not tackled directly for much of a decade—so many creative souls were lost. Similar things happened with the 2020 pandemic in the USA. Nonwhite workers in some cases (e.g., meatpacking plants) were designated essential workers but not given adequate protection from the COVID-19 virus, so many sickened and died.

Remember how when Native Americans first encountered Europeans, after a friendly welcome, they found the invaders to be soulless? Many Europeans exhibited the *wétiko* (a psychic virus), aggression against other living things to conquer, exploit, and ultimately destroy them.[16] It's a psychological disease running rampant in modern industrialized civilization characterized by an inability to recognize and receive the living other, whether human or other-than-human. The heart-sense is deadened. In my view, the heart-sense or heart-mind was not nourished in childhood by the evolved nest,[17] so individuals become more robopathic (emotionally empty, machinelike),[18] or even sociopathic,[19] in their orientations to life.

As philosopher and novelist Iris Murdoch described,[20] one's metaphysics (worldview) guides one's morals. Worldview guides awareness, which is value laden. Worldview draws our attention to some things and not others, shapes action possibilities (affordances), helps us evaluate what is good and not good. The Indigenous worldview we are discussing in this book is one of open possibility and ongoing self-transformation. Thus, when our conceptual structures or schemas about what it means to be a human being are challenged, we can regroup, regrow, expand. Murdoch writes: "But our freedom is not just a freedom to choose and act differently, it is also a freedom to think and believe differently, to see the world differently, to see different configurations and describe them in different words. Moral differences can be differences of concept as well as differences of choice."[21]

We can make the choice to let go of old ideas, misinformed ideas, exclusionary ideas, and open and expand our heart-sense. Everyone is welcome in the expanded, heart-connected community.

8

Nonmaterialistic Barter, Gift, and Kinship Economics

Rebecca Adamson (Cherokee)

*T*he interdependency of humankind, the relevance for relationship, the sacredness of creation is returning as a fact of life. It is ancient, ancient wisdom. More than any single issue, economic development is the battle line between two competing worldviews. Tribal people's fundamental value was with sustainability and they conducted their livelihoods in ways that sustained resources and limited inequalities in their society. What made traditional economies so radically different and so very fundamentally dangerous to western economies were the traditional principles of prosperity of creation versus scarcity of resources, of sharing and distribution versus accumulation and greed, of kinship usage rights versus individual exclusive ownership rights, and of sustainability versus growth.

In the field of economic development, economists like to think western economics is value-neutral, but the fact is, it is not. What does the finance system tell us about function and form, about our very values, when the same system pays a merger acquisitionist millions of dollars and a teacher $40,000? The Cartesian reductionist approach defined success according to production units or monetary worth. The contrast with successful Indigenous development is stark.

For example, because the Northern Cheyenne understand the environ-ment to be a living being, they have opposed coal strip mining on their reservation because it kills the water beings. There are no cost measure-ments of pollution, production, or other elements that can capture this kind of impact. There is an emerging recognition of the need for a spiritual base, not only in our individual lives, but also in our work and in our communities. Perfect harmony and balance with the laws of the universe means that we all know that the way of life is found by protecting the water beings. The Indigenous understanding has its basis of spirituality and recognition of the interconnectedness and interdependence of all living things—a holistic and balanced view of the world. All things are bound together, all things connect.

Source

Rebecca Adamson. "First Nations Survival and the Future of the Earth." In *Original Instructions,* edited by Melissa K. Nelson, 33–34. Rochester, VT: Bear & Co., 2008. Based on a talk given at Bioneers 2000.

Contextualized Biosketch

Rebecca Adamson, who holds an MS in economics, advocates for Indigenous rights and economic development. Growing up with her Cherokee mother and visiting her Cherokee grandmother in North Carolina, she absorbed the woman power of her matrilineal society. She implements Indigenous ways as "fundamental design princi-ples" for incentivizing good behavior. After studying philosophy and economics, she sought to bring about new models that integrate the approach and problem solving of Indigenous peoples with the tech-nology of the Western world, bringing about the First Nations Devel-opment Institute, which later birthed First Peoples Worldwide, which provides microloans to Indigenous communities to enhance their own sovereignty. She was a founding member of Native Americans in

Philanthropy, Funders Who Fund Native Americans, and International Funders for Indigenous Peoples. She seeks to build a global political machinery by interconnecting the thousands of Indigenous grassroots communities aiming for change. Sought widely as an adviser by politicians and Native peoples, she was named one of the most influential women in the USA by the PBS documentary *Makers: Women Who Make America.*

Indigenous Worldview Precept Dialogue

Darcia: Adamson speaks of harmony and balance, prosperity and sharing. In his book *The Gift: Imagination and the Erotic Life of Property,* Lewis Hyde begins by discussing the misunderstanding of gift exchange by Europeans who landed in the Americas, which led to the term "Indian giver."[1] Among gift economies like those of Native Americans, gifts are not considered private property but things that are always in the process of movement. A gift is *not* to be kept but is rather to be given to members of the community in the pattern the local group has established. Among gift economies, which occur all over the world, the cardinal property of a gift is for it to be given away, not kept, to keep the gift alive and the momentum going, a momentum of imbalance. A person who removes property from circulation is the opposite of an "Indian giver": a keeper (Daniel Quinn's "taker").[2] Hyde speaks of gift exchange as erotic (Eros), promoting involvement and union. Just as libido does not diminish when given away, so too is gift exchange enlivening, filling one with energy of connection. Capitalist economics, built on Logos (logic), work differently, whereby market exchange establishes an equilibrium or stasis. Money exchanged for a good cannot be a gift and adds nothing to the social fabric. In fact, when things are counted and priced, wealth cannot flow. Only a few people accumulate heaps of things. And market exchange builds an appetite for more and more.

I invite the reader to imagine *not* spending most of the time thinking about things—earning money to get stuff, shopping, organizing, arranging, using, cleaning, guarding, replacing stuff—what most people in consumerist cultures are encouraged to spend their time doing. Notice the dozens of messages a day that tell you that "everyone is doing it." There is little sense of how much harm such a lifestyle is doing. You are encouraged to admire the rich and famous as role models, fostering a hunger in you. You may notice that the more you focus on the things you have, the less rich are your relationships with others.[3]

The video *Enoughness,*[4] which Adamson's group First Peoples Worldwide funded, is helpful to watch to get a quick sense of the Indigenous way of approaching life. I'd also like to quote Yankton Dakota elder, Ella Deloria, who contrasts the two approaches:[5]

The aim of the old Dakota economic system and that of the white man's are one and the same, incongruous as that sounds when we compare the two systems for achieving it. Security, that was the aim: food, clothing, shelter, and an old age free from want. All peoples need that; it is what they struggle for in their respective ways.

But the two systems in question are irreconcilable. They go counter to each other. One says in effect: "Get, get, get now; all you can, as you can, for yourself, and so ensure security for yourself. If all will do this, then everyone will be safe." And it depends on things, primarily.

The other said: "Give, give, give to others. Let gifts flow freely out and they will flow freely back to you again. In the universal and endless stream of giving this is bound to be so." And that system depended on human beings—friends, relatives.

As Genevieve Vaughan points out, patriarchal capitalism parasitically relies on free gifts (e.g., Indigenous lands, natural "resources," laborer work, "housewife" work) to transform them into capital, turning gifts into forms of artificial exchange.[6] Vaughan notes: "Abundance is necessary for the successful practice of gift giving. Exchange competes with gift giving by capturing the abundance, channeling it into the hands of the few or wasting it, thus creating scarcity for the many. Gift giving, which is easy and delightful in abundance becomes difficult and even self-sacrificial in scarcity."[7]

Although gifting forms a hidden economy in market-based economies, matriarchal (matrifocal) societies operate according to gift economies and circles of gifting, following the patterns of nature's gift-giving, self-regulating system.[8] Among First Nation peoples, the gifting circle always includes other-than-human partners who sustain the community. Sacrifices or gifts are provided to natural entities in exchange for specific gifts or as general gratitude.

Adamson specifically mentions protecting the water beings. I think you have some firsthand experience with that.

Four Arrows: Yes, I relate to what Rebecca says about water. She talks about how the dominant approach to accumulation versus Indigenous sharing, a concept that you so eloquently address in terms of "gifting," results in the kind of greed that kills the water beings. The experience to which you refer relates to my four tours of duty at Standing Rock, where thousands protested against the oil pipeline going across the river. Everyone knew it would leak oil, as it wound up doing. We were there not just because of the repercussions for all the people who rely upon the Missouri River section for sustenance. People from around the world were also there to honor the *interconnectedness and interdependence of all living things.* Every morning the women would lead people, hundreds of us, to the river to offer the river tobacco and songs. The men would line up on the embankment forming two rows so the women could grab our hands to ascend to the water safely. They would do the ceremony at the water's edge and lead us all in singing the water blessing songs from various First Nations. Such spirituality is at the root of the nonmaterialistic worldview that once guided us. Your invitation to the reader to not spend so much time thinking about things is also an invitation to focus more on relationships. Giving significance to relationships is the essence of Indigenous spirituality. Replacing it with a need for more and more possessions replaces interconnectedness with stress and conflict.

Such gifting and enoughness within a materialistic culture are not easy. In fact, according to my research, it never was. The tendency to want to compete for and accumulate goods has always been an enticement for humans. We see this in how our origin myths, teaching stories, cultural mores, and ceremonial intentions attempt to overcome it. People came to understand that gift-giving was a reciprocal opportunity for building good relationships between people and other-than-human beings. They came to see the truth about how when one tries to enhance ego or fulfill discontent, accumulation of things created an unhealthy cycle of greed. Still, hinting that a child give its beloved new puppy to the child of a mother who died in an accident might be done with the understanding that it is not an easy thing for the child to do. Nor would it be easy to give the next-door neighbor your second car because he lost his job owing to COVID-19. Such acts require courage, which is why I have heard more than one Lakota say what my colleague Martin Brokenleg has said: "Generosity is the highest expression of courage."

How would you see us addressing the radical difference between Indigenous and dominant economic systems today related to land and "natural resources?" To me, this has become the most important target for a nonmaterialistic economy to consider.

Darcia: To keep us enchanted with the status quo, the dominant economic system and modern economics have to "externalize" (not take into count) effects on the natural world or on the health of individuals and communities. This kind of discounting of reality happens in education too. Elliot Eisner notes three types of curriculum in education:[9] the explicit (the topics covered), the hidden (the nonverbal expectations and values conveyed by rules, practices, physical environment), and the null (what is left out). Regarding what is left out, Eisner focuses on nonintellectual cognition (really, all the nonlinear intelligences) and various topics. From an Indigenous worldview, a lot is missing. Remember how Native American elders complained about the government or missionary schools that their communities' children were forced to attend? They said that the children did not learn much of anything useful, specifically, how to live on the earth—like how to find their way home from a great distance, how to recognize and harvest plants for food and medicine, and so on.

Dominant economic theory and education generally divorce themselves from the rest of life—from living well and wisely, from the development of heart-mindedness as well as the arts, from cultivating relationships and responsibilities to humanity and the other-than-human, and from guiding the transformation of the person to becoming a wise elder of the earth. Indigenous worldview and education keep all these things together throughout the life course. The learner is not separated from community to learn abstractions but learns within the community the personal knowledge needed for practical wisdom, the coordination and integration of all these areas. This is radically different from a dominating worldview that seems to use compartmentalizing and theorizing to justify acting like an ecological and relational sociopath.

Four Arrows: As I read your words about how children did not learn anything useful in the schools they were forced to attend, and as I reflect on Rebecca's reference to a more "holistic and balanced view of the world," I thought about the response of the Iroquois Confederacy to Virginia colonists offering free schooling for a number of young Indian men. In 1744, the Virginia Commission offered to pay for their attendance at Williamsburg College so they could learn the white man's way. After a day of reflection and discussion, a representative of the Indians penned this reply, as described by Benjamin Franklin:

> An Instance of this occurr'd at the Treaty of Lancaster in Pensilvania, anno 1744, between the Government of Virginia and the Six Nations. After the principal Business was settled, the Commissioners from Virginia acquainted the Indians by a Speech, that there was at

Williamsburg a College, with a Fund for Educating Indian youth;
and that if the Six Nations would send down half a dozen of their
young Lads to that College, the Government would take Care that
they should be well provided for, and instructed in all the Learning
of the White People. It is one of the Indian Rules of Politeness not to
answer a public Proposition the same day that it is made; they think
it would be treating it as a light matter, and that they show it Respect
by taking time to consider it, as of a Matter important. They therefore deferr'd their Answer till the Day following; when their Speaker
began by expressing their deep Sense of the Kindness of the Virginia
Government in making them that Offer, for we know, says he, that
you highly esteem the kind of Learning taught in those Colleges,
and that the Maintenance of our young Men while with you, would
be very expensive to you. We are convinc'd therefore that you mean
to do us Good by your Proposal, and we thank you heartily. But
you who are wise must know, that different Nations have different
Conceptions of Things, and you will therefore not take it amiss if our
Ideas of this kind of Education happen not to be the same with yours.
We have had some Experience of it: Several of our young People
were formerly brought up at the Colleges of the Northern Provinces;
they were instructed in all your Sciences; but when they came back
to us they were bad Runners ignorant of every means of living in the
Woods, unable to bear either Cold or Hunger, knew neither how
to build a Cabin, take a Deer or kill an Enemy, spoke our Language
imperfectly, were therefore neither fit for Hunters, Warriors, or
Counsellors, they were totally good for nothing. We are however
not the less oblig'd by your kind Offer tho' we decline accepting it;
and to show our grateful Sense of it, if the Gentlemen of Virginia will
send us a Dozen of their Sons, we will take great Care of their Education, instruct them in all we know, and make Men of them.[10]

I close with this telling quote about how the materialistic goals of
education, media, and the culture it creates contribute to nongener-
osity, envy, and possessiveness, priorities that detract from a holistic

life. Indigenous worldview emphasizes, as Rebecca Adamson says, "the relevance for relationship and the sacredness of creation." It is not about ascetic notions that do not enjoy the physicality of life and its pleasures, but rather about a flowing balance that has Nature-based priorities in place. All that is necessary to realize the dangerous impact of our materialistic world is to look around.

SEE BROTHERS SPRING IS HERE THE EARTH HAS TAKEN THE EMBRACE OF THE SUN AND SOON WE SHALL SEE THE CHILDREN OF THAT LOVE ALL SEEDS ARE AWAKE AND ALL ANIMALS FROM THIS GREAT POWER WE CONCEDE TO OUR FELLOW CREATURES EVEN OUR ANIMAL FELLOWS THE SAME RIGHTS AS OURSELVES TO LIVE ON THIS EARTH BUT HEAR ME BROTHERS WE HAVE NOW TO DO WITH ANOTHER RACE THEY WERE FEW AND WEAK WHEN OUR GRANDFATHERS FIRST MET THEM THEY ARE NOW MANY AN POWERFUL IT IS A STRANGE THING BUT THEY WANT TO PLOW THE EARTH AND GREED IS A DISEASE AMONG THEM THEY HAVE MADE MANY LAWS THESE THE RICH MAY BREAK BUT THE POOR MAY NOT THEY TAKE MONEY FROM THE POOR AND WEAK TO SUPPORT THE RICH AND POWERFUL THEY SAY THAT OUR MOTHER THE EARTH IS THEIRS TO OWN AND THEY FENCE OUT THEIR NEIGHBOURS THEY MUTILATE OUR MOTHER WITH THEIR BUILDINGS AND THEIR REFUSE THEY ARE LIKE A RIVER IN SPATE WHICH IN SPRING OVERFLOWS ITS BANKS AND DESTROYS EVERYTHING IN ITS PATH WE CANNOT LIVE SIDE BY SIDE SEVEN YEARS GO WE MADE A TREATY WITH THE WHITE MEN WHICH PROMISED US THAT THE LAND OF THE BUFFALO WOULD BE OURS FOREVER NOW THEY THREATEN TO TAKE THIS FROM US TOO SHALL WE YIELD TO THEM BROTHERS OR SHALL WE SAY TO THEM YOU MUST KILL ME FIRST BEFORE YOU TAKE POSSESSION OF MY COUNTRY

TATANKA IYOTAKE
HUNKPAPA SIOUX
1834 – 1890

Sitting Bull
Marble stonecut

Harriet Greene
Taos, N.M.

9

All Earth Entities Are Sentient

Robin Wall Kimmerer (Citizen Potawatomi Nation)

*C*ollectively, the Indigenous canon of principles and practices that govern the exchange of life for life is known as the Honorable Harvest. They are rules of sorts that govern our taking, shape our relationships with the natural world, and rein in our tendency to consume—that the world might be as rich for the seventh generation as it is for our own. The details are highly specific to different cultures and ecosystems, but the fundamental principles are nearly universal among peoples who live close to the land.

I am a student of this way of thinking, not a scholar. As a human being who cannot photosynthesize, I must struggle to participate in the Honorable Harvest. So I lean in close to watch and listen to those who are far wiser than I am. What I share here, in the same way they were shared with me, are seeds gleaned from the fields of their collective wisdom, the barest surface, the moss on the mountain of their knowledge. I feel grateful for their teachings and responsible for passing them on as best I can. . . .

The guidelines for the Honorable Harvest are not written down, or even consistently spoken of as a whole—they are reinforced in small acts of daily life. But if you were to list them, they might look something like this:

- *Know the ways of the ones who take care of you, so that you may take care of them.*

- *Introduce yourself. Be accountable as the one who comes asking for life.*

- *Ask permission before taking. Abide by the answer.*

- *Never take the first. Never take the last.*

- *Take only what you need.*

- *Take only that which is given.*

- *Never take more than half. Leave some for others.*

- *Harvest in a way that minimizes harm.*

- *Use it respectfully. Never waste what you have taken.*

- *Share.*

- *Give thanks for what you have been given.*

- *Give a gift, in reciprocity for what you have taken.*

- *Sustain the ones who sustain you and the earth will last forever.*

The state guidelines on hunting and gathering are based exclusively in the biophysical realm, while the rules of the Honorable Harvest are based on accountability to both the physical and the metaphysical worlds. The taking of another life to support your own is far more significant when you recognize the beings who are harvested as persons, nonhuman persons vested with awareness, intelligence, spirit—and who have families waiting for them at home. Killing a who demands something different than killing an it. When you regard those nonhuman persons as kinfolk, another set of harvesting regulations extends beyond bag limits and legal seasons.

Source

Robin Wall Kimmerer. *Braiding Sweetgrass: Indigenous Wisdom, Scientific Knowledge, and the Teachings of Plants,* 180, 183. Minneapolis: Milkweed Editions, 2013.

Contextualized Biosketch

Robin Wall Kimmerer, PhD, is professor of environmental and forest biology at the State University of New York College of Environmental

Science and Forestry and director of the newly established Center for Native Peoples and the Environment. Her work aims to integrate traditional ecological knowledge with modern science. Her book *Gathering Moss: A Natural and Cultural History of Mosses* (2003) won the John Burroughs Medal Award. She is also the author of the popular book *Braiding Sweetgrass: Indigenous Wisdom, Scientific Knowledge and the Teachings of Plants* (2013).

Robin grew up close to the land, with a father who led summer morning ceremonies of gratitude to the gods of the nearby mountain, Tahawus. She learned that "each place was inspirited, was home to others before we arrived and long after we left."[1] Feeling that she was born a botanist, that the plants had chosen her, when she was asked why she wanted to be a botanist in her college freshman intake interview, she told the truth. She had gathered collections of seeds and pressed leaves and had local knowledge about some plants and their habitats, but most especially she wanted to learn why asters and goldenrod grow together, why they "looked so beautiful together."[2] The interviewer did not write down her answer but told that her interest was "not science." Her adviser later told her that if she wanted to study beauty, she should go to art school. But she stayed in botany science and has worked to wed Western science, predominantly concerned with prediction, and Native science, predominantly concerned with relationships, along with her artistic prose. Her work "as an ecologist, a writer, a mother, as a traveler between scientific and traditional ways of knowing, grows from the power of those words,"[3] a daily thanksgiving to a sentient earth.

Indigenous Worldview Precept Dialogue

Darcia: I was not raised in the Indigenous worldview. However, I grew up with a sense of communion with and protection by the Great Spirit. I was not aware of the Indigenous idea about having reciprocity with the web of life. I did "hug trees," and on Sunday mornings I sat on the grass with my guitar among ancestors (in a cemetery) long before "earthing" became popular, but it was not until I first read Robin's work that I fully came to understand how all plants are community members, partners, persons with lessons from which we can learn. I had not considered how mosses, which have been around for over 300 million years, actually have much to teach human beings—like the virtue of humility.

I now keep in mind the honorable harvest principles she laid out. I ask permission if I want to pick lilies of the valley, only taking the ones that yield. I don't do a lot of harvesting for use; however, I do talk to the plants who start sashaying into the area reserved for a native plant and I will tell them they don't belong there. I look around to see what "weeds" the insects are liking and avoid removing them.

This whole way of being with plants (and all the other nonhumans) is so contrary to Western culture, especially during the last several hundred years. Robin graciously invites us into a different mindset, one infused with a sense of gratitude. In a May 2020 interview by James Yeh of *The Guardian,* Robin expressed her desire to foment a "contagion of gratitude," saying: "I'm just trying to think about what that would be like. Acting out of gratitude, as a pandemic. I can see it."[4]

Four Arrows: Robin's reference to a "contagion of gratitude" reminds me of a friend who ends all of her emails with "My only emotion is gratitude." All First Nations have songs and prayers giving thanks for the many gifts Mother Earth provides us. I especially appreciate the Haudenosaunee Thanksgiving Address. I even open my most recent book, *The Red Road,*[5] with a version of it. The prayer is a shared offering of appreciation, beginning with Mother Earth (who continues to care for us). Then it moves on to the Waters (who give themselves to us as food and purify the waters); the Fish; the Plants; the Food Plants; the Medicine Herbs (always waiting and ready to heal us); the Animals (who have many things to teach us); the Trees; the Birds; the Four Winds (bringing us messages and giving us strength); the Thunder Beings; the Sun; Grandmother Moon (who watches over the arrival of children); the Stars; the Enlightened Teachers; and the Creator. It is a beautiful thing to see a group of people to start with such a prayer each morning. Each person calls out one of these categories, with children often referring to a particular animal or plant. They describe what it does for us as a living, sentient, helpful being. At the end of each individual recognition, the group acknowledges that their minds are one with this affirmation. By paying homage to everything that sustains us and keeps us healthy, the prayer reminds us how important it is to take care of them.

Your reference to hugging trees when you were young reminds me of an exercise I have done over the years before I give a presentation. I will have scouted out a place outside the building where there are trees. If it's not too far of a walk from the room we are in, I ask the attendees to leave their things on the table and go out to touch a tree and then step back and count to ten. (Sometimes I have them come back to the room.) Then I ask them to do it again, but this time asking permission . . . and waiting for an answer before touching. People usually laugh when I give this instruction. Sometimes they go out of the room shaking their heads. When they come back, however, and I have done this close to a hundred times over the years, there is a different energy. When I ask people to report on the experience, invariably someone will cry. Disbelief is often mentioned, followed by, "But I truly felt it tell me." I conclude the exercise by saying, well, that is how we all lived in relationship to other-than-humans 24-7.

Darcia: I love that exercise. If we can respect the living nature of every plant and animal we meet, we can be more mindful of our actions. Our first instinct when we meet a spider or a dandelion should be a greeting, not getting them out of our way. I am writing songs for children to encourage an attitude of respect toward the living earth— one each for insects, water, birds, and plants—including one about the honorable harvest.

Inspired by Kimmerer's work, I wrote a bouncy children's song (and partner dance) called "Honoring Plants" (remember, it is for children).[6]

Chorus:
Give a little, get a little, like a friendship.
Give a little, get a little, with your partner.
Give a little, get a little, as we circle.
That's the gifting way.

Verses:
Don't be hurtful, don't be careless, they are creatures too.
"Weeds" or flowers, trees or prairie, they're full of life like you.
Ask permission, then you listen to the answer passed;
If it's yes you take a little, not the first or last.

Say hello and get to know them like a caring friend.
Don't be wasteful or unmindful of the offering.
Give to others and give thanks for every gift you get.
You will need them, they don't need you, so give them some
      respect.

Let's not poison plant or beast so all enjoy the feast;
Bee at breakfast, butterfly lunching, let's not choose to cheat.
Learn to know them and to love them every single day.
Keep them healthy watching carefully as you go your way.

Four Arrows: How wonderful. I think it is important to help children realize early on that the plants and animals we take for sustenance are sentient, so as to engender a more respectful, hence more balanced, spiritual approach to the "honorable harvest." Near the end of her quote, Robin says: "The taking of another life to support your own is far more significant when you recognize the beings who are harvested as persons, nonhuman persons vested with awareness, intelligence, spirit—and who have families waiting for them at home." How do we help children learn to do this? Schools certainly are not doing it.

I remember Jane Goodall, in her book *Reason for Hope,* tells a story about the first time a wild chimpanzee held hands with her and how deeply moved she was by the "soft pressure of his fingers."[7] She saw that moment as a "lifetime of research, for we are human-bound, imprisoned within our human view of the world that makes it hard to see the perspective of cultures other than our own, or from the point of view of a member of the opposite sex." She became the first person to photograph and thus prove that animals used tools, when the same individual who made friends with her was observed stripping leaves off of a stick and using it to poke into a termite hill and pick up termites to eat. The criticisms Goodall's publication on this received in the 1960s came from every direction, none grounded in science, despite being from scientists. She writes: "And in those days it was held (at least by many scientists, philosophers and theologians) that only humans had minds, only humans were capable of rational thought. Fortunately, I had not been to university, and I did not know these things. And when I did find out, I just thought it was silly and paid no attention."[8] To answer the title of Robin Kimmerer's quote, if universities cannot show people how to understand the world as a gift, then we must all take it upon ourselves.

The Sacred Nature of
Competition and Games

Sharon Firth (Gwich'in)
Shirley Firth (Gwich'in; 1953–2013)

Shirley: *When we twins first started skiing it was an experimental program called "Territorial Experimental Ski Training" to see if Natives could get ahead in the sport. My first reaction when I arrived from the North as a child in Banff was survival. How am I going to adapt to this place? Well, we did adapt. That's history. Thanks to so many who are part of our being in the 1976, 1980, and 1984 Olympic Games. Sure, we don't have any gold medals but we can sit down and tell lots of stories. I'll tell you one thing though. I had four Olympic jackets. And the first person who came by and said "I love it," I gave it to them. So I don't have any today. Maybe they will be inspired, those who have them, to be great athletes. What is important is that we continue to change people's lives.*

Sharon: *At a young age I promised myself when I was very young that I would be somebody. Skiing was not part of our trapping culture and I never dreamt of skiing. My competitive spirit to be our best was always there. We have to blossom where we are planted. And we blossomed in Banff, even though I had to be two people. I had to be strong with my native tradition while learning the white way, because that is the world we live in. Thanks to all our training buddies who pushed us on those tortuous hills on the back side of Sulphur Mountain, and around Mount Norquay, Sunshine Village, Lake Louise, the Bugaboos, the Caribou.*

Most of the time Shirley and I broke trail in the freezing weather. Oh, and how wonderful to have seen all the bears and wildlife we ran into. Even wild people! What sites we saw during our difficult training sessions. Memorable moments that we will cherish forever. And the mountains on which we skied are still there. They are eternal.

Most of all, we loved what we were doing. Competition and training were hard but so much fun. The combination of making lifelong friends while surviving on the trail and representing Indigenous people throughout the world has been a great honor. Although we have been told we have won 50 percent of all cross-country medals earned by Canadian athletes, it does not matter to us how many medals we have won. It is the way we do it that counts. If a kid got inspired because of my skiing, then I can call it "winning." They always told us we would never make it, but year after year we stayed on top. It was a good feeling because it showed Indigenous people can get ahead in life and live to their full potential. We did it mostly at first without sponsors. So we had to work double and sacrifice much. So that is it. To compete is to sacrifice, to have an open mind, to adjust and make changes. It is about learning everything you can about your pursuits or your sport. Competition is a way to learn to survive and love life and be your personal best person. You do it because you want to grow, not because someone else wants it for you.

Source

Nuvialuit Communications Society. "Walter Goose Interviews Sharon and Shirley Firth." June 6, 2012. Video, 9:26. www.youtube.com/watch?v=ZG0mA-KksuE.

Contextualized Biosketch

Twin sisters Shirley and Sharon Firth, members of the Gwich'in First Nation, were among the first Aboriginal athletes to represent Canada at the Olympics and were members of the first Canadian women's cross-country ski team at the Olympics. In total, they competed in four Olympic Winter Games. The Firth sisters were introduced to skiing through the Territorial Experimental Ski Training program and were members of the national cross-country ski team for an unprecedented seventeen consecutive years. Between them, the sisters won seventy-nine medals at the national championships, including forty-eight national titles.

Shirley and Sharon Firth were born in Aklavik, Northwest Territories, and spent their early years in a log house with their mother (a member of the local Gwich'in First Nation). Like many other children in the area, the twins were taught at an early age how to trap and hunt by their parents. The Firth sisters were introduced to cross-country skiing through the TEST program, which required the young skiers to train for hours outside; in winter, they skied in complete darkness in temperatures as low as forty degrees below zero, and in summer, they logged long runs across the tundra, battling fatigue and mosquitos. Motivated in part by their desire to see the world, the Firth sisters worked hard to make the elite team, coached by Norwegian Bjorger Petterson, and soon started competing in national and international competitions.[1]

Indigenous Worldview Precept Dialogue

Four Arrows: There are so many stories to tell about the sacredness of Indigenous sports and games throughout pre- and postcontact history. The Firth twins and their humble eloquence in this rare interview captures what our friend Greg Cajete writes about in his 2005 book *Spirit of the Game: An Indigenous Wellspring*. Competition held a special place in Indigenous cultures throughout the world, and although stifled in contemporary times in terms of recognition and resources, it remains a way to bind communities together. It develops survival skills, physical fitness, and spiritual interconnectedness. It helps reinforce the importance of honesty, fairness, and leadership. Dr. Joseph B. Oxendine, a Lumbee author, writes that the major factors that characterized traditional American Indian sports include: (1) a strong connection between sports and other social, spiritual, and economic aspects of daily life; (2) the serious preparation of mind, body, and spirit of both the participants and the community as a whole prior to major competition; (3) the assumption that rigid adherence to standardized rules and technical precision was unimportant; (4) strong allegiance to high standards of sportsmanship and fair play; and (5) the prominence of both men and women.[2]

Like most Americans, I grew up with a different perception about sports. I was extremely competitive in wrestling, football, running, handball, and equestrian sports. Until I was in my forties, I saw games and sports primarily about "winning" via outscoring or "beating" others. I was a "good sport," but it wasn't until my experience with the Tarahumara of Mexico that I truly awakened to the idea of competition being a sacred endeavor that was more about teamwork with opponents and teammates than about winning. In a remote place called Pino Gordo, located in the Chihuahuan Sierra Madre mountains, community members walked up to a hundred miles to watch a *rarajipari* race. The race begins when family members and friends of two competing teams of men start carving a round ball from a large fallen branch. When a team's ball is finished, they take off kicking it with the instep of their bare foot on a race that is usually between fifty and three hundred miles long, up and down rugged canyons that are thousands of feet deep. Many consider this to be the most strenuous event in the world.

The Tarahumara, who call themselves Rarámuri, which actually means "with running feet," exemplify the importance running has always played in Indian country.[3] As hunter-gatherers, they still can run a deer down until the animal can run no more. I sat with my friends for two days while people visited, drank corn beer, and wagered on which group or team would come out of the canyon first. When finally it happened, people smiled and yelled out praise while collecting whatever was betted. They continued to talk about the event while the runners were cared for by their families, waiting for the other teams to come across who received the same joyful exclamations. In awe of the event, and accustomed to seeing winning athletes celebrated in their victory, I was confused by the apparent indifference to who won, beyond the enjoyment of gambling over it. I asked my translator to ask the 102-year-old shaman I had been with for weeks why the winners were not being celebrated. I was told, "Well, someone had to come across first."

There are many other stories I could tell about how traditional Indigenous athletes have a different approach to competition from the dominant culture. They relate to football teams playing as hard as they can and then letting up just enough to allow teams to alternate touchdowns, or log-carrying races where members of the team with the lightest log drop off to help those with the largest one to catch up. However, Sharon Firth made the point well when she said, "Competition is a way to learn to survive and love life and be your personal best person." Darcia, I wonder if your work as a developmental psychologist can shed light on what aspects of the dominant worldview have led us to such attitudes as we have about competition. I'm thinking of the all-too-well-known credo in modern sports that says, "Winning isn't everything; it's the only thing."

Darcia: Sharon said, "It is the way we do it that counts." This is what virtue is all about, the manner of behavior. It's not enough to go through the motions, to do something that your heart is not into. This is contrary to the dominant view in Western scholarship that you must go against your inclinations for something to count as moral. It's so upside down. I think human beings are messed up in childhood in all sorts of ways through coercive force, a Western tradition with its most famous articulation given by philosopher Immanuel Kant. Philosopher John Watson (1847–1939) explained the perspective:

> At first everyone is under apparent bondage to his superiors in the family relation, but in reality this is the means by which a measure of freedom is attained. It is true that he must render implicit obedience to those in authority over him, but in so doing he learns to free himself from an undue accentuation of his own individual desires and to seek his freedom where alone it can be found—in the subordination of his own will to the good of others.[4]

So here we have the early divorce of self, intuition, and action. The child learns not to trust the self. It's hard to become virtuous if you were divorced from your spirit. We also have the training grounds for dominance-submission relationships—some people have power and others must subordinate themselves. We'll contrast the differences in child raising more specifically later.

"Competition is a way to learn to survive and love life and be your personal best person. You do it because you want to grow, not because someone else wants it for you." This matches up with the spirit of play. Peter Gray lists the characteristics of play identified by play scholars:[5] (1) self-directed and self-chosen; (2) intrinsically motivated for play; (3) guided by flexible, creative mental rules; (4) imaginative—separated from real-world serious activity; (5) conducted in a nonstressed but active and alert frame of mind. The more of these characteristics an activity has, the more playlike it is.

Gray suggests that Native peoples have a different orientation to dominance and competition because of play. We can get some insights from anthropologists and others who have studied small-band hunter-gatherer (SBHG) societies, which represent the social structure of 95 percent to 99 percent of human existence. SBHG societies are highly egalitarian. They do not tolerate power grabs. They use teasing and humor to keep each other humble and connected, and to suppress an inflated ego, such as that of a successful hunter. The result is usually laughter all around. Psychologist Peter Gray suggests that this emphasis on community egalitarianism in SBHG social life was founded on a spirit of play. Playfulness infuses SBHG life.

When social mammals play, they must cooperate, set aside dominance, and be fair. They don't compete or cheat, threaten or hurt. The focus is on enjoyment and extending their capacities, just as Sharon and Shirley demonstrate. As Gray explains: "Play always requires the voluntary participation of both (or all) partners, so play is always an exercise in restraint and retaining the other's good will. If one player fails at that, the other will quit and the play will end. Play very often involves animals that differ considerably in age, size, and strength. To keep the play going, the larger, stronger, or otherwise more dominant animal must continuously self-handicap, so as not to intimidate the other. Thus, play is always an egalitarian, cooperative activity."[6]

In a play-infused life that emphasizes egalitarianism and keeps the peace, competition is a violation of norms.

Four Arrows: I think we have to be careful when we separate "competition" from "play" or assume that competition cannot be egalitarian. You are correct, however, in that we have to take the time to redefine it. Most internet definitions reflect the negative connotation of which you speak. They are about "rivalry," or "the activity or condition of striving to gain or win something by defeating or establishing superiority over others," and so on. We must clarify that sports and games provide the structural opportunity to test one's own progressing skill levels in the spirit of egalitarianism and humility. We "compete" or "test" our skills best when pushed toward our potential in the "play" of the game or sport. Coming across the finish line before others, or catching the ball or throwing the spear, are all sacred efforts that only relate to "superiority" when we have bought into or are frightened by the prevailing worldview.

Note that in our quote, Sharon says, "Competition and training were hard but so much fun." For Indigenous people, competition is a form of play, whether a game or a sport. The rigor and challenge of the competition originally helped prepare individuals for "competing" with the elements or wild animals in order to survive. This is the perspective we want to put forth for this precept. Sure, it is likely that for each title and medal they won, there were likely others who felt defeated, inferior, sad, angry, etc. If so, however, it was because of their holding onto the dominant worldview.

We also must distinguish when we are participating and competing in a sport or a game and when we are trying to successfully survive with our hunting, fishing, or gathering skills. The latter is also a form of competition, and as I've mentioned, our success can relate to the more playful forms of competition in games. We must also know when an activity should have nothing to do with competing, such as education, music, art, and collaborative problem-solving. Service to others rather than competition is the focus in such activities. Greg Cajete, who writes that education "must engender a commitment to service rather than competition," also refers to competitive sports and games as "a way of making one's own medicine" in behalf of service.[7]

Valery Krasilnikov, a professor of physical training in Russia, concluded a study of Siberian Indigenous competitions by saying, "We consider that traditional games and competitions can be that link between culture of the past, the present and the future."[8] Perhaps if we see competition as ceremony rather than just play, and prepare and pray accordingly, the problems relating to corporations, professional sports, governments, schools, and just about any other institution that emphasizes the dominant interpretations of competition would quickly change for the better.

Darcia: You are remininding me of anthropologist Colin Turnbull,[9] who contrasted his own British upbringing with the Mbuti, hunter-gatherers of the former Zaire (now the Democratic Republic of Congo), with whom he lived and studied. They demonstrated a playful orientation to life and reached adolescence full of life and readiness for more. Turnbull described reaching his own adolescence empty and unconfident. He was raised with harsh nannies and then in boarding school, where he was severely criticized for not doing well in competitive sports, and even for being a coward because he did not assert himself nor take his punishment "like a man." Developing "team spirit" meant training to punish and be violent toward others. Corporal punishment of children has a long history in England (and the USA). The competitive dominator culture displayed is so much the opposite of a play-based culture.

I like your idea of Indigenous "competition" as ceremony. Turnbull describes one such ceremony among the Mbuti, a tug-of-war between the sexes:

[When the men and boys start to win], one of them will abandon his side and join the women, pulling up his bark-cloth and adjusting it in the fashion of women, shouting encouragement to them in a falsetto, ridiculing womanhood by the very exaggeration of his mime. . . . [Then, when the women and girls start to win] one of them adjusts her bark clothing, letting it down, and strides over to the men's side and joins their shouting in a deep bass voice, similarly gently mocking manhood. . . . Each person crossing over tries to outdo the ridicule of the last, causing more and more laughter, until when the contestants are laughing so hard they cannot sing or pull any more, they let go of the vine rope and fall to the ground in near hysteria. Although both youth and adults cross sides, it is primarily the youth who really enact the ridicule. . . . The ridicule is performed without hostility, rather with a sense of at least partial identification and empathy. It is in this way that the violence and aggressivity of either sex "winning" is avoided, and the stupidity of competitiveness is demonstrated.[10]

Here, playfulness, Indigenous competition, and humor are all mixed together with ceremony. It becomes a sacred time of bonding among community members. It illustrates another form, apart from individual endeavors like skiing, of Indigenous competition.

11

Nonanthropocentrism

Terry LeBlanc (Mi'kmaq)

*B*eginning with its philosophical underpinnings in a progressively
developed series of dualisms, and its biblical foundation in Genesis 3,
*Western Christian theology has, with some notable exceptions, histori-
cally focused its inquiry on the restoration of relationship between God
and humankind—the salvation and recovery of the lost human soul. . . .
The emphasis has almost entirely been exclusively on the restoration of the
human relation with God first, then with others in the human community.
As history will attest, we have failed miserably on the latter and we've
struggled to give effective evidence to the former. . . . The Christian scrip-
ture are abundantly clear that redemption through Jesus's work on the
cross, if we take the time to reflect on them, has implications far beyond
our limited focus on the restoration of human beings alienated from their
Creator. There is this interrelatedness that Western theology has not
explored. The creation itself, Paul makes quite clear, "groans in travail
awaiting its own redemption." Yet even as we give tacit assent to this in
our Christian theology, we fail miserably to account for the work of the
Spirit, dare I say the gifts of the Spirit, so abundantly evident in the rest
of creation, through which that groaning is becoming increasingly unmis-
takable, and from which we might learn something about the means and
trajectory of salvation were we able to actually listen more carefully to
those groans. Most times the best we seem able to offer is to ensure there is
a pastoral scene of the rest of creation projected on a church screen behind*

the lyrics of the hymns and choruses we sing. That is often the extent of our creation theology. Seldom in evangelical writing does the idea that Jesus came to give his life so that the rest of creation might also be redeemed find its expression. When I teach about this, I tell my students that if at the conclusion of my course they do not believe that Jesus died for your dog, they need to think again about the nature of their creation theology.

The creation itself is groaning. This, Native people would argue, characterizes the lived theology of the majority of the evangelical church, even today, as it has done through the ages. It is precisely this framework that allowed Christian missionaries to cross large bodies of water to where, if they had not brought God, God would not have been present. . . . How is it that the Christian church could articulate this principle of the omnipresence of God and yet call us Godless heathens in a Godless heathen land? . . . If I had a platform to do so, I would want to cry loudly that it is in the rest of creation then that we find the gifts of the Spirit most consistently manifest, to teach us, to talk about the past, and the present. We find this expression in the natural way of life, which creatures living in a more intuitive relationship with their Creator tend to express. . . . Why don't you ask the birds in the air, the fish that swim in the sea, the animals that walk on the land, speak to the Earth itself. . . . Which of these do not know that the hand of the Lord has done this? . . . My grandfather and people of his generation used to say that animals are indeed persons, they're just not people.

Source

Terry LeBlanc. *Native American Theology.* June 17, 2015. Video, 39:26. www.youtube
.com/watch?v=5UyMhwYN0jM.

Contexualized Biosketch

Professor Terry LeBlanc, a Mi'kmaq-Acadian, holds an interdisciplinary PhD from Asbury Theological Seminary in Orlando, Florida, and he specializes in theology and anthropology. In addition to serving as an adjunct professor at Tyndale University in Toronto, Ontario, he also teaches at George Fox University and Seminary in Portland, Oregon, and Acadia University and Divinity College in Wolfville, Nova Scotia. For over four decades, he has worked in American Indian and global Indigenous communities as an educator in theology, cultural anthropology, and community development practice. He is the executive director of Indigenous Pathways as well as the founding chair and current director of the North American Institute for Indigenous Theological Studies (NAIITS). NAIITS is dedicated to working together with the Indigenous community to develop and articulate Indigenous perspectives in theology and practice. Its goal is to facilitate the development of a body of written work addressing biblical, theological, and ethical issues from within Native North American and other Indigenous perspectives.

Indigenous Worldview Precept Dialogue

Four Arrows: I realize that naming this precept by saying what it is *not* is inconsistent with the other chapter titles. However, finding antonyms for anthropocentrism and choosing one is not easy for me. Biocentrism is a good choice. Deepak Chopra's back-cover quote for Berman and Lanza's book *Biocentrism* asserts that the authors' theory is "consistent with the most ancient traditions of the world which say that consciousness conceives, governs and becomes a physical world." However, after having read the book, I find that "ancient" for the authors refers to early Western civilization. Plato did write that the world is "a living being endowed with a soul and intelligence . . . a single visible living entity containing all other living entities, which by their nature are all related."[1] As close as this seems to be, well, consider that the authors of *Biocentrism,* who never mention the word "Indigenous" in their book, put more emphasis on consciousness being a "projection from inside our minds, where experience begins"[2] than I would argue (if I had more space) truly fits my notion of what we mean by Indigenous "nonanthropocentrism."

Ecocentrism might be thought of as an antonym, but humans claiming that the ecosystem is the entire focus is not quite right. Also, such an authoritative (anthropocentric?) claim by humans seems to miss the importance of the sentient beings. I discovered the phrase "metaphysical anthropocentrism," which is about humans seeing nature as a "meaningful context to which a person should attune his or her life." This fits, but not holistically, the Indigenous way as I perceive it. Maarten Drenthen describes how philosopher Arnold Burms understands metaphysical anthropocentrism as believing that "the divine that manifests itself through nature to humans and speaks to humans."[3]

Two other terms that reflect nonanthropocentrism are pantheism and panentheism. As I understand them, pantheism makes a supreme energy the single agent that moves all of life, whereas panentheism allows for individual souls, that are expressions of the "Creator," to also have individual agency. The latter comes closest to our Indigenous worldview precept by incorporating animism. Indeed, anthropologists usually refer to Indigenous cultures as being animistic, given that they see—as we have seen in this book—that we are surrounded by nonhuman sentient beings of all sorts. Animism is about believing that everything has a soul, just as humans do.[4]

Still, none of these terms are quite adequate for how my research and experience have brought me to understand Indigenous spirituality. Notwithstanding that all the terms were created and defined by Western or Eastern postcontact philosophers, religious scholars, and anthropologists, there is something missing. The best I can do to briefly explain the nonanthropocentric Indigenous worldview precept is to simply list my own descriptors:

1. The precept is place-based, with place uniquely mirroring its own version of the cosmos. So each nonanthropocentric understanding is similar in terms of the common Indigenous worldview, but different in terms of details relating to unique location on the earth.

2. In essence, humans belong to the land, not vice versa.

3. There is a mysterious, loving, creative force who, with helpers from the nonhuman world, created an interconnected world.

4. This original sacred energy pervades everything, making us humans—along with all other forms of life—family or kin. This comes with responsibility for caring for all members of this family.

5. Every element of creation has a spiritual presence that we all share but also has its own agency and unique wisdom designed to foster flowing balance in the universe.

6. All elements, including rocks, water, mountains, and thunder, are animated with individual personalities.[5]

7. Humans cannot fully explain any of this, but they use reflection upon lived experience and wisdom stories handed down generationally to guide other humans to find their own way.

Darcia, I have a feeling you will be a little puzzled that I chose for this important spiritual precept an Indigenous person who is Christian, knowing the concerns I have expressed in papers I have written, so feel free to guess why, or ask me to explain.

Darcia: "Panpsychism" is a term that aligns with animism but puts the power of being into everything instead of putting it in the perception of human beings. But I think you are right: there exists no term from Westernized scholarship that can cover the deep, place-based, reciprocal, relational, sacred, loving individuality that is the nature of the dynamic, living world. It is an Indigenous spirituality. To perceive the world this way represents an ecological intelligence that unfortunately is missing in most Westernized adults. Children raised in a traditional Indigenous way, close to the earth, would develop this intelligence to great heights over time. It is squelched in Westernized cultures.

It is sad and frustrating that if you talk to most people with the assumptions of what I just named as Indigenous spirituality, they think you are naive or Disney romantic. Initially my white husband rolled his eyes when I spoke of insects as kin whom we should honor, for whom we are responsible. Little by little he has come around to accepting my partnership view, letting go a little more of his ingrained dominator view. Although I know that life will continue after this world passes, I cry virtually every day over the mistreatment of the earth, the loss of species and individuals, the silencing of birds, the missing insects, the disrespected waterways. Heart-impaired, ecologically awkward people mindlessly carry out the destruction.

Regarding the quote, in my view, patriarchy and its wedding with Judaism and Christianity have *caused* the groaning of the earth. Even though I was a devout Christian when I was young, raised in an evangelical household, I did not know alternatives, I did not know the history of destruction, I did not have much ecological attachment, I did not know of Christianity's supremacist orientation—to make everyone believe the same and do as the Europeans wanted or be killed in body and/or spirit. And now capitalism/globalization has the same attitude. This is evil in action, promoting suffering instead of life. Such beliefs have torn up the earth and the deep sacred wisdom of Indigenous peoples everywhere. Indigenous spirituality is life giving, life honoring. It is an expression of the songs of creation—each people's expression unique, but with the same underlying heartbeat of Mother Earth.

I got rather carried away on Christianity's history. There are exceptions to the history I could bring up (e.g., Matthew Fox's creation spirituality, Jesus's statements as recorded). I appreciated LeBlanc's attempt to wed the worldviews and honor the earth, but I was surprised you selected this quote. Do you want to say more about that?

Four Arrows: I wrestled with the choice to use a Christian American Indian only because of a concern my intent might not be understood, so thank you for asking. According to the NAIITS website for its journal,[6] LeBlanc's organization "seeks to bring together men and women of varied experience and background in mission, ministry and community service from within the mainstream of evangelical Christian faith, intentionally providing a forum for the development of biblical and theological thought from within Indigenous North American points of view." For many years I have pondered, studied, and written about whether such a merger between Christianity and Indigeneity is possible. For example, the journal *Critical Education* published my article titled "'False Doctrine' Christianity and the Failure of Indigenous Political Will."[7] In the collection of essays I edited, *Unlearning the Language of Conquest: Scholars Expose Anti-Indianism in America,*[8] I wrote a chapter on this topic in which I offer an argument for a way Christianity and Indigenous worldview might be compatible. Near the end of the chapter, I write: "Or maybe this theory of the twin relationships is no more than a wistful hope for a partnerships between the dominant religion of the United States and the Indigenous spiritual philosophies of the land. In his article, 'Canaanites, Cowboys, and Indians,' published in *Christianity and Crises,* Robert Allen Warrior, a member of the Osage Nation, tends to agree that the Bible will always be incompatible with authentic Indigenous ways of seeing the world."

Warrior's position is that "we will perhaps do better to look elsewhere for our vision of justice, peace and political sanity." I end the chapter with reference to the overwhelming influence of Christian fundamentalism and how its "subtle power continues to suppress a worldview that may be our only true 'salvation.'"[9]

Still, LeBlanc's eloquent call for understanding the teachings of Jesus as being nonanthropocentric offers possibilities. Perhaps he is helping Christians learn how Jesus was trying to bring the world back to our original way of being in it, and that his intent and words have been misinterpreted and used by the prevailing dominant worldview in ways that contract his teachings. In the meantime, I close my part of our dialogue with this song by Australian Aboriginal activist Hyllus Maris, which represents what I mean and which I hope LeBlanc would support as part of his "cry for the rest of creation."

Spiritual Song of the Aborigine

I am a child of the Dreamtime People
Part of this Land, like the gnarled gumtree
I am the river, softly singing
Chanting our songs on my way to the sea
My spirit is the dust-devils
Mirages, that dance on the plain
I'm the snow, the wind and the falling rain
I'm part of the rocks and the red desert earth
Red as the blood that flows in my veins
I am eagle, crow and snake that glides
Thorough the rain-forest that clings to the mountainside
I awakened here when the earth was new
There was emu, wombat, kangaroo
No other man of a different hue
I am this land
And this land is me
I am Australia.[10]

Darcia: Lovely and deep. In my book *Neurobiology and the Development of Human Morality: Evolution, Culture and Wisdom,* I mentioned the characteristics of group psychopathology: extreme in-group loyalty and scapegoating of outsiders; big group ego; desire for group dominance; dogmatism rooted in either/or thinking; in-group hoarding and exploitation of natural resources; and vicious imagination (using planning skills for control or harm to others). These reflect a deep disconnection from the community of life. I noted: "Christianity describes separation from God as the ultimate punishment, but according to an Indigenous perspective, Western culture has created its own separation from God (Nature). And by its separation from Life in every corner of creation, Western culture has created its own hell."[11]

I also listed some of the beliefs that must be altered for Indigenous wisdom to take root. For example, that nature is malevolent rather than benevolent; that nature is dumb or dead rather than full of sacred,

sentient beings; that human nature is evil and to be coerced into goodness; and that we are all just waiting for the afterlife instead of finding
eternity now. The alternatives match up well with the list you gave of
the characteristics of the nonanthropocentric Indigenous worldview.

As I documented in my book, many of the anthropocentric assumptions have roots in preverbal early life, based on how a child is treated
and which capacities are grown from which kinds of experiences. For
example, early toxic stress (degraded evolved nest or trauma) can
create a disposition toward distress, shifting the developmental trajectory toward an egocentric, self-protective orientation to life, undermining learning and openness to others, especially to difference. This
makes one susceptible to the group pathologies I mentioned. Without
intervening experiences like nature immersion, there will be a disconnection from the rest of life. As mentioned in our discussion of precept 1, there are ways to feel more connected to the natural world and
become less anthropocentric.

The child treated with respect and shown the ways to connect to
All will have healthy right hemisphere development, which grows
capacities for connections to higher consciousness and sense of Spirit.
Back to Turnbull's observations of the Mbuti, who are deeply cooperative and inclusive without any coercion: "For them, at least, it is that
awareness of Spirit that enables them to accept differences of manner,
custom, speech, behavior, even of belief, while still feeling an underlying unity. It is awareness of Spirit that enables them to avoid the conflict and hostility that arise so easily from such differences."[12]

An awareness of Spirit, then, is key for Indigenous nonanthropocentrism. It is nurtured in early life with the evolved nest and nourished in a community that attends to the transpersonal nature of the
living relational web that includes ancestors and other-than-humans.
Life begins and ends in connection, in Spirit.

12.

Words Are Sacred (Truthfulness)

Ed McGaa, a.k.a. Eagle Man (Oglala Lakota)

*N*ature is very, very truthful. Does not a ball always fall toward the earth? Does not the sun rise in the east and set in the west and always on a daily basis? Does the cold come from the north in the northern half of the planet? Do streams flow toward the lower places? Do the animals not always direct their lifestyle toward the direction that the Higher Power has given them?

Therefore, Nature can be depended upon as being supremely truthful. Nature does not lie!

I believe that unless modern day two leggeds can learn that high state of truthfulness, eventually we will lose the planet and we will suffer a great amount of disharmony before we arrive at that fateful destiny. We really do not deserve this planet unless we can return to that state. I have a strong supposition; all that Nature exhibits is pure, unalterable Truth. I also believe that Nature will exact some severe, corrective measures if we humans cannot take charge of our errant conduct and destructive values.

Source

Ed McGaa, Eagle Man. *Native Wisdom: Perceptions of the Natural Way*, 19, 22. Minneapolis: Four Directions Publishing, 1995.

Contextualized Biosketch

Ed McGaa (Eagle Man) was the last of thirteen children born in his family during the Depression on the Pine Ridge Reservation in South Dakota. He joined the Marine Corps and served in Korea and Vietnam, where he flew 110 missions, as many as five in a twenty-four-hour period. For his distinguished record, he earned eight Air Medals and two Crosses of Gallantry and was nominated for a Distinguished Flying Cross. He has participated in six Sun Dances under Chiefs Fools Crow and Eagle Feather. After earning a bachelor's degree and a law degree, he became a published author of fiction and nonfiction, depicting the history and experiences of his people. In his later years, he led workshops and wrote books on Native spirituality. His book *Mother Earth Spirituality: Native American Paths to Healing Ourselves and Our World,* published by HarperOne, is in its forty-fifth printing.

Indigenous Worldview Precept Dialogue

Darcia: Truthfulness is fundamental, yet Western scholarship for centuries has moved against natural law, thinking that their human powers (their truth) were superior to nature (nature's truth) and that they needed to conquer nature. So, I believe dishonesty has been part of civilization generally. To harm our animal and plant partners with little conscience takes a denial of relational connection. That can be called a lie.

As Thomas Cooper learned from his interviews and observations of multiple North American Native American tribes, lying was considered a sign of insanity:[1] "A person who does not speak truth must not know reality, and thus is to be pitied." Tadodaho Chief Leon Shenandoah put it poetically:

The Creator made us for honoring Him.
He put in us the ability to work for the good of all.
One of the things He did

Was give us ears, and ears are not mouths.
Ears were put on the side of our heads
So that we would hear all that goes on around us.
That's to let us know things before we talk.
Our mouths are on the front of our face so that our words can be
    directed.
We're to use that gift of speech for specific purposes.
It should be limited, otherwise we can mislead.
When we mislead, we can influence the people
To take a wrong direction or course of action.
That can cause a lot of harm. . . .
Watch what you say. Somebody is always listening.
It could be another human being
And that person could turn your words around on you,
Especially if you talk about somebody.
It's not just human beings who may hear you.
Spirits are always about, and they hear you, too.[2]

Among First Nation communities, honesty is expected from every-one. E. Richard Sorenson summarized his experiences living with peoples around the world whom he described as having a "preconquest consciousness." These were communities where babies had priority and were continuously carried or held, extensively breastfed, and responded to quickly, and eliciting delight from them was a norm (all elements of humanity's evolved nest):[3]

> I was astonished to see the words of tiny children accepted at face
> value—and so acted on. For months I tried to find at least one case
> where a child's words were considered immature and therefore disre-
> garded. No luck. I tried to explain the idea of lying and inexperience.
> They didn't get my point. They didn't expect prevarication, decep-
> tion, grandstanding, or evasion. And I could find no cases where they
> understood these concepts. Even teenagers remained transparently
> forthright, their hearts opened wide for all to gaze inside.[4]

I think deception in civilized countries starts with poor baby care, where the baby is told "I love you" by a parent and then left alone, left to cry, or forced into an adult schedule. That doesn't feel like love. It's a lie. The baby will feel subconsciously disconnected from self, others, and the world and will have to find an outlet for deep anxiety, and sometimes a target for rage. Then as the child grows older, the child is punished for following urges to learn and grow, so the child starts to lie to avoid punishment. I think this sets people up for believing and living in a world of deception and falsehoods. They get thrown off their natural development and have an impaired sense of reality. They become easily manipulated by half-truths by master manipulators.

The amount of lying that has gone on in the USA recently is astounding. In his book *Fantasyland,* Kurt Andersen argued that Europeans were lured to the Americas with false advertising, and he thinks that has made Americans susceptible to fantasy ever since.[5] In the USA, people are constantly manipulated, smothered in propaganda from corporations primarily, and now significantly so by politicians funded by oligarchs.

Four Arrows: Twice I have read your words about how people might learn to be deceptive initially via a contradiction early on between a parent's overt promises of love and the subsequent lack of evidence of caring. I remembered that *Paths of Learning,* a journal I wrote for years ago, had a themed issue titled "Do Americans Really Care for Their Children?" All the contributors wrote articles in the affirmative. Then I thought about people I know closely, and I found tears forming. It was not so. Truly, Eagle Man has it right. It is not natural to be dishonest. He reinforces your words about a disconnect from Nature being at the root of dishonesty in a passage he wrote for a chapter in one of my books: "The Natural Way of spirituality is a matter of living your beliefs according to what you know, understand and feel in the presence of that which is Nature. It is a lifetime of moral and ethical application of integrity and caring for others."[6]

This contention that honesty is rooted and demonstrated in our other-than-human environment and practiced under our original worldview is not something our educators teach us, despite the rhetoric about the importance of truthfulness. Instead, our best-selling philosophers tell us that "Mother Nature has seen to it that the conscious mind is relatively blind to the nuances of social behavior."[7] Worse, our neuroscientists, using brain scans and laboratory studies on honesty and deception, generally conclude that deception is a higher-order brain function that evolved to help humans survive. In the book I coauthored with him, Greg Cajete responds to the studies we cite that come to this conclusion:

> This does not make much sense to me. There can be little doubt
> that deception has "evolved" to play a large role in the world today.
> However, in Indigenous ways of thinking, we learn to observe and
> listen carefully so as to understand physical reality and experience,
> not to find ways to misrepresent it! . . . Learning how differing real-
> ities interact is real understanding. Our knowledge comes from
> our stories that mirror the way the human mind works. They echo
> a truth lived and remembered because their roots go beyond the
> context processes of the brain. . . . If deception, not right thinking
> and remembering, were tools for social cohesions, as these studies
> conclude, it seems survival would be compromised, not enhanced.
> Moreover, Nature is the first and foremost teacher of how things are
> in the world. This is why animals and plants are considered to be
> teachers for us. Neither Nature nor animals lie about reality.[8]

"Survival would be compromised, not enhanced" shouts out for us to look around. Is there a connection between human dishonesty under the dominant view of the world being more about dog-eat-dog competition than cooperation and mutual aid? Look around, I say.

Darcia, as a world leader on human development, your references that connect Indigenous worldview to child-rearing throughout our chapters continue to give richness to the worldview discussion. With this in mind, and going back to how the relative mistreatment of children creates habits of dishonesty, I want to share a story about my grandson. When he was six years old, my daughter sent him to be with my wife and me for a few months while she suffered through a difficult divorce. On his second night in our little Mexican fishing village, I took him to a small outside restaurant on the ocean to have dinner. After we finished, I went to pay the bill. When I came back, he had taken all the napkins out of the napkin holder on the table and had torn them into little pieces. He was sitting innocently at the table, looking at the ocean.

I said, "Hey, grandson, who did this?" and pointed at the torn paper. Without hesitating, he pointed at the waitress.

I was surprised at such a bold lie. I was not concerned about the napkins. I would just have had him apologize to the waitress and would have made my tip larger to replace the napkins. But I was concerned about such a blatant lie and thought I might be able to prevent it from happening again during the rest of his stay. I told him he would not have gotten in much trouble for tearing the paper, but that telling a lie and blaming an innocent person are a bigger problem. I told him if he lied again, he would not like the consequences. I said I would walk away and come back and ask him again who did it, expecting he would confess honestly.

True to my word, I walked away, came back, and said, "Wow, what a mess. Who did that to the napkins?" Then he looked around. A man at a table nearby had just gotten up to pay his bill. My grandson pointed at him and said, "He did it."

I usually laugh when I tell this story, especially since at this writing he is a very squared-away, generous, and honest young man of seventeen in addition to being a nationally ranked gymnast with universities trying to recruit him. I think living with us for the next six months turned him around. His life with us did not have the constant manipulative half-truths common in his world, guided mostly by the dominant worldview.

Darcia: Ha! I have several reactions as an armchair analyst. First, this is a boy coming from a troubled place—he was probably made afraid early on or from trauma—and so the world would seem untrustworthy. Why should he trust you? I suspect he was punished, either intentionally or unintentionally, seeding his self-hiding. He may have felt betrayed so frequently that he had no sense of safety, putting him into a self-protectionist disposition, which operates according to what worked to bring about a sense of safety in the past—like lying. At the same time, by tearing up the napkins he acted out in frustration, destroying something to try to alleviate his anxiety. Then he rationalizes the action so as to protect himself from punishment. On a more optimistic note, your grandson may have been teasing you, trying to play, perhaps not knowing how to do so appropriately. I'm sure you taught him many other ways to be, other than destructive and self-protective.

I think it is important to understand how detrimental fear in childhood is. Fear makes it hard to learn truthfulness. I like what Jiddu Krishnamurti says about fear:

> It is really very important while you are young to live in an environment in which there is no fear. . . . Most of us have fear in one form or another; and where there is fear, there is no intelligence. And is it not possible for all of us, while we are young, to be in an environment where there is no fear but rather an atmosphere of freedom—freedom, not just to do what we like, but to understand the whole process of living? Life is really very beautiful; it is not this ugly thing that we have made of it. . . . To live is to find out for yourself what is true, and you can do this only when there is freedom. . . . We must create immediately an atmosphere of freedom so that you can live and find out for yourselves what is true, so that you become intelligent, so that you are able to face the world and understand it, not just conform to it. . . . It is only when you are constantly inquiring, constantly observing, constantly learning, that you find truth, God, or love; and you cannot inquire, observe, learn, you cannot be deeply aware, if you are afraid. So the function of education, surely, is to eradicate, inwardly as well as outwardly, this fear that destroys human thought, human relationship and love.[9]

In early childhood (before age six), life should be worry-free so that the child's neurobiology grows in a healthy manner. Otherwise, fear is like a poison to a young animal. The animal might survive but it will not reach its full potential, without some healing experience or intervention.

Four Arrows: Thanks for your "armchair analysis" about the source possibilities of my grandson's blatant lie when he was six. I would agree it was fear of punishment; however, I believe a sense of punishment begins with a sense of authoritarian hierarchy as an intrusion on authentic love. He was being sent to his grandfather, whom he knew as the person his mother always used as an authority figure. I believe, notwithstanding the possible effects of historical trauma, that children are born as pure egalitarians and have a strong sense of altruistic generosity. They naturally desire both belonging and independence. In fact, in my experience, a healthy, happy, cared-for and dry-diapered baby is hard to scare. Larry Brendtro once told me a story about an experiment long ago that used surprise, loud noises, ugly masks, and all sorts of methods to get such a baby to cry. The only thing that worked was a recording of another baby crying.

Any sensibility that allows for seeing another as somehow superior creates a defensive consciousness. R. Michael Fisher calls it a "defense intelligence" or "DI."[10] Once a child's psyche perceives a real threat from another, the brain invokes one of two main avoidance strategies: submissiveness or deception. More than ever before in our post-truth world, we can see that over time these strategies become more and more a part of the fabric of living under our misguided dominant worldview. In closing I share some thoughts I wrote for a chapter in the collection of essays we helped to edit, *Indigenous Sustainable Wisdom: First Nation Know-How for Global Flourishing.* As you will recall, the title of the chapter was "Truthful Communications as a Sacred Practice":

Indigenous communication was inseparable from the spiritual sense of interconnectedness to all things visible and invisible. There was a kind of telepathic interplay with other-than-human sentience that seemed to be mutually understood. This telepathy also worked between humans and co-existed with verb-based languages that stemmed directly from the sacred places in which Indigenous tribes lived. Words were understood as sacred vibrations that continued to vibrate into the universe. The idea of intentionally speaking untruthfully was, by all accounts, unthinkable. Then came the conquerors who had long since departed from original ways of being in the world. With their noun-based languages, greed, and strategic lies, communication lost its sacredness.

13

Mutual Dependence

Jack Forbes (Powhatan-Lenape, Delaware-Lenape; 1934–2011)

*T*_{*he fact of our absolute, utter, complete dependence upon the earth is used by native teachers as a part of self-understanding. It is empirically obvious that we are not only children, sucking at our earth-mother's breast all of our lives, but that we are also mixed with, and part of, that which Europeans choose to call the environment.* For us, truly, there are no "surroundings."}

I can lose my hands, and still live. I can lose my legs and still live. I can lose my eyes and still live. I can lose my hair, eyebrows, nose, arms and many other things and still live. But if I lose the air I die. If I lose the sun I die. If I lose the earth I die. If I lose the water I die. If I lose the plants and animals I die. All of these things are more a part of me, more essential to my every breath, than is my so-called body. What is my real body?

We are not autonomous, self-sufficient beings as European mythology teaches. Such ideas are based upon deductive logic derived from false assumptions. We are rooted, just like the trees. But our roots come out of our nose and mouth, like an umbilical cord, forever connected with the rest of the world. Our roots also extend out from our skin and from our other body cavities.

Nothing that we do, do we do by ourselves. We do not see by ourselves. We do not hear by ourselves. We do not breathe, eat, drink, defecate, piss, or fart by ourselves. We do not think, dream, invent or procreate by ourselves. We do not die by ourselves.

That which the tree exhales, I inhale. That which I exhale, the trees inhale. Together we form a circle. When I breathe I am breathing the breath of billions of now-departed trees and plants. When trees and plants breathe they are breathing the breath of billions of now-departed humans, animals, and other peoples. As Lame Deer said, "A human being, too, is many things. Whatever makes up the air, the earth, the herbs, the stones is also part of our bodies. . . ."

Who was my mother? An egg? Who was my father, a little animal called a sperm? But where did this egg and this sperm come from? They grew inside a woman and inside a man, but they had their own life-paths distinct from those of the man and the woman. Their bodies, that flesh, my ancestor, grew inside of them and what was it? It was the earth, it was the sky, it was the sun, it was the plants and animals. We are very lucky to have so many wonderful mothers and fathers!

I live in a universe. I am a point of awareness, a circle of consciousness, in the midst of a series of circles. One circle is that which we call the body. It is a universe itself, full of millions of little living creatures living their own separate but co-dependent lives. They live, fight, make love, split, and die independent of my consciousness, most of the time. If some of them get disturbed or get hurt they might tell me about it so that I can help them, so that I can get them some food, or scratch them, or get rid of their left-overs.

Another circle is all of the other things which I am completely dependent upon—Gishux, the sun, the air, the water, and so on. Another circle is all of the things that fill my consciousness—the things I see, smell, hear, and so on. Another circle is the source of my dreams, consciousness, insights, gifts or powers, ideas, and "intuitions."

But all of these "circles" are not really separate—they are all mutually dependent upon each other, they are all mixed up with each other, they all overlap and move in, and out, of each other.

And that mutual dependence blurs into the circle of love, that mystery, that glue that holds all of this together. Scientists may call it attraction, or affinity, or magnetism, or gravity, as well as affection, symbiosis, kinship, community, family, compassion, or whatever. But there is that circle, that mysterious circle, that makes life possible.

Source

Jack D. Forbes. *Columbus and Other Cannibals: The* Wétiko *Disease of Exploitation, Imperialism, and Terrorism,* 181–83. Rev ed. New York: Seven Stories Press, 2008.

Contextualized Biosketch

Jack D. Forbes, PhD, earned degrees in philosophy, history, and anthropology. In the early 1960s, he was an activist in the newly emerged Native American movement that asserted Native rights to sovereignty and resisted assimilation into the dominant culture. After he joined the faculty at the University of California, Davis, he helped found a Native American studies program there. In 1971, he helped found Deganawidah-Quetzalcoatl University, the first tribal college in California. In his writing, both fiction and nonfiction, he explored the confluence of Native, African, and European histories. Among his books are *Columbus and Other Cannibals, The American Discovery of Europe,* and *Apache, Navaho, and Spaniard.* His signature work is considered to be *Africans and Native Americans: The Language of Race and the Evolution of Red-Black Peoples,* in which he studied the fluidity of race in US colonial history. The book remarked on how Natives who were part Black were classified by authorities as Black, subverting their Native culture. Among his awards are the American Book Award for Lifetime Achievement from the Before Columbus Foundation, Writer of the Year from Wordcraft Circle, and a Lifetime Achievement Award from the Native Writers' Circle of the Americas. The library at UC Davis has a special collection of his papers.

Indigenous Worldview Precept Dialogue

Darcia: When I first read this years ago, it was like being struck by lightning, restoring a truth known deep in my bones—my dependence on the earth. The feeling of deep connection with the earth is sometimes called an oceanic feeling (Freud) or peak experience (Maslow). Interestingly, in his research, Maslow found that not all people have peak experiences.[1] But I think he was referring to civilized people who grow up away from the rest of the natural world, encouraged to feel disconnected from and superior to it, which civilization has seeded over millennia and accelerated in the last few hundred years.[2] In the last couple of millennia, European people, their colonies, and their international networks have had their attention pushed-pulled to strivings, advancement, and conquest. Because of their restlessness, they have a hard time being still enough to feel deep connection to place, especially to relationships in a particular landscape. In contrast, among First Nation peoples traditionally there is daily attention to the rest of nature, and daily practices like ceremonies of gratitude enhance opportunities for peak experiences.

Forbes makes me reflect on the question: who are we really? Asian and African societies traditionally don't conceive of a person as an individual, but as a relation. The Nguni Bantu term *ubuntu* is translated as "I am, because you are," a reference to relational connection. Among Confucians, a sense of oneness extends to the entire universe. But in these cases, they mostly discuss the relational web among human persons. What I like about Forbes' statements is that he gives us the language to discuss our dependence on the wider web of life—who are we without the sentient earth? Although Forbes doesn't mention it here, I'm sure he would agree with an even wider circle that includes our being made from stardust (Carl Sagan's common phrase). Remembering that I am always in a web of "all our relations," grand and small, lifts my spirit, pulls me out of my self-concerns, for I am never alone. I am a wave on an ocean of life. How can you be lonely nestled in the arms of Mother Earth?

Four Arrows: When I read the part of the quote saying "nothing we do, we do by ourselves," I was still high from having just played a few games of one-wall handball with a friend. I smiled at the realization that this phrase pervaded this experience. Allow me to think this through with you to see if I can make some relevant connections. I start by noting that playing handball with someone else was far more fun than just hitting the ball against the wall by myself. As the Firth twins say in our chapter on sport and competition, it is the interaction with others that allows us to excel. No runner ever broke a world record without racing someone else.

In handball, the interaction with the person you are trying to keep from hitting the ball back to you is more holistic. Body, mind, and spirit all come into play. I think of the Maya hero twins, Hunahpu and Xbalanque, who many say invented one-wall handball three thousand years ago. The twins represent solar and lunar symbiosis and the flowing balance between the sun and moon energies. One can only play handball well when the right and left hands work equally in harmony.

Mutual intimacy with the ball comes to my mind next. Because no racquet or paddle is separating it from one's hand, there is something magical about the interdependent physics. Keeping your eye on the ball is crucial because the slightest deviation from a perfect connection sends the ball where you did not want it to go. This means working in harmony with gravity and the remarkable interplay the ball has with the ground. After the initial impact, the ball rapidly decelerates from the speed coming of the wall, but miraculously it then accelerates in a negative direction. I have always thought of this as "becoming one with the ball."

Forbes also talks about the exchange of air with the trees. A large tree to the left of our court has a branch coming out over its center. If we hit the ball too high and hit the branch, we lose the point. So our awareness of it is continual, as is our appreciation that at the same time, it shades us from the hot Mexican sun. Although there is no time to be conscious that the tree is also sending me the oxygen needed for this highly cardiovascular event, I am sufficiently aware of the partnership, and it makes the game all the more delicious for me.

I'll stop now, but I could go on and on. My point is that, indeed, "I am a point of awareness, a circle of consciousness, in the midst of a series of circles. One circle is that which we call the body."

Darcia: Nice description of some of the complexities of dynamic interconnecting flow. Unless we are in a logical thinking/problem-solving mode or in considerable distress, we reside in such a connected flow of existence, a receptive, creative liminal space. How wide our perception is will depend on such things as brain development, trance-based experiences, and current activity, but also the stories that your culture has taught you. It was called "participation mystique" by anthropologist Lucien Lévy-Bruhl,[3] labeled "primitive" in contrast to Western logical thinking, and taken up by Carl Jung as part of an earlier evolution of human consciousness. Historian Marvin Bram calls this connected flow state "polysemy,"[4] interconnecting with the supernatural and the dynamic flux of other beings, and he describes how the Western world shut it down more and more over time due to an emphasis on work and the control of nature and people, increasingly focusing on the narrow logical-problem solving mode he calls univocity. Flow is taken more seriously in positive psychology, but it usually only refers to one's body performing an activity (e.g., playing golf), not to broader interconnectedness with the rest of nature, both manifest and unmanifest. This kind of receptivity is still viewed with suspicion by Western science, apart from physicists like David Bohm. We will need to restore polysemy if we are to survive as a species.

But I'd like to go more deeply into our mutual dependence in everyday life. Did you know that 90 percent to 99 percent of the genes that a human being carries in her body are not human genes?[5] They are the genes of the microbiome—the community of bacteria, viruses, fungi, and protozoa that keep us alive. They do such things as digest our food, manufacture vitamins we need, and keep our immune systems in working order. So, there is no such thing as an "individual." Each human being is a community of beings. This is another arena of vast cooperation, the kind of mutualism that is dominant in the natural world, with competition being a smaller component. When our "community of beings" gets out of balance, we get symptoms of being ill. Our microbiome keeps us healthy if we treat it properly, for example, taking in more *pro*biotic substances rather than *anti*biotic ones (which kill off "bad" and "good" bacteria). Notice that we all carry viruses, just like all animals. This new awareness calls into question the idea that we should seek to exterminate a particular virus when we get sick. Better to get things back into balance.

Four Arrows: Our opening quote references, albeit indirectly, how everything we do is orchestrated via our microbiome: "We do not breathe, eat, drink, defecate, piss, or fart by ourselves." Making connections between this worldview precept and viruses is also most appropriate considering we are in mass communication now with the COVID-19 virus. I believe this messenger is trying to tell us about mutual dependence. It is not a coincidence that the most polluted places are getting hit the worst. This applies to the Navajo Nation, and to North and South Dakota, all of which have among the highest death rates in the world. In addition to poor health care resources and lower immunity potential, all three places suffer from industrial pollution forced upon the reservations. The Navajo have been dealing with water and air pollution from uncapped uranium mines since the 1960s. Air pollution in North Dakota comes from thirteen thousand active oil and gas wells and processing plants.[6] South Dakota has been suffering from poor air quality owing to forest fires. A simple Google search reveals the relationship between air pollution and COVID-19. However, sources of the pollution remain in full swing. Deforestation and pollution have increased. As journalist Beth Gardiner puts it: "The popular notion that the COVID-19 pandemic has been 'good for the environment'—that nature is recovering while humanity stays at home—appeals to many people grasping for some upside to the global tragedy. Reality, though, may not cooperate with such hopes."[7]

Air pollution is not the only factor in the deadly spread of this novel coronavirus. Cutting down forests and subsequent development is increasing extinction rates of mutually dependent species. Those that survive are hosting new and dangerous pathogens. As humans encroach into their territories, our exposure to these pathogens is inevitable. However, instead of focusing on these causes of the pandemic, we focus only on vaccine development, diagnosis, and containment. We treat the symptoms and ignore the cause. "We've been warning about this for decades," says ecological modeler Kate Jones. "Nobody paid attention."[8] We are not paying attention because our dominant worldview gets in the way. For all of us living amid and largely supporting settler colonialism, we must begin to recognize what Forbes tells us: "Nothing that we do we do by ourselves." Once we realize this truth, mutual aid will become our banner in life. What happened and is happening to Indigenous peoples is beginning to happen to everyone as earth systems are breaking down everywhere. Let's join together in a unified commitment to helping one another, remembering that "other" includes even the dust particles on which we walk (if you are fortunate enough to walk on unconcretized land.)

Speaking of dust particles, I just thought of a good way for me to conclude our dialogue that connects mutual dependence to the "circle of love" that Forbes describes. Last year I was on a panel with three soil experts talking about the soil crises facing our world. Each of the scientists spoke articulately about the importance of soil health for human survival. I learned much. I went last. I stood up and thanked them for their significant knowledge and recommendations, but then added, "It won't make a difference, I'm afraid." I proceeded to show a slide that had similar affirmations from three people in history that I respect for their concern about "the environment." The largely ignored quotes were:

> "A nation that destroys its soil, destroys itself."—Franklin Delano Roosevelt

> "To forget how to dig the earth and tend the soil is to forget ourselves."—Mahatma Gandhi

> "Without proper care for the soil, we can have no life."—Wendell Berry

After everyone studied each quote for a minute, I asked them to compare it to this one:

"Every part of this soil is sacred in the estimation of my people. Even the rocks thrill with memories of stirring events connected with us, and the very dust upon which we stand responds lovingly to our footsteps."—Chief Seathl (Suquamish)

I think this is what Jack Forbes means by mutual dependence blurring into a circle of love.

14

Complementary Duality

Barbara Alice Mann (Seneca)

*H*ere is the first truth: Nothing in the European mindset prepares Westerners for anything in the Turtle Island mindset. . . . Here is the second truth: The only way to grasp Turtle is to take Her on Her own terms. . . . In truly traditional thought, there is no dichotomous Good and Evil duking it out for supremacy. The whole point of the Twinned Cosmos is to achieve balance, not the victory of one over the other. Third, either Blood or Breath is capable of injuring the cosmos if used without balance. Lack of balance requires rebalancing, not the obliteration of one half in favor of the other. . . . One of the most important of the iconic references to pairing comes in the Twinship of "Blood" and "Breath" (also rendered "water" and "air," respectively, typically west of the Mississippi River). I know that, when Europeans hear Blood, they immediately think, "death, **destruction, Murder Most Foul!**" but Indian traditionals think, "menstruation, **conception, Successful Childbirth!**" Blood is creativity, and creativity is life, which is forcefully expressed by women through their twinned ability to bleed without dying and to pull new life from their wombs. Thus, Blood goes beyond the simplistic Western definition of physical lineage, and deeply into the realm of cosmic potency.

Clans spring from the Blood half of physical birth through their mothers, with Blood (and water) very obviously connecting to childbirth. This is why most North American groups are matrilineal, with some downright matriarchal. . . . Blood's creativity belongs exclusively *to women. Male bleeding is destructive. Men who bleed are injured and may die, so that what men create from the Blood half is death. Death is not as powerful as life, so that women are in ascendency in the Blood half of the cosmos. . . .*

*Men are in the ascendency with Breath. Westerners associate Breath with "air quality, **ozone**, **EMPHYSEMA**," whereas traditionals think, "wind, **wings**, **SPEECH**." If women work from watery caves up to level, then men work from airy heights down to level. . . . Men's special creativity is their ability to set up physical vibrations in the air, a medicine which, in powerful shamans, can be harnessed to extract things through the orifices, the reason that chants and blowing medicine are always male-practiced, at least in traditional circles.*

Source

Barbara Alice Mann. *Spirits of Blood, Spirits of Breath: The Twinned Cosmos of Indigenous America*, 41, 47–49. New York: Oxford University Press, 2016.

Contextualized Biosketch

Barbara Alice Mann is a professor of humanities at the University of Toledo. She lives and works in Ohio, traditionally the Land of the Three Miamis (which refers to three of Ohio's rivers). Her scholarship uses tools of ethnography, oral tradition, history, and sharp humor in her pioneering work in Native American history, women's studies, and literature. She has published hundreds of papers and over a dozen books, including *Iroquoian Women: The Gantowisas; Native American Speakers in the Eastern Woodlands; Native Americans, Archaeologists, and the Mounds; George Washington's War on Native America; Daughters of Mother Earth: The Wisdom of Native American Women; The Tainted Gift: The Disease Method of Frontier Expansion; Spirits of Blood, Spirits of Breath: The Twinned Cosmos of Indigenous America;* and *President by Massacre: Indian-Killing for Political Gain.*

Indigenous Worldview Precept Dialogue

Darcia: To read Barbara Mann is to be led into the Indigenous world of complementarity, with a special emphasis on the importance of the balance between men and women. The violence perpetrated against Mother Nature via the relatively recent dominant worldview and the poor treatment of women in cultures that follow it represent disregard for such balance. Paula Gunn Allen discusses this violence:

> The physical and cultural genocide of American Indian tribes is and was mostly about patriarchal fear of gynocracy. . . . The colonizers saw (and rightly) that as long as women held unquestioned power of such magnitude, attempts at total conquest of the continents were bound to fail. In the centuries since the first attempts at colonization in the early 1500s, the invaders have exerted every effort to remove Indian women from every position of authority, to obliterate all records pertaining to gynocratic social systems, and to ensure that no American and few American Indians would remember that gynocracy was the primary social order of Indian America prior to 1800.[1]

This kind of fear of women seems to have led European Christians to instigate inquisitions and "witch" burnings.[2]

Patriarchal dominator cultures have put us out of balance in many ways. However, I think understanding the positioning of women under the dominant worldview is most vital. Most of us have recognized or experienced the great power imbalance between men and women. In my family, my mother was the most bullied member of the family, and my father was the key role model, based on his own socialization. You can see such husband-wife dynamics in early television shows like *The Honeymooners*. At our church, women were second-class members who could not hold power over men. When there are no role models for women's creative strength but a denigration of them as inferior, girls can grow separate from their feminine nature. It happened to me. I was the only girl for nine years and my father's favorite. In adolescence, I refused to follow the dictates of the culture's view of womanhood, such as wearing makeup. I taught myself not to move my hips much when I walked and to carry my books like a boy (arm straight instead of hooking them on my hip). It turns out that my path reflects what Maureen Murdock calls the heroine's journey.[3] *The first step in that journey is a separation from the feminine, and the next is to identify with masculine values.* (Many women continue, sadly, to live in this space.) Multiple steps in my journey finally led to an embrace of the feminine and an integration of masculine and feminine aspects of the self.

Perhaps my journey is why I am passionate about my studies relating to mothering and especially to traditional Indigenous approaches to mothering. I see such mothering as a preliminary step in preparing people to seek complementarity in others, no matter how different they seem. This essentially is what Indigenous mothers (and those who intuitively mother accordingly) do. They are all about engaging and growing full human capacities in the other, including fostering a deeper sense of connection with others and with the larger All.[4] To rebalance the world by seeking complementary duality, we must return to honoring mothering and mothers who essentially teach such seeking under our original worldview. Sadly, as Mann says in her quote, European men were frightened to see the power of women in the Indigenous cultures they came upon, and we continue to live with this tragic legacy. Men from dominator cultures generally do not seek complementarity with women, and perhaps women no longer do so with men as a defense. Four Arrows, what from the Indigenous worldview do you see as it relates to the masculine-feminine pairing and the "twinning" phenomenon that relates to complementarity?

Four Arrows: As you will see, I address male-female duality and other gender dualities by not using gender terms, but I'll get to that shortly. The main point for the worldview precept reflected in Dr. Mann's quote resides in her assertion that "the whole point of the Twinned Cosmos is to achieve balance, not the victory of one over the other." She refers to the "twinning" of air and water, breath and blood, to illustrate the Western world's imbalance, especially as it relates to male and female power dynamics. Exposing the disregard for the traditional balance between men and women in Indigenous cultures and how it contrasts to dominant cultures has long been her academic domain. However, it is not the male-female dynamic per se that I wish to address in this section. As reflected in Indigenous worldview and the great diversity of Indigenous cultures under its umbrella, complementary duality is a broader and a deeper conversation.

All cultures worldwide identify binary pairings such as male-female, sky-earth, hot-cold, dry-wet, spirit-flesh, up-down, etc. Differences between dominant and Indigenous orientations relate to the degree to which people seek complementarity or not. I think we know about oppositional dynamics and emphasis in our dominant worldview-based societies. However, traditional Indigenous societies "see their binary systems as involving them in a constant effort to harmonize with these forces and to hold them in dynamic tension," as David Maybury-Lewis puts it.[5]

Regarding the male-female problematic, my work with Dr. Howard Teich over many years has brought me to see that a better way to discuss it uses "solar-lunar" language.[6] Teich has studied twin-hero stories from around the world. He finds that coincidental with humanity's separation from Nature and its establishment of more hierarchal, patriarchal nation-states, the original Indigenous archetype for twins is modified in the Western myths. Like Jung, he saw constrictions implicit in assigning gender labels to solar and lunar principles. Over the years I have found that replacing "masculine and feminine" with "solar and lunar" when helping clients with related problems has significant benefits.

The reason for this is that the twin archetype embodies the fundamental dichotomy Jung describes as "the primary pair of opposites, consciousness and unconsciousness, whose symbols are Sol and Luna."[7] Joseph Campbell, referring to the Navajo twin story about Monster Slayer (solar) and Child Born of the Water (lunar), described how the myth teaches that a union of these two brings solar/lunar ego into a union of opposites.[8] When this happens, according to Campbell, the life-supporting, mysterious lunar energy tempers the solar fire. (You can see the relevance of this to the male-female dynamic). This means that each of us has to find our own internal balance between our solar and lunar energies, before we can seek complementarity with others who must have also accomplished this.

More significantly for this chapter's worldview precept, the Indigenous twin-heroes always work in complementarity, whereas twin hero stories after our "point of departure"[9] from our Indigenous ways changed so that the solar twin emerged as superior in one way or the other, often killing the lunar twin. Teich explains this on his website:

> We find this solar/lunar dialectic duplicated over and over in Twin myths. The patriarchal myths with which we are most familiar, such as Romulus and Remus or Jacob and Esau, usually portray the Twins as antagonistic. Typically, the Lunar Twin is slain in favor of the Solar Twin. The dominant culture, up to now, has hailed only the Solar Twin as its prototype of masculinity, consigning the Lunar Twin to impotence and oblivion. . . . The sacrifice or suppression of the Lunar Twin runs so deep in our culture that most of us are unaware that nearly every central male hero figure was originally a Twin. Even Hercules, the quintessential patriarchal Solar hero, was born with a powerful (but largely dismissed) lunar Twin named Iphicles.[10]

Darcia: Several things strike me in what you said. I think the twinning references by you and Dr. Mann are similarly represented by the ancient Chinese tradition that also emphasizes balance, although the Indigenous stories refer to the solar-lunar binary, whereas yin-yang generally uses the masculine-feminine binary you critique. In any case, the idea is that when the two forces are out of balance, illness occurs. Whatever analogy is used to describe the imbalance, it has caused a virus that that cannibalizes life and has taken over our planet like a pandemic as a result of "exploitation, imperialism and terrorism" *(wétiko).*[11] *Wétiko*-solarity seems to be intertwined with left-brain dominance, associated with masculinity and patriarchy, over right-brain processing, which the Western world has overemphasized to the detriment of human and earth well-being.[12] Even the Native American twin stories have been masculinized, or to use your reference, have taken power away from the lunar, through hundreds of years of colonization and patriarchalization.[13] I think that the evidence shows that with proper support (the evolved nest), humans grow up with complementary duality intact, with occasional imbalances that their communities help heal. But the world has moved far from supportive childhoods and healing communities due to colonization and other global invasions disrupting healthy societies.

I think in Native communities, it was assumed the *wétiko* virus could be caught by an individual and then could be spread to others. But it is different today. Today, *wétiko*-solarity is infused into most world systems at sociopolitical levels, so people are born into a world of *wétiko*-solarity. They are undercared for and so are susceptible individually to *wétiko*. There are now so many ways to get stuck in *wétiko*-solarity: disconnection, fear, self-protectionsim, cultural stories, lack of attention, inability to perceive, inexperience, ego inflation, and/or poor role modeling that is imitated mindlessly. Children are also taught to believe *wetiko*-solarity is a normal human orientation or even "human progress." The world is currently stuck in an inflamed *wétiko*-solarity cancer.

In my view, the Indigenous worldview and the dominant worldview are not complementarities. The Indigenous worldview and matrifocal culture, with all the nurturing it offers, represents the grounding for the twinned solar-lunar aspects that each person carries, according to Mann. In contrast, the dominant worldview and the culture that brings it about have thrown out the grounding of life on the earth, removed nurturing and nesting. It's as if *wicasa* (protector, man) is trying to murder *winyan* (First Spirit, woman). It leaves people distressed from the beginning, pushing them into *wétiko*-solarity, accompanied by a great deal of anger toward the lunar principle for failing to "show up"—mothers cannot nurture their children properly in a *wétiko*-solarity world. The constant denigration of the lunar twin makes it hard for the return to a matrifocal culture and the grounding for true complementarities.

The notion that the Indigenous and dominant worldviews form a duality I think represents a shifted baseline for what is normal human functioning. "Shifting baselines" is a notion from marine biology, where it was noted that scientists were assuming that the state of the ocean when they were children was its normal (optimal) state.[14] This tyranny-of-the-contemporary assumption led to the inability to perceive the ocean's decline over generations.

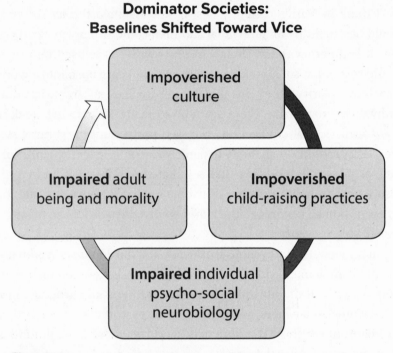

Figure 14.1

Similarly in the human realm, one has to zoom out and take a cross-century view to avoid the same blindness. We have forgotten what children need to thrive, what normal child and adult behavior are, what a healthy society looks like.[15] Figure 14.1 shows how I think of it.[16] We are now into generations of disorder, disorder that starts from the ground up neurobiologically, leading to dysregulated, suboptimal human functioning. For example, coercion like spanking is one of the worst things to do to a young child—it disorders the mind, wounding the spirit/soul/psyche, and makes the child susceptible to *wétiko* and other psychic viruses. Then the impaired adults, from the top down, make poor judgments about how to run society to keep the same cycle of undercare and disorder going (or going worse), because they have not experienced better, and because the cultural stories that those with power tell are that this is the best it can be and that we must "eliminate" the problematic elements (humans or viruses).[17] To get out of the cycle of decline, we must decolonize our minds and our practices to restore a true complementarity.

Four Arrows: All dualities, according to our Indigenous worldview, play a vital role in teaching us about who we are and how we can learn to live as interconnected beings. Hillary Webb's research with Andean Quechua people focuses on *yanantin,* a concept that is about the Quechua's emphasis on seeking complementary dualism.[18] She concludes that complementarity does not require harmony, but it does require recognition. She says the Quechua shamans, who were her research participants, explained to her that those who seem very different from us can serve to help us see ourselves more clearly. She says a complementary worldview that tries to bring antagonisms into interrelationship forces us to go deeper into ourselves to learn what must be learned to live in flowing balance.

I think the best way to understand complementarity is to spend several hours watching a space in the wilderness, a tide pool, or a garden. After a while, the symbiosis of life begins to appear. With the lessons we can take away from such observations, we can be more open to being symbiotic with those we dislike or with whom we feel uncomfortable. Webb told me in an email (or I read it somewhere in her book) that some polarities are so difficult to see as complementary forces that people leave them alone or consider the difference as sufficiently inappropriate that they should focus on better options. This is how I feel about the duality between dominant and Indigenous worldviews. Whether or not we find *yanantin* or pairing between them, we can still use the *yanantin* principle to better understand where we are and where we need to go by seeking to understand the various positions.

THE GREAT SPIRIT MADE US BOTH. HE GAVE US LAND AND HE GAVE YOU LAND. YOU CAME HERE AND WE RECEIVED YOU AS BROTHERS. HE MADE YOU ALL WHITE AND CLOTHED YOU. HE MADE US WITH RED SKINS AND POOR. US MADE YOU TO EAT TAME GAME, AND US TO EAT WILD GAME.
YOU DO NOT KNOW WHO APPEARS BEFORE YOU TO SPEAK. HE IS A REPRESENTATIVE OF THE ORIGINAL AMERICAN RACE. WE ARE GOOD AND NOT BAD. ALL I WANT IS RIGHT AND JUSTICE. I REPRESENT THE WHOLE SIOUX NATION, AND THEY WILL BE BOUND BY WHAT I SAY.

MAHPIYA-LUTA
1822-1909
OGLALA SIOUX

RED CLOUD AND WIFE, PEACE CRUSADE COOPER INSTITUTE NEW YORK CITY - 1870

Red Cloud
marble stonecut

Harriet Greene
Taos, N.M.

15

Generosity as Way of Life

Martin Brokenleg (Lakota)

*W*e *were taught much about generosity in my Lakota society because it was so molded into our social system. For example, if you were visiting someone and you openly admired a possession of theirs, they would probably give it to you. Giving in this way would make them happy. Of course, real giving entails sacrifice—if it doesn't cost you something, it is not generosity. Thus, if I were to give away that necktie that Aunt Mildred gave me last Christmas—the one that I was never going to wear in public—it would not be generosity, it would be recycling!*

In many tribal cultures, giving away possessions is part of an entire way of life—one that creates powerful social bonds. Young children learn that it is not always easy to give things away. The Lakota say one should be able to give away anything "without the heart pounding."

Unfortunately, not many examples of such total generosity exist in our largely materialistic Western culture because of a preoccupation with acquiring possessions. This stockpiling of stuff is related to individualistic thinking, excessive materialism and conspicuous consumption—the cultural thinking error that flaunting wealth is a testimony of a person's worth. We should not make a show of generosity and recipients do not have to fawn in obeisance. Sharing is just what relatives do.

Generosity comes in many forms. To be patient, to listen, to share a smile, a joke or even a tear are powerful gifts. An apology to one we have offended can be a form of generosity, because it puts one in a position of humility. Even more powerful is the generosity of forgiveness extended to

*those who have hurt us. . . . As we see in our Circle of Courage work, the
highest expression of courage is generosity, such as when children learn to
show compassion for others and to give a higher priority to relationships
rather than possessions. Unfortunately, such altruism is contradicted by
cultural traditions of dominance, exploitation and selfish materialism.*

Sources

Martin Brokenleg. "Native American Perspectives on Generosity." *Reclaiming Children and Youth* 8, no. 2 (summer 1999): 66–68. http://martinbrokenleg.com /wp-content/uploads/2016/02/08_2_Brokenleg.pdf.

Larry Brendtro, Martin Brokenleg, and Steve Van Bockern. *Reclaiming Youth at Risk: Our Hope for the Future.* 3rd ed. Bloomington, IN: Solution Tree Press, 2019.

Contextualized Biosketch

Martin Brokenleg is Sičáŋǧu Lakȟóta. His generation learned from
those who lived most of their lives before treaties and reservations and
who were at the Little Big Horn in 1876. He is a descendant of Wažáža
medicine men and Isáŋti singers. He is also Wi'í'iŋkte and grew up a
traditional dancer carrying the teachings of his people. With degrees
in psychology and theology, he taught Indigenous studies for fifty
years and maintained a psychotherapist practice. He is retired and
now belongs to the Kyaanuuslii Raven House of Haida Gwaii, Canada.
He is coauthor of *Reclaiming Youth at Risk: Our Hope for the Future,*[1]
which draws on traditional Indigenous teachings on youth survival
and resilience and is based on his work with the Circle of Courage as
illustrated in the figure below.[2]

Indigenous Worldview Precept Dialogue

Four Arrows: Based on Indigenous worldview approaches to raising
and educating children as sacred beings, Martin's work with his Circle
of Courage, as depicted in Figure 15.1, balances independence with

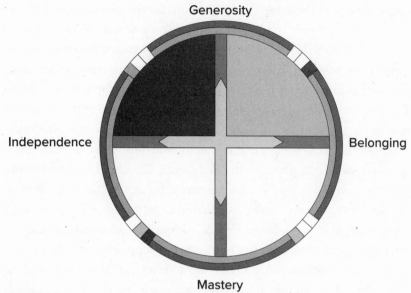

Figure 15.1

belonging, and generosity with mastery. In this medicine wheel, health depends upon finding the center among the four directions. As Martin says in his quote, the highest expression of courage from his Lakota perspective relates to authentic, unhesitating generosity. I have found this same conviction in all of the Indigenous cultures I have studied, as did Christopher Columbus with the Indigenous people of the Americas he first met. He wrote in a letter to King Ferdinand of Spain about them, saying, "They are so naive and so free with their possessions that no one who has not witnessed them would believe it. When you ask for something they have, they never say no."[3]

This trait among traditional Indigenous cultures is evidence for asserting that generosity is an expression of a deep biological instinct for giving and receiving that represents natural reciprocity. Greg Cajete agrees: "Giving and receiving emulates the central animating dynamic of life itself. Indigenous mind mirrors Natural mind. And so, it is the Indigenous way to emulate the ways of Nature in the social ways of community."[4]

Even if generosity and reciprocity are innate in human biology, without a worldview that sees the earth living its own harmonizing consciousness, I think human civilizations for the past 1 percent of our history have been overriding this innate instinct somehow. Greg and I learned this during the research for our book on neuroscience and Indigenous wisdom. After reading the research on such Indigenous precepts as prioritizing generosity, we changed the name of the book to *Critical Neurophilosophy and Indigenous Wisdom,* coining the first term to express the idea that we should be critical of how neuroscientific conclusions often reflect the dominant worldview. Then, in turn, those conclusions help to promote it. Greg Cajete, Jongmin Lee, and I wrote the text with the help of twelve neuropsychology doctoral candidates. The students gathered neuroscience studies on generosity among other Indigenous worldview-based virtues. Although a few studies supported our assumptions, the majority of the studies supported a reward-based theory of generosity. After reviewing a variety of laboratory studies, they concluded that the "underlying neural explanation behind generosity related to how the brain processes acts of generosity in terms of reward. . . . The brain processes acts of generosity in ways that encourage future acts of generosity in order to obtain additional rewards."[5]

I had and have several responses to such conclusions. First, I believe they come from scientists who view their results via a dominant-worldview lens. Second, I think we put too much emphasis on brain activity imaging. Brain activity during staged acts of generosity showing up in the same place where previous selfish activities also show up is a small part of the larger picture of mind/brain/consciousness. Third, references to "primitive centers of the brain" that assume animal behavior is purely reward/punishment-oriented are not well-founded. There are countless acts of animals acting in altruistic ways with no reward or punishment perspectives involved.[6] Our Indigenous stories have long been about the generosity of animals and other Spirit beings providing us with goods, clothing, and advice.

Once again, Indigenous wisdom about the natural world is missing from the Western scientific equation. Without it, the generosity mandate is, as Brokenleg writes, "contradicted by cultural traditions of dominance, exploitation and selfish materialism."

Darcia: I thoroughly agree with everything you've said, including the critique of brain scans. A recent review indicates that studies summarizing brain scans across participants are highly unreliable—they are not getting replicated. This is no surprise if you know that every brain is different and that the researchers are ignoring the many differences and looking for sameness. Moreover, it is hard to know what brain activation means, because experts often have *less* activation than novices; plus it is hard to examine deeper brain areas. Also, these are brains that have likely been raised in stressful situations, outside of our species's evolved nest, so you have to be careful about generalizing to human nature.

To add to what you have already discussed, I was struck by Brokenleg's statement that "the highest expression of courage is when children learned to show compassion for others and to give a *higher priority to relationships rather than possessions.*" This prioritizing of relationships starts with early life experience. Do parents, family members, and the community give higher priority to a relationship with the child than they do to their possessions or seeking possessions? Do they give themselves over to the young child's needs? Healthy, holistic child development depends on the generosity of caregivers and community members humbly providing for the needs of the child.[7] Babies need their caregivers to yield to meeting their needs and to have the know-how to provide the appropriate type of care needed for the moment.[8]

This kind of baby care likely goes along with what anthropologists call "demand sharing"[9]—the common view among egalitarian hunter-gatherers that all is to be shared. "Sharing is just what relatives do," Brokenleg reminds us. This basic form of generosity mimics the mutualism of the rest of the natural world. Ants and flies come to share your picnic with what looks like an assumption that they have a right to take part. Explorers to what became the Americas were astounded that people with few provisions would always share what they had with others. Members of traditional collectivist societies often are highly generous. Hospitality means not only welcoming strangers, but giving guests possessions they indicated they like. I've experienced this in

South Korea, which has parallels with US culture but maintains hospitality traditions like other non-Western societies.

The view of generosity common among Western civilizations accords better with Aristotle's view. He lived in a highly unequal society (90 percent of the population was underprivileged, consisting of women, slaves, children, and less fortunate men) and assumed that the highest form of existence was in "reason" (thinking). Generosity referred to someone with greater possessions who decides to give to others as a noble act. Instead of being heart-centered or driven by a sense of solidarity, generosity was driven by reason. When actions are guided by reason, it is always easy to rationalize the opposite behavior, as has happened in the USA in the last fifty years, as neoliberalism[10] and Ayn Randism[11] took over political discourse, convincing most people, starting with the wealthy, that it is good to be selfish. The rich cover up their hoarding by throwing scraps to foundations and toward endeavors to help the less fortunate while at the same time ensuring that the system upholding inequality doesn't really change.[12] The masses are told that they too could be millionaires or billionaires if they just try harder, similar to the Christian promise of heaven if you just believe and behave correctly. In the USA, you really have to be immersed in a strong counterculture to resist the constant chatter about making more money and getting more possessions to keep up with the Joneses. In this stressful environment, it may be hard to be generous in a heartfelt way because you think there's not enough for everyone—the scarcity mindset that capitalism has promoted—and you think everyone else is your competition.

Four Arrows: If we are ever to bring back the Indigenous worldview, it will occur because parents use it for child-rearing. This is why your ability to orient the worldview precepts accordingly is so vital for this text. I have a student now doing focus groups on what it would take to bring Indigenous precepts such as generosity into American societies. Early understanding comes up as a priority.

I found your comment about South Korea interesting. I agree that despite its many parallels with US culture (such as patriarchy and capitalistic priorities), it maintains hospitality traditions that stand apart from the US. I spent time there also and came away with a similar feeling. I suggest that this might relate to South Korea having more unconscious and conscious respect for Indigeneity and our Indigenous worldview precepts than is generally typical in the US, where anti-Indianism is foundational.[13] Its society is based on the coevolution of "shamanism and Indigenous folk beliefs, sharing a fundamental belief in the existence of a myriad of gods, such as the mountain gods, the house gods, the fire gods and the spirits of the dead."[14] With its wide range of religious beliefs, there is also a strong focus on the meditative traditions of Korean Buddhism, the human-heartedness of Confucianism, and the bodhisattva of compassion.

Although I see South Korea as part of the increasing corporatizing occurring around the world, I think if Indigenous worldview catches on it will happen in places where Eastern religions prevail. Hinduism, the oldest of organized religions, is closest to its Indigenous roots. For example, it believes in sentience and souls existing in all living creatures. I have a pet theory that, starting with Hinduism, all of the organized religions have a foundation that relates to original Indigenous worldview. I propose that the enlightened founders, all the way up through Jesus Christ, saw the devolution of human civilization and created ideas for returning to our original loving nature. My theory is that religions are an effort to rectify the horrors of hierarchy and the loss of egalitarianism and Nature-based thinking. Indigenous worldview is thus prevention oriented, knowing about the potential but not experiencing life based on greed and division. Over time, the teachings of the religious founders were modified by the political and social mores of the times to create orthodoxy that weakened the original intent. Post-contact efforts became conventional for maintaining the religion itself.

If generosity is learned by observing the natural world and our place in it, as I believe it is, Indigenous worldview is a necessity for returning to life based on generosity, it seems.

Darcia: I agree with you that the Axial Age religions that started in the first millennium BCE—Confucianism, Daoism, Hinduism,

Buddhism, monotheism in Israel—have roots in Indigenous sensibilities of respecting the earth.[15] At their inception, they all focused
on rituals and behavior, not beliefs, including practices for self-
transformation. Striking are the long-standing differences between the
Western Roman Catholic Church and the Eastern Orthodox Church,
which finally officially split from each other in 1054. The Western
church dove thoroughly into the thinking mind, whereas the Eastern church continued to emphasize self-transformation via religious
practices enhancing the mind-in-the-heart.[16] At least daily spiritual
development is expected, unlike in the West. Significantly, however,
Eastern Orthodox hesychastic practice—referring to retreating inward
to find union with God (divinization)—contrasts with Indigenous
practices of going out into nature to find union with the Spirit of the
earth. This might be a critically important difference. The separation
of thinking from existing/being/heart and the separation of individual
faith from community relations are characteristic of Western church
and culture.[17] The result of the West's divorce from heart and relationship may have contributed to the rabid fever to conquer, colonialize,
and consume life forces (wétiko)—all the opposite of generosity.

Research into generosity, funded by the John Templeton Foundation and related entities, has been ongoing for a couple of decades.
I find it ironic that Western social science is conducting research
into human virtues, such as generosity, after noticing their weakness
among the populace. Of course, virtues would be weak when young
children are undercared for and forced into early "independence"
instead of being provided the support of the evolved nest that fosters the natural development of virtue![18] Research findings show that
babies and toddlers are instinctively generous, people are more generous when they feel attached to individuals or the community, and
role models facilitate generous behavior.[19] Those with an Indigenous
worldview would not be surprised at any of this except the neglect
of attachment to and generosity toward other-than-human persons.
To return to such attitudes and behaviors, apparent in all our ancestors, it helps to notice throughout the day how our lives are full of gifts

from the other-than-human, our kin network. A few examples: air to breathe; water to drink; plants for our meals; soil, rain, and sun that grow the plants; pollinator insects who help plants bear fruit; plants that feed the animals we consume; animals who give their lives for us. We can grow habits of enhancing and not harming the well-being of all these entities. This is generosity in action.

16

Ceremony as Life Sustaining

Linda Hogan (Chickasaw)

*W*e remember that all things are connected. Remembering this is the purpose of the ceremony. It is part of a healing and restoration. It is the mending of a broken connection between us and the rest. The participants in a ceremony say the words "All my relations" before and after we pray; those words create a relationship with other people, with animals, with the land. To have health it is necessary to keep all these relations in mind. The intention of a ceremony is to put a person back together by restructuring the human mind. This reorganization is accomplished by a kind of inner map, a geography of the human spirit and the rest of the world. We make whole our broken-off pieces of self and world. Within ourselves, we bring together the fragments of our lives in a sacred act of renewal, and we reestablish our connections with others. The ceremony is a point of return. It takes us toward the place of balance, our place in the community of all things. It is an event that sets us back upright. But it is not a finished thing. The real ceremony begins where the formal one ends, when we take up a new way, our minds and hearts filled with the vision of earth that holds us within it, in compassionate relationship to and with our world.

We speak. We sing. We swallow water and breathe smoke. By the end of the ceremony, it is as if skin contains land and birds. The places within us have become filled. As inside the enclosure of the lodge, the animals and ancestors move into the human body, into skin and blood. The land merges with us. The stones come to dwell inside the person. Gold rolling *hills take up residence, their tall grasses blowing. The red light of canyons is there. The black skies of night that wheel above our heads come to live inside the skull. We who easily grow apart from the world are returned to the great store of life all around us, and there is the deepest sense of being at home here in this intimate kinship. There is no real aloneness. There is solitude and the nurturing silence that is relationship with ourselves, but even then we are part of something larger.*

Source

Linda Hogan. *Dwellings: A Spiritual History of the Living World*, 40–41. New York: W. W. Norton, 1995.

Contextualized Biosketch

Linda Hogan, former faculty at the Indian Arts Institute, is writer in residence for the Chickasaw Nation and professor emerita at the University of Colorado. She is an internationally recognized public reader, speaker, and writer of poetry, fiction, and essays. Her poetry book, *The Book of Medicines,* was a finalist for the National Book Critics Circle Award. Her lyrical work is considered to be writing of literary quality that illuminates a new environmental and Indigenous activism, as well as Native spirituality. It is included in anthologies not only in literature but in works on nature, science, and the environment, including animal studies. Hogan was inducted into the Chickasaw Nation Hall of Fame in 2007 for her contributions to Indigenous literatures.

Indigenous Worldview Precept Dialogue

Four Arrows: Darcia, before I came back to edit this part of our dialogue, I initially used this space to share with our readers about how I elected to use ceremony in place of chemotherapy for the aggressive return of my non-Hodgkins lymphoma and my stage IV diagnosis. I wrote about being told that a second spontaneous remission was unlikely at my age of seventy-four and with a highly aggressive return of the lymphoma. Now I return three months later for our final editing to tell the reader that ceremony worked. My organ tumors disappeared, and the large abdominal one shrank significantly. In fact, I just raised money for the Rarámuri rainwater harvesting project by stand-up paddling in the open ocean for six hours.

Well, as Linda Hogan says: "The intention of a ceremony is to put a person back together by restructuring the human mind." This seems to possess more healing truth than poisoning cells throughout one's body with chemotherapy. For Hogan, ceremony and ritual provide opportunities to reconnect to food relationships. In my case, ceremony—particularly *inipi* ceremony (purification lodge)—helped me conceive of the cancer as a gift. Hogan believes ceremony takes us toward the place of balance with all life. This is how it helped me with my motivation to be grateful for all my relations, to honor my body with exercise and good food, to control my mind with self-hypnosis and meditation. I believe my confrontation with a prognosis of death— coupled with a commitment to facing it in ways that align with trees, fish, animals, birds, and insects more than with human technology— worked. I offer this small part of a poem by Linda Hogan that I think is about the history of Western medicine. I lean toward the magic side, and this means toward Spirit.

> Then there was medicine, the healing of wounds.
> Red was the infinite fruit of stolen bodies.
> The doctors wanted to know what invented disease
> How wounds healed from inside themselves
> How life stands up in skin,
> If not by magic.[1]

Darcia: All of life on Earth has membership in Spirit, making it possible to communicate with one another, whether human or other-than-human. Most Westerners do not learn schooling's null curriculum: the fostering of innate feeling, intuition, and intelligence that is receptive to the dynamic world of Spirit. Many do not know how to follow or pick up its nonintellectual signals. They do not think that knowledge can be gained from sacred experience, from ceremony. You do. So I trusted your sensibilities on how you should treat the visitation of the tumors.

Dreams, visions, songs are access points to the sacred. Ceremony is our form of communicating back, requiring a feeling of reverence and attention to respectful relationship with the other-than-human, and the merging of self with All in an intimate kinship, as Hogan describes. But for the dominant worldview, which aligns with Western history, ceremony typically involves human community and a particular notion of the divine as outside the self. If the rest of Earth's persons are included—the other-than-human—it occurs superficially. There is no sense of nations of bear, wolf, oak, pine, or water spirits. Nature is more like wallpaper than a complex set of communities with which humans interact.[2] The discussion may be of the "way of the heart" as perceptive of Spirit, as an antenna for it. But the human heart is perceived to be different from the animal heart, in contrast to the Indigenous worldview, and Spirit is something apart from the self, and not part of the nature of the world.[3]

Tadodaho Chief Leon Shenandoah warns that, although everyone's ancestors had original instructions that included ceremonies, a person or group needs to understand the ceremonies to practice them, or else they can be dangerous and harmful.[4] He says that everyone needs to return to their circle.[5] This may be hard for non-Natives because their ancestral ceremonies were last practiced so many generations ago that they were forgotten. What do you think, Four Arrows?

Four Arrows: Thank you for your beautiful and supportive words about my decision to use my ceremonial and nature-based approach as an alternative way to heal. You are correct in saying that someone without a deep understanding of Indigenous spirituality may not understand. Ceremonies are at the heart of First Nations spiritual practices. To do them effectively, one must know about related ancient stories, symbolic items, songs, and language. Being far away from the Lakota culture here in Mexico, the *inipi* ceremony is one of my primary practices. In the purification lodge *(initi)*, purification leads to healing, rebirth, and a reconnection with the Spirit world on behalf of all life. *Inipi,* the word for the ceremony, means "to live again." With my ceremonial communications, whether in the lodge or on a mountaintop, I learn important information about my health more deeply than when in the doctor's office. It is important to seek the complementarity between both, but the priority is what I gather from my communing with the spiritual energies. They help me see cancer as a teaching gift, not an enemy to kill.

Although, as I said, there is no question about the importance of understanding a ceremony, one can take this too far. Many American Indian traditionalists have forgotten how to conduct a number of their original cultural ceremonies. There is still interpretive variation in conducting ceremonies for those where people still remember origin stories, songs, and protocols. Ceremonies are living, changing entities. Ceremonies are like rivers and change here and there, and whoever leads their own ceremony often has their own version of it. Furthermore, ceremonies are not somber events. A sacred ceremony is not sacred without humor prevailing, for example. Mistakes are made and corrected. This said, it can be dangerous to participate in a ceremony led by someone who does not have sufficient knowledge. An extreme example of this is the non-Indian who made millions of dollars leading Lakota *inipi* ceremonies without sufficient knowledge. He actually was responsible for the deaths of three people who died from the heat in the purification lodge.[6] In 1998 a number of Lakota spiritual leaders published their statement about "War against Exploiters of Lakota Spirituality."[7] Further proclamations by Lakota spiritual leaders have said only Indigenous People can participate in Sun Dances and that in order to pour water in an *inipi,* one must have fulfilled their Sun Dance vows and at least know the prayers and songs in the Lakota/Dakota/Nakota language.

However, it is important to note here that Indigenous spiritual leaders are divided down the middle on such mandates about who can

participate in ceremonies. As an Irish man with "unproven" Cherokee heritage, I was made a relative of the Oglala Lakota. (The "making
relative" ceremony is one of the seven sacred Lakota ceremonies that
includes the Sun Dance and the purification lodge). I have completed
my Sun Dance vows, I am a pipe carrier, and I know my songs and
prayers in Lakota. However, I am on the side that says what Fools Crow
said long ago: "These ceremonies do not belong to Indians alone. . . .
We are keepers of certain areas of knowledge, which we are to share
for the good of mankind. . . . If we don't the whole world will die."[8]

Darcia: I appreciate your discussion of Lakota ceremony, which I
have not experienced. I think ceremony is needed to nourish our spirits. Growing up going to church, then later becoming a church organ-
ist, then a seminarian practicing ministry, I was always lifted by the
worshipful attitude that some ministers had—those who did not just
go through the motions but acted as if their actions were sacred and
connected to a universal holiness. I think we can apply this to everyday
life. We can infuse ceremony into what we do each day. Zen Buddhists
ask the vegetables they are cutting for dinner how they would like to
be cut. Former Uruguayan president José Mujica, who spent a decade
in solitary confinement, kept his sanity by sharing his meager meals
with the mice and cockroaches in his cell. This is a kind of ceremony.
We can all find times and places for ceremony in our daily lives.

But we also need to pay attention to the signals we get about
respecting others, including other-than-humans. Here is a recent
example. When I was spreading fall leaves on the gardens to protect
them from winter chill, I saw a newly arrived rock. I connected with
it and felt moved to pick it up. I brought it inside, rinsed it (which I
later regretted—why remove some of Mother Earth?), and put it on
my desk. A few days later I had a dream where a statement was made in
outrage: "She treated it like a pet rock!" I got the message. I apologized
and ceremoniously, with a song, returned the rock to the garden.

Now that many of us have lost awareness of our ancestors' ceremonies, it is important to remember that ceremonies emerge from the
landscape. When we listen to the living world around us, ceremonies

will find us if we are still and listen. What does the land call forth? During sunrises or sunsets, what song or prayer of gratitude rings in your heart? When the birds sing, do you stop and listen and give thanks? How can you honor the foods that compose your meal?

Daniel Wolpert offers a helpful guide that can be used to create our own ceremonies.[9] He selects five elements as a framework for learning an embodied appreciation of the earth through ceremony for each element, propelling self-transformation away from ego and toward wisdom. In daily experience, we can express appreciation for each of these: *space,* for spacious hospitality instead of ignorance; *water,* for vision instead of judgmental arrogance; *air,* for compassionate action instead of aggression and anxiety; *earth,* for abundance and generosity instead of a sense of poverty and grasping action; *fire,* for warm relationships instead of loneliness and insecurity. Wolpert gives guidance on how to experience each of these elements through reverent attention and apply them to one's relationships and behavior. These concrete ways to revamp ourselves align with what Hogan says: "The intention of a ceremony is to put a person back together by restructuring the human mind."

17

Humor as Essential

Charlie Hill (Oneida-Mohawk-Cree; 1951–2013)

*P*ilgrims came to this land four hundred years ago as illegal aliens. We used to call them "whitebacks." They started unloading the boats, building houses. The first thing we asked is, "Are you guys going to stay the night?" Doesn't that just burn you up when people come over and they never leave? "Yeah, we'll leave after Thanksgiving," they say. You have a lot of holidays, but this is Indians' country. There's no Indian holidays; there's Thanksgiving, Columbus Day . . . oh, no, there's one holiday we do celebrate with white people. It's Halloween. Every year, we dress up like white people and knock on doors saying, "Trick or treaty?"

They call us now Native Americans, which is a generic term I never liked, but we are older than America, so how can we be native to something we are older than? Call us by who we are. But then I met someone who is Chickasaw, Potawatomi, and Paiute, and he got his enrollment card and it said "Chicken Pot Pie." The bylines of the Iroquois Confederacy is what Franklin and Jefferson lifted to use what they call democracy here. So the idea of democracy—that's not imported, that's Indigenous, and that came from us.

I had a heckler the last time I did a show. I'm on stage; he goes, "I don't want to hear that crap, Injun! I'm an American. Why don't you go back where you came from?" So I camped in his backyard.

I just want to say—white folks, what we're doing up here tonight? We're not white bashing. This is just a little spiritual spanking you should have got four hundred years ago.

When you get a lot of Indian people together, there is always laughter, even in times of stress, sorrow, sadness. There is always that undercurrent of humor. It's something spiritual. There is always something funny about it because joviality, lightness, laughter—they say laughter is the language of God.

We're doing pretty good with our casinos, folks. Some day we're going to buy our land back—from the Japanese. White folks, you wouldn't even be here if it wasn't for Indian people. You came to this country. We taught you about democracy. We taught you how to fight the British so you could be free. "Hide behind the trees!" So come to us now. We can fix this country. All the problems it has. We can fix it because we have the owner's manual. Everything you are going through now. We survived it already. The economy. What economy, you know? The war on terrorism. Hell, we've been fighting terrorism since 1492. If we only had metal detectors on Plymouth Rock, that shit would have been nipped right in the bud.

Sources

Charlie Hill. *American Indian Comedy Slam: Goin Native No Reservations Needed.*
    Directed by Scott Montoya. Laugh Out Loud Comedy Inc., aired December 2009
    on Showtime, filmed during the Laugh Out Loud Comedy Festival. Quoted in
    Laugh Out Loud Flix, "Charlie Hill: Remembering a Native American Comedy
    Legend." October 14, 2019. Video, 12:21. www.youtube.com/watch?v
    =RaWTGnA9xrY.
Charlie Hill. *The Richard Pryor Show*, episode 4, aired October 20, 1977, on NBC.
    Quoted in Laugh Out Loud Flix, "Charlie Hill: Remembering a Native American
    Comedy Legend." October 14, 2019. Video, 12:21. www.youtube.com/watch?v
    =RaWTGnA9xrY. ·

Contextualized Biosketch

Charlie Hill grew up in Detroit for the first ten years of his life; then he moved to the Oneida reservation. He majored in speech and drama at the University of Wisconsin and was involved with the Broom Street

Theatre Group. His first network appearance was on *The Richard Pryor Show* in 1977, and he later became the first American Indian comedian to appear on *The Tonight Show* and made a number of appearances thereafter. He was chosen to host the First Americans in the Arts awards show three times. He died of lymphoma at a nursing home on the Oneida reservation. His philosophy can be summed up by what he once said in an interview, "My whole thing is to get people to laugh *with* us, not at us."[1]

Indigenous Worldview Precept Dialogue

Four Arrows: Although all cultures appreciate and use humor, under the dominant worldview humor is too often merely for entertainment rather than for helping us understand the world better. Humor has always been fundamental to existence in Indigenous communities. It serves to bond people together. It encourages social harmony and complementarity work. It is vital for education in all forms. Joseph Bruchac, an Abenaki storyteller, says: "Humor can be used to remind people—who because of their achievements might be feeling a little too proud or important—that they are no more valuable than anyone else in the circle of life."[2]

American Indian humor postcolonization has focused especially on survival, politics, and walking in two worlds, in precontact times and among remote tribes today. Thomas King, a retired Cherokee/German professor in Canada, is one of the great Indigenous storytellers who focuses on humor with these goals in mind. A scholarly article about him argues that "King deploys a more comprehensive and diverse strategy of humor, ingeniously synthesizing the tragic and the comic to call attention to the perils of environmental degradation."[3] Jaroslav Tuček's doctoral dissertation proposes a theory about King's "strategies for decolonizing Canada": he hypothesizes that "through the use of humor and irony Native artists can explore the alternative space where through the process of hybridization new possibilities and meanings can be carried out."[4]

Whatever is happening in your individual, community, or universal world, the Indigenous worldview approach to humor is a vital thing to reembrace along with all the others. With our current existential crises it is past time to remember that, as Charlie Hill says, "We've been fighting terrorism since 1492." Darcia, are there any studies in your field that talk about the importance of humor in early childhood?

Darcia: There are not a lot of studies on humor in early childhood per se, but there is a lot of research and advice on social play that brings about laughter. One of the books I recommend to parents is called *Playful Parenting,*[5] a fantastic suggestion-filled guide for how to raise children to feel connected and confident through play. It has a chapter titled "Follow the Giggles" that emphasizes the importance of laughter in childhood and techniques for getting children to laugh: "Laughing can be a sign of connection between people, a sign of successfully completing a challenging task, or a sign that a child no longer feels miserable or hurt. Giggles and belly laughs are the natural way that children and adults release fears and embarrassment and anxiety."[6]

For babies, it's important to remember that they need to be kept optimally aroused (contented) generally so they grow well and develop a pleasant personality. Colwyn Trevarthen suggests that babies under natural conditions are often ready to play from birth—to move with others in a physical "communicative musicality," an "exchange of feelings-with-awareness" in proto-conversations with proto-gestures, and even a banter back and forth with sounds.[7] "In the first year, intense sharing of familiar situations with favorite persons who offer affectionate intimacy starts to build a child's 'proto-habitus,' or personal life story in company."[8] In fact, traditionally the Hopi honor the first person to make a baby laugh. Laughter is "joy juice" that revs up the personality to be a happy one.[9] Among hunter-gatherer groups a great deal of time is spent in joking, playing, and laughter, which Peter Gray contends promotes bonding and peaceful cooperation.[10] Although there is teasing, it is not put-down humor. Humor and laughter seem to foster peaceful personalities and peaceful societies.

Four Arrows: Indeed, I found when I lived on Pine Ridge that teasing actually made me feel more accepted. I was teased often by my Sun Dance brothers! This happened especially when I tried to speak Lakota, which I knew everyone appreciated despite my difficulties with the language. Once I was going to a gathering to join some Sun Dance brothers for a dinner at Rick Two Dog's home. I wanted to memorize a sentence in Lakota that I might offer during our dinner. Memorizing sentences was the main way I was learning the language. I wanted to say something about my having trained wild mustangs. Everyone knew I rode my horse to the college and, being horse people, they loved it. I thought I would gain points by telling about my experience with wild horses. Because my wife was having a difficult time getting accepted by the wives of the men, I wanted to bring her into the conversation too. The day before the dinner, I asked a student to write down how to say "I trained wild mustangs with my woman for many years" (or something like that). I repeated the sentence over and over on the way to Rick's house. That evening I waited for an opening in the conversation to blurt it out. When I did, everyone started laughing. Eventually, after I begged to know why, they told me. Instead of *winyan* for woman, I said *wisan* which means "vagina." Instead of using *sungwathogia,* which is Lakota for "mustang," somehow I put together *wisan wathogla,* which translates to "wild vagina." Essentially, I was telling everyone that I used to train wild vaginas.

The laughing and teasing about this went on for many months. When I brought my wife, Bea, to her first *yuwipi* ceremony, everyone smiled or giggled when she walked into the room. However, as you said, it was not put-down humor. In fact, it wound up helping Bea feel accepted and loved, not ridiculed. Twenty years later and we still laugh about it.

Indigenous teasing is a way to let someone know when they are out of step with cultural norms. Ironically, at the same time it increases mutual acceptance and bonding. It would be interesting to see how today's comedians, who give us more insightful commentary about what is happening in the world than the news does, could use the

Indigenous teasing of wrong-minded politicians and world leaders in ways to get them to see how they are out of step in ways that would allow for an eventual bonding.

Darcia: Oh, that's hilarious! I can't stop laughing. Yes, that's bonding humor—laughing together at life's stumbles or unusual events. Steve Allen, a popular comic in the middle of the twentieth century, pointed out the different pathways that television comedy could go—toward focusing on human foibles and such, or toward put-down humor. To his unhappiness, put-down humor became dominant. Steve Allen also said that groups in the USA who have had a history of oppression in some manner—such as Jews, Blacks, and Natives—are often funnier than the dominant group, white people, but they only are heard after whites give them the freedom to speak out.[11] Since the 1960s, more minority groups have gotten the chance to be publicly funny. I like how Charlie pokes fun at the European invasion. He is joking about unfairness, disrespect, and racism. Being an outsider enables one to see alternatives, multiple perspectives. So does social play.

The dominant culture generally has undermined childhood—thereby, play and silly humor—for many generations. In their book *The Art of Play: Helping Adults Reclaim Imagination and Spontaneity,* Adam and Allee Blatner asked and answered the question: if free playing is so beneficial for brain development and socioemotional intelligence, why are so many adults uncomfortable playing (and joking in a non-put-down manner)?[12] They mention causes like mild depression, play experiences being restricted to competitive or structured activities, and lack of experience with singing, dancing, or enacting drama. Other psychological reasons include fear of being vulnerable, needy, or silly; fear of being shown to be ignorant of anything, or making mistakes; or fear of having qualities assumed to be of the opposite gender. To me this sounds like they were made fun of, perhaps bullied, at significant times growing up, which shut them down. Of course, it would be hard to play when you feel so guarded. The other key reason the Blatners mention is envy of children's vitality, a threat to the fragile character of the adult. Instead of letting go and playing in response to energetic children, adults punish them for their playfulness. Victorian asceticism was extended to babies, denying them pleasure or attention on request, which Victorians thought was dangerous. To many adults, playing looks like being out of control or even like aggression.[13]

The Blatners point out that the Western world's intellectual history of simplifying reality also suppresses play. This includes dualistic belief systems, both religious (something is good or is evil) and scientific (something is true or is false). Other dualistic pairs that straitjacket people's orientation and behavior include adult/childish, male/female, serious/foolish, civilized/primitive, strength/weakness. According to Steve Allen, humor rarely comes from the conservative side of the political spectrum because conservatives traditionally prefer to support rather than make fun of society's institutions. Neurobiologically, conservatism often represents inflexibility of one kind or another, focused on keeping the structure of things as they are rather than attending to living beings themselves. Imaginative play is about interacting with one another as living beings, disregarding the boundaries of conformity culture, challenging black-and-white categorizations. It prepares people to understand reality as a gray, overlapping, interpenetrating mixture of fuzzy, shifting categories.

In the modern world, children are controlled much more by adult needs than in our ancestral context, leading to a lot of frustration of child autonomy. Parents can use play to help them through these challenges, or any time when jealousy or fears arise (though the playtime needs to be when the child is not upset). For example, power-reversal play, as with pillow fights where the parent falls down dramatically each time they are hit to elicit laughter from the child, is especially useful at letting out tension and building attachment bonds.[14]

Experiencing the evolved nest, an attachment-supporting system, sets up the neurobiology from the bottom up that supports social enjoyment and the development of capacities to be flexibly attuned to others—the socioemotional intelligence to be able to play. The Indigenous worldview, from the top down, offers a wide-scope view of life that supports playing, kinship humor and the deeper bonding that ensues from the "laughter [that] is the language of God."

18

Conflict Resolution as Return to Community

Wanda D. McCaslin (Métis)

*N*on-Aboriginal *people tend to consider our Indigenous restorative processes as simply a matter of the community putting social pressure on an offender to correct his or her ways, essentially by shaming the person into compliance. They assume Indigenous processes work similarly by using force and coercion—albeit a sociological, shaming kind rather than a physical, punitive sort to make offenders change. This is not how we understand healing processes. Community pressure does play a role since their relatives share responsibility for harms done. But sharing is not the essence of our healing processes. Force and coercion are not how we make our societies and people harmonious; therefore they cannot provide the means we use to repair harms.*

Instead, when hurts occur, we are instructed to go back to what makes our families and communities strong in the first place: we work to rebuild the bonds of mutual responsibilities that hold us together in a good way. These bonds are forged not in force but in respect, in an honest appreciation of each person as a valued member of the community, and in a trust that we each have a sacredness that guides us. Law is far more than rules to be obeyed for Indigenous peoples. It is embedded in our ways of thinking, living and being. It is found within the carefully balanced relations of our clan systems and our extended families. It is also found in ceremonies and rituals. Law is a whole way of life. Through countless means, our

*traditions teach us how to be respectful of others and mindful of how our
actions affect them. . . . It is modeled for us daily through our languages,
customs, behavior and relationships. The closer we stay to our traditional
ways, the more we internalize what it means to be a good relative, not
only with each other but with all beings . . . through everything we do.*

*Looking beyond those immediately involved, Indigenous people tend
to interpret hurtful actions less individualistically and more as signs of
imbalances within the community as a whole—imbalances that affect
everyone. In this sense, offenders help the community by drawing attention to imbalances. Their actions tell us that the essential fabric of the community is starting to unravel and needs mending. . . . Instead of placing
all the blame on the offender, our traditions acknowledge that everyone
in the community has played some role in the patterns that culminated in
hurtful actions. The responsibility for harms is distributed and shared.*

Source

Wanda D. McCaslin. "Introduction: Reweaving the Fabrics of Life." In *Justice as
Healing: Indigenous Ways,* edited by Wanda D. McCaslin, 89–90. St. Paul: Living
Justice Press, 2005.

Contextualized Biosketch

Wanda D. McCaslin is a Métis woman from northern Saskatchewan
and a graduate of the University of Saskatchewan with a BA, an LLB,
and a master's in laws dissertation. After being accepted as a member
of the Law Society of Saskatchewan, she worked with a private law
firm and later with Legal Aid Saskatchewan. She served as research
officer for the Law Foundation of Saskatchewan with the Native Law
Centre of Canada and lectured at the College of Law. Her portfolio
includes editing the text *Justice as Healing: Indigenous Ways,* editing a newsletter on Aboriginal concepts of justice, and coordinat-
ing the Young Professionals International Project. Throughout her
career, Aboriginal rights have been central to her work. McCaslin has

presented in the area of Aboriginal justice, case law analysis, and international Indigenous matters. She has also been actively involved with Aboriginal community empowerment initiatives in the areas of healing, Indigenous justice, housing, and youth. She has received awards and recognition for her work on a variety of Aboriginal initiatives and has recently completed research projects on identity, membership, and kinship; duty to consult and accommodate; First Nation communities at risk or in crisis; and other projects specific to the quality of life for Aboriginal women in Canada.

Indigenous Worldview Precept Dialogue

Four Arrows: This Indigenous worldview precept prioritizes community harmony over punishment or revenge. McCaslin describes it beautifully as being about expanding the circle of blame and benefit when dealing with hurtful actions. This is done with the understanding that the community has played some role in the injustice or conflict. When I was director of a large residential school and treatment center for adjudicated youth in Idaho, I successfully employed this philosophy. It was referred to at the time as the "restorative justice" model. Most people think this concept emerged in 1974 with the first victim-offender reconciliation program in Ketchener, Ontario, Canada. It was based on a probation officer successfully getting teenage vandals to work with their victims to agree to restitution. However, Indigenous cultures have used restorative justice for thousands of years, not as an intervention, but as a way of life.[1]

Traditional Lakota/Dakota approaches to conflict resolution started with a council of elders and those involved, directly or indirectly. All would sit in a circle to discuss the incident, and everyone would contribute and learn. From the start, the perpetrator was thus put on equal footing with all others in the community, including those harmed. Perpetrators were considered to be an integral part of the community because of their important role in defining what was inappropriate behavior and pointing out weak spots in the community that influenced it. The ultimate goal of the process was not punishment, but rather to restore peace and harmony in the community. In an article titled "Decolonizing Restorative Justice," Denise C. Breton refers to Dakota scholar Ella C. Deloria's 1936 notes about what the Dakota saw as the most powerful outcome such a council could achieve:

> It was for the family of the murdered person to adopt the murderer as a relative to take the place of the one killed. If this path was chosen, the murderer was not treated as a despised slave to the family but was given the finest gifts and treated with all the kindness and respect that the dead relative would have received. By so doing, both the family of the murdered person and the murderer would spend the rest of their lives committed to healing a harm that might otherwise have divided the community.[2]

Vine Deloria Jr., who was Ella's nephew, once told me about such an incident, as conveyed to him by his aunt. I told the story often when trying to defend my program at the youth ranch, something I had to do often. It was about a teenage boy who killed a friend of his in a fight. After many days of council, the decision was made: the parents of the deceased boy would adopt the boy as a replacement son. The community came for the adoption ceremony, bringing many gifts for the boy who did the killing and his new family. Although I do not remember his name, the boy became one of the great Dakota leaders. I usually ended the story with the rhetorical question, "What do you think would have happened to the boy, the family of the boy he killed, and the community at large had he been put in prison?" As you can imagine, most people are shocked by this story. Indeed, such an approach scared the Mormon community around the residential school I directed so much that they got me fired when we proved our program worked so well that we reduced physical restraints where counselors brought children to the floor from 144 per quarter to twenty-two, and we reduced attempted escapes to zero.

Darcia: When I first heard of restorative justice, it was the watered-down version that takes up only part of the whole process and ignores its grounding in the Indigenous worldview. Rupert Ross, retired Canadian Crown attorney who worked over many years with hundreds of First Nation communities across Canada, finally listened to elders telling him that carting offenders to jails did not help, did not heal the underlying trauma. In several books, he depicted his own journey of learning why the Canadian (and generally Western) justice system does not heal but makes things worse within Native communities. He obtained elders' permission to share what he learned about their conflict resolution approaches.[3]

Ross described the holistic traditions that heal instead of punish, that connect instead of maintain disconnection, that regenerate trust instead of allowing distrust to fester. Ross summarizes the characteristics of programs that were successful. They differ from dominant (Western European) approaches that assume as baselines for normality individualism, innate badness, hierarchy of value of people (some more valuable than others), emphasis on verbal communication, and human separation from nature. To add to what you've already described, here are some of the understandings and practices he learned for restoring the community from an individual's damaging behavior:

> **Focus on Spirit:** Aboriginal communities believe that all beings are sacred, and as part of healing ruptured relationships they connect to forces larger than the self. Hard work is needed to manifest Spirit, honor one's gifts and responsibilities, and develop more respectful relationships.

> **Definition of a healthy person:** Health involves establishing good relationships with everything in nature, accommodating with openness, humility, and respect. A healthy person understands his nestedness, interconnectedness, and interdependence, and the responsibilities he has to fulfill to the whole.

> **Group healing:** People sit in a circle as equals with others suffering from the same abuse or abuse of others. People share personal

stories as they will, passing the talking stick around the circle. The process of sharing and being listened to, of listening to the unique journeys of recovery, promotes healing and self-confidence. When offenders, who often do not realize the harm they have done, sit in a circle of those harmed by other offenders, they begin to let themselves start to understand and feel the suffering they have caused.

Individual health is grounded in social healing: Aboriginal communities have been damaged as a whole, and so it is vital that they recognize group trauma. The community participates in the healing of relations, providing a bedrock for recovery. Every person's healing is socially situated in the nest of relationships and responsibilities.

Restoring the emotional: One's emotions are central to being human and for tuning into spiritual and relational responsibilities. Healing comes through "heart learning" rather than through thinking. Having a pure heart is central to living properly, relationally connected and tuned to Spirit.

Respect for everyone's worth: Aboriginal communities separate the person from their acts. There is no diagnosing or labeling of people (e.g., alcoholic, offender, freak). Each person is considered "born into sacredness, goodness and kindness," with "the potential to be strong creators of harmony in our relations with all of Creation, though few of us will ever achieve anything close to full relational harmonies."[4] The view is that "with hard work we can nurture our spirit, learn to recognize our gifts and being to honour our responsibilities."[5] Instead of trying to change the person, the focus is on helping the person change ways of relating.

Talking is not always necessary to get back to health: The primary focus of healing is on emotional and relational discernment, not cognitive understanding. The direct way to do this is in concrete activities like berry picking, making art, or storytelling. The indirect way would be through talking, which is considered less effective.

The importance of land for healing: The best place to learn accommodation to all one's relations is on the land. You cannot defy the weather. One must compromise to survive and thrive. Experiencing the landscape helps one connect to something greater than the self, a "cathedral, full of life, promise, openness and blessedness."[6] The largest lesson is that "humans are small, unskilled, dependent *and* blessed with everything they'll ever need."[7]

What a different world we'd have if everyone followed these kinds of practices!

Four Arrows: The Spirit world brings things to us for seeing and understanding our relationships with self and others all the time. Your offering Ross's Indigenous ways for restoring relationships might be one of those gifts for me. I just now set up a Zoom call with a man I met in flight school back in 1969. We were Marine Corps officers living in a beach house near the Pensacola Naval Air Station. When we got out of school, we had adventures that are still legendary. Like most relationships, we had some bumps and cooling-off periods, but the last one has lasted for well over a decade. We exchanged positive emails this month, reestablishing our bond. We will talk for the first time this coming Tuesday. While reading Ross's list, I pondered how things might not have put us out of community if we had done the following (using Ross's list):

- Brought Spirit into the conflict that parted us

- Given more responsible consideration to health and interconnectedness factors

- Gathered friends, wives, and neighbors for a council to help understand what happened and to recognize their pain as well as ours

- Identified the social situation with others and the challenges associated with it better

- Put heart ahead of head during the arguments

- Accepted one another while working on improved ways to relate

- Played music or sailed or walked in the desert together instead of "talking"

- Emphasized the earth connection to learn compromises in our positions

If we are truly spirits living in these bodies to have experience on this beautiful planet and learn from it, then my reflections are "better late," as they say. I have no doubt when we talk next week it will seem as if we just got back safely from a wild sail on our sailboat and no time has passed at all. I think we both have learned what McCaslin writes in her quote. We have learned not to interpret hurtful actions individualistically, and we know what happened was a reflection of many imbalances within our community, imbalances that affected not just us. So the question I leave for you, Darcia, on behalf of our dear readers is a tough one: in light of our existential global situation, with climate change, pandemics, extinction rates, pollution, and violence, what kinds of conflict resolution can occur throughout the world to start bringing us back into community after we suffer through the sixth mass extinction?

Darcia: You like to pitch me the easy questions, eh? Just to clarify our situation, the four horsemen of the environmental apocalypse are upon us, one of which is mass extinction; the others are massive toxification of earth systems, degradation of the atmosphere, and global warming.[8] Because of various tipping points being reached, the planet's overall temperature may suddenly soar, so we are living on the edge already. And I am afraid that the sixth mass extinction may include us.

Here are few things to get in the habit of doing now which will help immediately and during future challenging times (more techniques are discussed in my book *Neurobiology and the Development of Human Morality: Evolution, Culture, and Wisdom*). To build capacities for getting along with others in a kind, cooperative manner, you need to calm yourself, feel connected, and expand your imagination.

These are routine Indigenous ways of being that we can pull out to practice:

Practice self-calming. Find different techniques to calm your body (e.g., lying on the earth, lying in the sun, taking a hot bath, cuddling with others) and to calm your mind (meditation/prayer, chanting, visualization, reminding yourself of why you are here). Group ceremony, practiced in the Indigenous way, calms us together.

Practice social joy. Find ways to connect with people, plants, and animals. One of the best ways to connect is to play, which we discussed in the humor chapter. Singing and dancing with others also helps. You can sit in silent enjoyment of a plant and even have a conversation with a stone.

Expand your communal imagination. Remember that you are a part of the web of life, and what you do affects all your human and other-than-human relations. It is important to decolonize your mind of Western root metaphors that straitjacket imagination: human separation from and superiority to the rest of nature, progress as overturning traditional knowledge, and individualism.[9] To this list of ideas to be cleansed, we could add the opposites of all the precepts we are discussing.

It's also helpful to learn specific ways to avoid or resolve conflicts, such as learning nonviolent ways to communicate.[10] Marshall Rosenberg, who developed the Nonviolent Communication approach, suggests that when you meet a person you ask yourself, "What is alive in us?" and "What can we do to make life more wonderful?"[11] These are Indigenous ways of relating that are learned automatically from growing up in traditional Indigenous communities. As Sorenson noted in living around the world with Indigenous peoples, they enriched his life without needing to be asked.[12] Rosenberg lays out steps for people for whom smooth cooperation is not a habit and with the more direct way of relating to others that Americans have. Specifically, he has four steps for nonviolent communication: *observe* the actions that affect our well-being; name our *feelings* in relation to those observations; name the *needs* or values that create those feelings; and *request* concrete actions to "enrich our lives."[13]

Learning nonviolent means of group protest is also useful. The Albert Einstein Institution has a document listing 198 forms of civil disobedience;[14] other resources are available at the International Center on Nonviolent Conflict, including the film *A Force More Powerful*.[15] The Standing Rock water protesters used nonviolent civil disobedience, bringing attention to the importance of sacred water and the dangers of the oil industry, and sacred prayers that vibrated across the world.

Of course, your CAT-FAWN work, which teaches people how to use natural trance-based learning to dehypnotize themselves and use Indigenous understandings about Fear, Authority, Words, and Nature, can be a tool for helping people in conflict return to positive relationships. We'll discuss CAT-FAWN in more detail in chapter 21, "Nature Is Benevolent."

As we face the environmental apocalypse, we must understand that "the responsibility for harms is distributed and shared." But the responsibility for *healing* is also distributed and shared. We can acknowledge our oneness with all human and other-than-human persons and act to enrich the lives of all as the foundation for using our differences, conflicts, and crimes to discover ways to come back into community.

Laws of Nature as
Highest Rules for Living

Winona LaDuke (Ojibwe)

*T*hat *is our biggest teaching, that natural law is the highest law, and it would be folly to figure that you can outwit natural law. . . . You can change the terms, you can change the allowable limits, you can do the risk assessment—all these things—but in the end, the fact is that you and I drink that water. You and I breathe that air. You and I live here.*

So we can say whatever we want to in our little human minds, but in the big picture of things, it is natural law in the end. We all walk down the same path. We all have to live here. So we say that natural law is the highest law, higher than the laws made by nations, states, and municipalities.

How do we know what is natural law? Two sources of our knowledge. . . . First, intergenerational residency. Observe nature over a long period of time. I laugh because in northern Minnesota we have this argument about wolf reintroduction. These guys come up there, and they have all their scientific models. They figure out what's going to happen with the wolf. They know how many wolf packs there are, how many wolves can be here, and they've got it all projected over a ten-year period. Do you know what happened? About five years in they had to toss their model out. That was just totally great, guys, great model. A wolf is a wolf. They're going to go where there's something to eat. They're going to go where they like it. That's what they're going to do. We could have told them that, but they didn't ask us. They came up there with their models. Intergenerational residency: you observe how your relatives live. That's a good way to know what natural law is.

Another source of our knowledge is spiritual knowledge, spiritual practice. . . . We all have our own wellspring of our spiritual practice and that's a good thing. But what I would say is that in our community, I think it is really important to always emphasize that, because a lot of times it is associated with a place. We practice our religion at a certain place, a sacred site; a lot of the sacred sites are endangered in this country today.

Source

Winona LaDuke. "Honor the Earth: Our Native American Legacy." Speech delivered at the Ninth Annual Westheimer Peace Symposium, Wilmington College, Wilmington, Ohio, October 20, 1999.

Contextualized Biosketch

Winona LaDuke is an activist, environmentalist, and writer known for her work on sustainable development and tribal land claims. She is executive director of Honor the Earth, which creates awareness and support for Native environmental issues, such as the Dakota Access Pipeline, and develops needed financial and political resources for the survival of sustainable Native communities through the arts. She ran for vice president of the United States as the nominee for the US Green Party in 1996 and 2000. In 1989, LaDuke founded the White Earth Land Recovery Project to buy back reservation land from non-Natives, reforest the lands, revive cultivation of wild rice, and market traditional products. The project is administering an Ojibwe language program, managing a herd of buffalo, and running a wind-energy project. She is the author or coauthor of over a dozen books, including *All Our Relations: Native Struggles for Land and Life; The Militarization of Indian Country;* and *Recovering the Sacred: The Power of Naming and Claiming.* She is a popular speaker and has received many awards, including the Thomas Merton Award, and she has been inducted into the National Women's Hall of Fame.

Indigenous Worldview Precept Dialogue

Darcia: LaDuke writes that one way to learn natural law involves "intergenerational residency." Through this place-based orientation, we learn to master our social and moral sensibilities in healthy, balanced ways. For example: "The Lakota way of dealing with their landscape is not going to work for the Hopi in Northern Arizona, and vice versa. We have to pay attention to the context of their specific models and their moral metaphor and their moral landscapes, or what Leslie Marmon Silko referred to as their cognitive journeys across a landscape. We all have to find our unique ways of taking our cognitive journeys on our landscapes. . . . Dennis [Martinez] suggests a great way to do this: find the plants. Connect with them and your cognitive journey begins, and next your metaphors will begin, and that place becomes your moral landscape."[1]

Those raised in the dominant worldview are not taught to focus on the laws of nature. They lack a landscape-grounded morality. It's not just scientists who have this moral blindness, but humanitarians too. A common problem among Western-educated folks who travel to low-income parts of the world to "help" them—the so-called "white man's burden"—often cause more havoc than help, wasting billions of dollars, because they interfere with long-standing, sustainable, socially cohesive practices.[2] They are acting out another form of colonization, fueled by what I call "detached imagination," practiced too often by highly educated people.[3] There is also a vicious form of imagination represented by the US government agents who collaborate with multinational corporations to purposefully "help" a country's economy through shenanigans like arranging loans with the elite class, loans that can't be paid back, and then taking "natural resources" as compensation.[4] David Korten pointed out that the West has imposed economic development on societies all over the world at the expense of social and ecological wealth.[5] Spiritual, psychological, and physical health too!

Four Arrows, you and I were raised in the dominant worldview. We obtained doctorates from institutions and curricula based on the dominant worldview. What caused us to be able to do our best to embrace the Indigenous worldview and challenge the dominant one in ways that honor the laws of nature?

Four Arrows: Your general question, interestingly, is one a doctoral student of mine just an hour ago decided to use for her dissertation research question! "What can be learned from focus groups of teachers about how to work toward decolonizing education?" As for your more specific question about our particular motivations, the obvious answer might be growing up with a sense of—and, for me, a disregard of—our Indigenous identity. I don't think this is sufficient, however. I know a number of enrolled tribal members who are as colonized and unaware of nature's laws as any white person. We must keep in mind, though, that in the United States, American Indians and Alaskan Natives are taught via colonized curriculum and teachers. So your claim that Western education is the culprit stands. For me, reading some of the early work of Indigenous authors and others that promoted Indigenous worldview before I started studying it gave me some "aha" moments. My near-death experience in Mexico and my time with the Rarámuri people are what pushed me to go full-tilt with Indigeneity, and even that took a number of years.

I think the solution is in doing what we and many others are doing to promote Indigenous worldview. The 2019 United Nations *Global Assessment Report on Biodiversity and Ecosystem Services* references Indigenous worldview as a vital consideration to rebalance life systems. The decolonizing education movement is growing. Indigenous activists are being heard. I get letters from people around the world saying that their lives have been transformed by realizing the kind of information we are offering in this book. We both have students and scholars coming to us to learn about Indigeneity. More and more respected personalities are shouting it out. Just consider some back-cover endorsements of my book, *Teaching Truly: A Curriculum to Indigenize Mainstream Education:*

"[It] offers a way create a better world—before it is too late."
—Thom Hartmann

"The grim prognosis for life on this planet is the consequence of a few centuries of forgetting what traditional societies knew."
—Noam Chomsky

"Educators need to be paying attention [to Indigenous knowledge]."—Bill McKibben

I think an equally if not more important question than what can we do to bring forth Indigenous worldview is what can we do to stop the hegemonic and violent efforts to kill it once and for all. On many fronts, including COVID-19, status quo institutions and governments continue to oppress and even murder Indigenous peoples around the world.

To honor natural laws as the highest rules for living, we must support traditional Indigenous peoples who are still living accordingly. We must learn to *listen* again to the animals and plants. We must feel the wind and honor the bodies of water around us. Using my visionary mnemonic, CAT-FAWN, can be a powerful way to immediately start using an Indigenous worldview approach to Fear, Authority, Words, and Nature with natural trance-based learning/self-hypnosis. It does not take long for the "laws of nature" to start talking to us.

Darcia: The laws of nature are yelling "climate emergency," though it may be too late to do much about it.[6] The last three decades of fossil-fuel burning has put reversal of global warming out of reach. Too much carbon has been put into the atmosphere, so we are reaching several tipping points. The only things preventing superescalating global temperature are the particles that fossil-fuel burning produces. They act like an umbrella, keeping sun rays from heating the planet further.

We are all subject to natural law, Mother Earth's laws. Those laws include participating in the cycle of life. We all die but then regenerate into new life. Matrifocal societies followed the cycle, but patriarchy acted against the cycle, shaping a linear worldview taken up by capitalism's endless growth, bringing us to the climate emergency underway.

What has gone wrong that one human culture has taken over to destroy most of the biocommunities on the planet? How does one species (or part of a species) come to believe and act as if they alone should live on the earth? My answer: species-abnormal upbringing— unnested care. Critical in early life—when neurobiological, social, and moral foundations are being established—is maintaining the continuum of feeling one with Life,[7] with mothers and others, bonded to and embedded in the natural world—the traditional Indigenous way. In industrial-colonialist-capitalist societies like the USA, there is a massive breakdown in children's continuum of connection, often forced by culture and authorities. No other animal intentionally breaks that continuum, introducing toxic stress. In this way a "schizoid" personality develops when, according to R. D. Laing, "experience is split in two main ways: in the first place, there is a rent in his relation with his world and, in the second, there is a disruption of his relation with himself. Such a person is not able to experience himself 'together with' others or 'at home in' the world, but on the contrary, he experiences himself in despairing aloneness and isolation."[8]

Actually, the Indigenous Worldview shows us that there is a third split, hard for dominator culture to perceive: the split from the rest of nature. The person is split from self, social relations, and a sense of communion with Nature.

Whatever is ahead, the planet's physical life will continue (most of the planet is biomass that will survive what comes) and our particles will be part of it. We can let go of ego and embrace Spirit, and help others do the same.

Four Arrows: I am convinced that the "split from self" to which you refer is the consequence of humanity's split from nature. I just took a look at the various definitions of "nature" on the internet. They included phrases like the following:

- as opposed to humans or human creations

- the material world surrounding humankind and existing independently of human activities

- all the processes not caused by people

- the external world

- all things predating or unaffected by human technology

Why would a human operating under a worldview that sees nature this way care about following its laws? As the eloquent quotes throughout this book reveal, we *are* nature. We *are* the land, the sky, the oceans, and the wind. Our minds and the mind of Mother Earth are inseparable. We are as integral to nature as it is to us. When LaDuke refers to practicing Indigenous "religion" in a sacred place, she is referring to this intimate relationship. Of course, Indigenous languages, as far as I know, do not have an original word for "religion." Nor do we have words for "nature" or "environment." Usually when such language is being used, it is a dominant worldview guiding it. Moreover, it is probably related to some form of colonization, even if it is environmentalists who are using the words. LaDuke was speaking to an audience of non-Indians to offer an alternative view of what they perceive as religion. She knows that no organized religion is higher than natural law that is understood most clearly in the observation, interaction, and assimilation of all that is of Mother Earth.

Western academics, philosophers, and theologians have written about "natural laws" for centuries. I have a copy of Martin Rhonheimer's 2000 book titled *Natural Law and Practical Reason: A Thomist View of Moral Autonomy.* I recall from it the debates of philosophers from Aristotle to Aquinas, and how Aquinas stood somewhat apart from the others with his claim that the foundational rule in natural law was about loving one's neighbor. I remember it as a positive takeaway that recognizes the symbiosis and mutual-aid orientation of all life. Aquinas still put the supernatural world above the natural world, however. I view this as a misunderstanding of nature's law of interconnectedness. It is akin to thinking of water as something out-side of living. Ask people what they think the most important things in their life are, and seldom will anyone refer to water. Separating water from life, according to Indigenous understanding of natural law, is impossible. In Lakota, *mni,* our word for water, is "the first conscious-ness" and "the womb of all creation."[9]

This brings us full circle to the opening sentences in Winona's quote: "Natural law is the highest law, and it would be folly to figure that you can outwit natural law. . . . You can change the terms, you can change the allowable limits, you can do the risk assessment—all these things—but in the end, the fact is that you and I drink that water."

20

Becoming Fully Human

Greg Cajete (Tewa, Santa Clara Pueblo)

*I*mbued with the perception that all things were sacred, traditional education, from the moment of conception to beyond the moment of death, is considered a time of learning the true nature of one's spirit. That learning begins with reflecting on the spirit's expression in the human and natural community through the understanding and use of "breath" in all its forms, an understanding that includes the physical nature of breath as well as the perception of thought as a kind of "wind" and a unique variation of breath. Language and song are other forms of breath that create a holistic foundation for communication. Language is an expression of the sacred because it contains the power to express human thought and feeling and to emotionally affect others. Breath consciously forms and activates the parameters of communication in traditional tribal education through language, thought, prayer, chanting, ritual, dance, sport, work, story, play, and art. . . . For American Indians, what is called "education" today was traditionally a journey for learning about being fully human while living in a relational universe. Learning about the nature of the spirit was considered central to learning the full meaning of life. . . .

The Indigenous goal of living "a good life" is sometimes referred to by Native American people as striving "to always think the highest thought." This metaphor refers to the framework of a sophisticated epistemology of community-based, spiritual education in which the community and its traditions form the primary support for its way of life and quality of thinking.

Thinking the highest thought means thinking of one's self, one's community, and one's environment "richly"—essentially, a spiritual mindset in which one thinks in the highest, most respectful, and most compassionate way, thus systematically influencing the actions of both individuals and the community. It is a way to perpetuate a "good life," a respectful and spiritual life, and a dynamic wholeness. Thus, the community becomes a kind of center and context for learning how to live spiritually. . . . Each Indigenous community is considered a sacred place, a place of living, learning, teaching, healing, and ritual—a place where the people share the breath of their life and thought. The community is a living, spiritual entity supported by every responsible adult. In striving to "think the highest thought" and reach "that place that Indian people talk about," each adult becomes a teacher and a student—because to learn to think the highest thought and teach that place is a step-by-step process that begins at birth, and each individual, from youngest to oldest, has a role to play.

Source

Greg Cajete. *Native Science: Natural Laws of Interdependence,* 262, 276–77. Santa Fe: Clear Light, 2000.

Contextualized Biosketch

Gregory Cajete, a Tewa from Santa Clara Pueblo, has dedicated his life and work to the foundations of Indigenous knowledge in education. He was director of Native American Studies and a professor in the Division of Language, Literacy, and Socio-Cultural Studies at the University of New Mexico. Dr. Cajete is extensively involved with art and its applications to education. He is also a scholar of herbalism and holistic health, designing culturally responsive curricula based upon American Indian understanding of the "nature of nature." He utilizes this foundation to develop an understanding of the science and artistic thought processes that are expressed in Indigenous perspectives of the natural world. He has authored seven books, including *Look to the Mountain: An Ecology of Indigenous Education; Igniting the Sparkle: An Indigenous Science Education Model; Spirit of the Game: Indigenous Wellsprings; A People's Ecology: Explorations in Sustainable Living;* and *Native Science: Natural Laws of Interdependence.* With Don Jacobs (Four Arrows) and Jongmin Lee, he also coauthored *Critical Neurophilosophy and Indigenous Wisdom.*

Indigenous Worldview Precept Dialogue

Darcia: Indigenous learning is about the growth of the self in a more holistic manner than in the learning common in the dominant culture. With this broader interconnectedness in mind, learning is not focused on just one form of self-development, as often occurs in Western societies, through school-book learning of abstract semantic knowledge. Such a focus is not useful for embracing what Cajete refers to as "becoming fully human." Instead, he points out how learning is considered to be a lifelong, whole-community process that enhances the well-being of the individual and the community, who are considered to be spiritual entities.

Some Western philosophers have focused on self-actualization in ways that touch upon some of the holistic Indigenous considerations. For example, Abraham Maslow's interest in human potential intrigued him the most, and so he did some investigation of what it looks like. In comparison to other members of (US) society, he described self-actualizers as having the following traits:[1]

- A more efficient perception of reality

- Greater acceptance of self, others, and nature

- More spontaneity, simplicity, and naturalness

- A problem-centered orientation

- Greater autonomy, will, and active agency, including being independent from culture

- A continued freshness of appreciation

- Common mystic or peak experiences

- Feeling of kinship with all of humanity

- Deeper interpersonal relations

- A more democratic character structure

- Discriminatory view of means and ends, between good and evil

- A philosophical, unhostile sense of humor

- Creativity

- Resistance to enculturation and transcendence of any particular culture

- A quality of detachment and need for privacy

Such characteristics describe the average traditionally raised Indigenous child!

Four Arrows: It is not a coincidence that you refer to Maslow and his list of optimal attributes for becoming a "true human." Maslow got his ideas directly from his observations of the Blackfoot understandings about self-actualization. In 1938, he spent several weeks doing research on a Blackfoot reservation in Canada. His experience "had a powerful impact on him, and completely overturned his socially conditioned view of Indians."[2] In fact, Indigeneity and the innate positivity in humans was the basis for his "humanistic psychology." There is evidence it was also foundational for his hierarchy of needs.[3] University of Alberta professor Cindy Blackstock refers to his work as "a rip-off from the Blackfoot nation." Blackstock is a member of the Gitksan First Nation and is a recipient of the Nobel Women's Initiative and

Aboriginal Achievement Foundation recognition. She says Maslow's famous triangle was originally a tipi and that self-actualization is supposed to be at the base of the tipi, not at the top where Maslow placed it. "In the Blackfoot belief, self-actualization is the foundation on which community actualization is built."[4] The highest form that a Blackfoot can attain to be "fully human" is "cultural perpetuity," or what the Gitksan people call "the breath of life."[5]

Maslow is not the only Western psychologist or philosopher whose wisdom is founded upon Indigenous worldview. I have written about how Henry David Thoreau's philosophy stems from his intense studies of the Indigenous perspective.[6] His major publications were based on almost three thousand handwritten pages in his "Indian Notebooks." His goal was to write a book from these notes that would help stifle the ignorance and anti-Indianism of his era, a book he never wrote. He also spent much time learning from his Penobscot friends, including learning their language that he thought was "less artificial than English."[7]

After writing the above paragraph, I co-presented to ecoversities groups from around the world with a young Guaraní shaman from Brazil named Verá Tupã. The questions I received about Indigenous worldview were the best I've ever received from an audience. The quote about Thoreau saying the Indigenous language is less artificial than English was brought to light by both of us. I spoke about how Indigenous languages grew from the world of nature, and the European languages grew from the world of human society disconnected from nature. I said the pronouns alone are "it-ing" the world to death. Then Verá spoke about how the words "doubt" and "love" do not exist in the languages of Brazilian Indigenous people. (I looked to see if I could find them in Lakota, and they also do not exist as nouns.) He says if we stopped using the word and let feeling, tasting, observing, touching, and other flourishings from the four directions be what they are in us and with us, we would share more loving (as a verb). As for "doubt," he said when you listen to the wisdom of the ancestors about their observations of Nature passed down for many centuries orally, there can be no doubt. I think Greg Cajete would agree that such awareness is crucial in self-awareness and becoming a true human.

Darcia: I appreciate you pointing out how much of Indigenous wisdom was culturally appropriated—taken and presented as "new" theory in the dominant culture. I did not know this about Maslow, but the source of his theory makes perfect sense. Tadodaho Chief Leon Shenandoah said, "The thing wrong with the world is that people don't have instructions. We were told almost three hundred years ago that people would be coming to us and asking for our instructions. We were told back in the 1700s that there'd be a day when white people would be coming to us, asking for instructions and finding out the way we think."[8]

I think Maslow was looking for such instructions, though he did not credit his mentors. And I think we are trying to be mediators of those instructions.

Western Indo-European languages, which emphasize nouns, can give us a static view of life, making the world seem full of objects we manipulate, whereas Native languages typically emphasize verbs, emphasizing the dynamic beingness of all. For Indigenous peoples, living life is perceived as an ongoing unfolding organic change, a "continuous birth. . . . One is continually present as witness to [the] moment, always moving like the crest of a wave, at which the world is about to disclose itself for what it is."[9] When asked how to recognize if someone is a human being, Chief Shenandoah said, "You just know. They know the Creator. They work for the benefit of the people, and they walk so softly on Mother Earth they don't even leave any foot-prints."[10] Commenting on this and other insights from anthropologist Tim Ingold into Native ways, I wrote: "This is a different form of being—rather like an ongoing *becoming*—from what is expected and fostered in modern civilizations."[11] In these challenging times a new becoming is required. As Stephen Buhner writes: "As this egg of the new time cracks open, we must rebirth ourselves into lifeways that are in good relationship and will sustain all life over time."[12] The arts help us revamp our minds, releasing them from dominator consciousness to be able to co-create a transformed future. Melissa K. Nelson writes:

> One of the ways we can invite this trickster consciousness or coyote way into our lives and decolonize our minds is through traditional cultural arts: music, dance, weaving, carving, beading, regalia-making, sculpting, painting, and other mediums. By engaging the hands with natural materials—wood, plants, stone, pigments, leather—or engaging the mind with song, music, and sonic imagination, we can disrupt our Eurocentric conditioning. There is something about the rhythm of using our whole bodies and other parts of our minds that opens up a more fluid way of knowing and being. All artists know that when you are "in the groove" or "in the flow"—using your hands, bodies, and minds in creative ways—that the trappings of Cartesian logic fall away. We are not thinking of the past or concerned with the future. We are present in the moment as an integral part of creation. This creative liberation is a foundation and form of cultural sovereignty."[13]

We can encourage readers to immerse themselves in the arts to find the flow of being, self- and world-transformation.

Four Arrows: This idea of "becoming human" as an ongoing process is often referred to by Indigenous peoples. Steve Wall's book about Leon's call to the world is even titled *To Become a Human Being: The Message of Tadodaho Chief Leon Shenandoah*. In his speech to the United Nations, the chief made it clear that Indigenous peoples today hold the wisdom for becoming human again, something most *Homo sapiens* seem to have forgotten: "Why are such elemental deductions beyond the understanding of the leaders of governments, when we, the people, so easily understand? We must gather the mothers of the nations and hear their outrage at the senseless expenditure of their children's lives for profit, power and the supremacy of any ideology, whatever it may be."[14]

Most people who talk about "becoming human" are referring to the evolution of *Homo sapiens,* or perhaps the ontology of human characteristics such as use of emotions. They would question the idea of a human needing to "become human." However, all one has to do is look around at what we do to one another and to Mother Earth to realize we have forgotten how to be human beings. For Indigenous people this is about living according to the precepts put forth in this book. For example, the Lakota say in order to be a human being we must learn to authentically and consistently practice the following virtues:

Wóčhekiya—Prayer

Wičákha—Honesty

Wahwala—Humility

Waúnšila—Compassion

Waóhola—Respect

Wawokiye—Generosity

Wóksape—Wisdom

The capability of humans to lose their humanity seems to be a unique trait of our species. Although any animal can become insane owing to a variety of environmental conditions, such as being put in a cage, or losing habitat, it seems we are the only ones who create such conditions intentionally. In addition to people like us claiming that traditional Indigenous wisdom is key to living life in balance, we must realize that Indigenous people also are susceptible to whatever happens that causes us to separate ourselves from natural law and the practices that stem from it, like those listed above. According to Hopi and Maya origin stories and prophecies, what is happening in our world today has happened before when humans forgot who they were and used their special powers without regard for the Laws of Nature. Thomas Banyacya, a Hopi spiritual leader, says it this way in a presentation taped in 1995:[15] "They began to develop power for themselves to do anything, not caring what they would do with the power. [There was] no spirituality, no balance, all wide open. . . . Gambling, money, fighting, quarreling, disputing, destroying one another. No stopping, much dishonesty, no corrections."

In the same presentation, referring to a famous petroglyph on a rock near his home, he talks of three previous human worlds that were destroyed when people became greedy and worshiped technology, forgetting the original, sacred instructions for being human. Three apocalypses purified the world. The first time the Creator used fire, then ice, and the third was a great flood. I know a number of Indigenous elders from around the world who believe that we are at the threshold of a fourth or a fifth world. No one knows how the Creator will end this one or when it will happen if we cannot do enough to rebalance life systems. I personally do not believe we can, though I do believe in miracles. I recently shared this at a presentation at the University of British Columbia, and someone asked why I am still doing this work if I believe there is little chance to turn things around. I responded, "Because I want to become fully human before my spirit moves on, a spirit that will likely be back to help future generations rebuild."

21

Nature Seen as Benevolent

Basil Johnston (Wasauksing)

*W*e owe the earth our all, more than we can take in, more than we can say. We can never return anything but our respect and thanksgiving.

In offering a whiff of incense in the Sacred Pipe ceremony to Mother Earth we acknowledge that.

When we hunger, Mother Earth nourishes us. Whatever we need is there in abundance, more than enough to fill the wants and needs of every insect, bird, animal, fish, man and woman with fruit, vegetables, seeds and nectar.

When we need to clothe our bodies from the sun, wind, rain, snow and insects, Mother Earth provides the means to cover our bodies. She gives fat and pelt to the deer, beaver, moose, buffalo, rabbit and bear. They, our older brothers and sisters, lend us their coats. To care for ourselves, our families and our communities, Mother Earth yields the means by which we make our weapons, canoes, snowshoes, clothing, utensils, adornments, and our homes.

When we need shelter from the winds, snows, storms, rains, cold and heat, there are woods, forest, valleys, mountains, bays, and inlets where insects, birds, animals and humans may find harbour, build their nests and dens, or erect their dwellings and found their villages and towns.

When we are sick and need care to nurse us back to health, Mother Earth's meadows, forests, and shorelines are lush with berries, plants, roots, seeds and resins that bear the elixir of health and life. Our ancestors called medicine "Mashki-aki," the strength of the earth for its capacity to infuse the enfeebled sick with energy and vitality.

When our spirits flag and are burdened with cares, worries, losses and sorrows, Mother Earth comforts us. She whispers and chants to the downhearted and dispirited through the tree tops, over the meadows, in cascades and rapids. It is a mother's soothing voice offering solace to the low in spirit. She whispers, "I love you. I care."

Source

Basil Johnston. *Honour Earth Mother: Mino-audjaudauh Mizzu-Kummik-Quae*, vii–viii. Lincoln: University of Nebraska Press, 2003.

Contextualized Biosketch

Basil Johnston was born on the Parry Island Indian Reserve in Ontario. At first, he was educated in reserve schools in Cape Croker but later was sent to a residential school, which he wrote about in his book *Indian School Days*. He was his high school class valedictorian, graduated with honors from Loyola College in Montreal, and earned a certificate to teach high school. He taught high school before taking a position in the ethnology department of the Royal Ontario Museum in Toronto, where he stayed for twenty-five years. His focus was the restoration of the language, values, and beliefs of the Anishinaabe. Through the museum, he developed Ojibway language courses, believing that Indigenous culture was best understood through traditional language. He published many books, including *Ojibway Heritage; The Manitous: The Spiritual World of the Ojibway; How the Birds Got Their Colours; Moose Meat and Wild Rice; Ojibway Ceremonies;* and *Hudson Bay Portraits: Native Peoples of the Hudson Bay Watershed*. He received several honors, including honorary doctorates, the Order of Ontario, the National Aboriginal Achievement Award for Heritage and Spirituality, and the 125th Anniversary of the Confederation of Canada Medal.

Indigenous Worldview Precept Dialogue

Darcia: These are the words of a wise elder. The abundance of Mother Earth's gifts is something we lose track of in scarcity-producing (capitalist) societies, where our attention is often on keeping our place in the line toward success.

To *feel* the nurturing that Mother Earth provides may require a reverence for it. Among First Nations, this grows from modeling the elders and listening to their stories. Immersion in its beauty also plays a role. I like Luther Standing Bear's reflections:

> "The character of the Indian's emotion left little room in his heart
> for antagonism toward his fellow creatures. . . . For the Lakota,
> mountains, lakes, rivers, springs, valleys and woods were all fin-
> ished beauty. Winds, rain, snow, sunshine, day, night, and change
> of seasons were endlessly fascinating. Birds, insects, and animals
> filled the world with knowledge that defied the comprehension of
> man. . . . The Lakota was a true naturalist—a lover of Nature. He
> loved the earth and all things of the earth, and the attachment grew
> with age. The old people came literally to love the soil and they sat or
> reclined on the ground with a feeling of being close to a mothering
> power. . . . It was good for the skin to touch the earth, and the old
> people liked to remove their moccasins and walk with bare feet on
> the sacred earth. . . . Their tipis were built upon the earth and their
> altars were made of earth. The birds that flew in the air came to rest
> upon the earth, and it was the final abiding place of all things that
> lived and grew. The soil was soothing, strengthening, cleansing, and
> healing. . . . This is why the old Indian still sits upon the earth instead
> of propping himself up and away from its life-giving forces. For him,
> to sit or lie upon the ground is to be able to think more deeply and
> to feel more keenly; he can see more clearly into the mysteries of life
> and come closer in kinship to other lives about him."[1]

Neurobiologically speaking, going barefoot or sitting on the earth with no synthetic barrier causes physiological changes in our bodies.

Cortisol, the mobilizing and stress hormone, decreases, and oxytocin increases, making one feel more relaxed, more open.[2]

The sense of earth-nurturing might also increase when we learn about its deep kinship networks. For example, plants have tiny mouth-like openings in their leaves (stomata) that exchange mists with the surrounding atmosphere, allowing them to feed off the atmosphere; this is enabled by particular kinds of music that resemble birdsong. Just think, birds and plants coevolved to enhance one another in the ecosystem over thousands of millennia.[3] In fact, scientists are discovering that forest trees form symbiotic relations with hundreds of fungal species and use fungal networks to connect to other trees and plants, helping one another when needed.[4]

We evolved with plant intelligence too. Monica Gagliano records phytobiographies of plants as persons, conveying that they expect nonhierarchical respect and partnership.[5] Stephen Buhner says of plants: "By partaking of their vibratory intelligence through ingestion as well as through communion, we can become more whole and integrated ourselves, and thus extend a healing vibration to the life around us. For it is in the emotional healing of our relationship issues that the world will become whole. . . . It is very hard to cut down a forest when we experience it as alive and intelligent and as an elder to the human."[6]

Of course, Indigenous cultures have understood and learned from the intelligence of plants long before Western science.[7] If we take the time, all of us can feel the vibrations of Mother Earth all around us in wild nature—in the plants, the waters, the wind, the animals, the soil. They heal and restore us.

Four Arrows: I think it is essential to note the risk that what Johnston, Standing Bear, and you are saying is dismissed as idealizing nature unrealistically, making it something more perfect or appealing than it is or can be. Such romanticizing of nature and Indigenous peoples who live according to what the quote conveys is, as we both know, almost as dangerous for landscapes and their original human inhabitants as is the blatant disregard for them. It creates boundaries, hierarchies, and illusions that create situations that ultimately can lead to some form of violence against the land and its people. Navajo weavers warn about the problem of seeking or claiming perfection by intentionally putting a knot or two in their weaving. One can know if a rug is truly one woven by a Navajo traditionalist by searching for its imperfection.

The Indigenous worldview precept that sees even the worst of nature's forces—whether droughts, storms, cold, burning heat, or other challenging conditions—as essentially benevolent, is very different from the dominant worldview that separates humanity from nature and sees it as dangerous or inferior to humans. It also contrasts with what I believe to be the foundational philosophy supporting capitalism and its dependence on its externalities, which are the side effects of economic degradation. Walter Block articulates this philosophy in a book where he and I argue cooperatively about our worldview differences. A well-published scholar and Loyola University economics professor, Block was surprised that anyone could see animals or trees as having intrinsic value. He writes during one of our exchanges:

> "Yes, of course, everything on Earth should exist solely for human exploitation. . . . What other reason do the fauna and flora of our planet exist? That is, in my view, the earth and its accoutrements exist solely for our sakes, and for no other reason. They do not at all have intrinsic value, only instrumental value, as a means toward *our* ends. As I hope I have demonstrated to you, there really is no incompatibility between benefits for human beings, and survival of other species if we adopt laissez faire capitalism and free enterprise, where private enterprise and the profit and loss system mitigate against extinctions, via barnyards."[8]

This is the dominant view writ large. I am convinced that Block's position, coupled with the competitive orientation of capitalism, illustrates the source of violence among humans and between humans and nature—the result of a worldview that misunderstands nature and human nature and does not see nature as ultimately benevolent. I also believe that Darwin's emphasis on natural selection and his willingness to accept the term "survival of the fittest" (coined by Spencer) showed the bias of the dominant worldview he held. His thinking was grounded "scientifically" by Hobbes, who saw human beings as ferocious beasts engaged in constant wars with one another in need of sociopolitical control.[9]

The failure of social scientists, educators and contemporary philosophers to embrace Pyotr (Peter) Kropotkin's perspective, which better aligns with the Indigenous worldview, has given support to modernity assuming nature to be cruel.[10] Kropotkin, who studied Darwin deeply, mostly agreed with his understanding of natural selection, but critiqued his presentation and the interpretations of it by subsequent scientists and social Darwinists. He found that Darwin's work, as well as his own studies, actually proved that mutual aid, rather than fierce competition, defined the natural world.[11] Kropotkin based his conclusions on many years as a scholar, analyzing university lectures and doing fieldwork in geology, geography, biology, and botany, especially in wilderness areas throughout Russia. He was convinced that Darwin's writing and the interpretations of it overemphasized the role of competition in nature and in human nature, serving to rationalize human behaviors on behalf of the misguided emphasis on "survival of the fittest" and the Hobbesian view of nature.[12] The question is, what will it take for contemporary and future educators, psychologists, philosophers, and scientists to teach how science supports the Indigenous worldview precept this chapter describes?

Darcia: Most scientists are focused on their silos and not oriented to the big picture, and those who are tend to be afraid to say anything that sounds religious. The science world is still largely positivistic (you only can know something after an experiment gives you measurable, statistically significant results). Once you invest in a particular worldview upon which your work and lifestyle rely, it is hard to shift to another worldview. But biological scientists have been getting more and more in tune with nature's inherent cooperation.[13] Lynn Margulis was a proponent of symbiosis, mutualism, being the driver of evolution.[14] Scientists are also starting to acknowledge that our bodies are communities themselves, with only 1 percent to 10 percent of the genes we each carry being human (most are those of our microbiome).[15]

The dominant voices in scientific circles, propelled by the dominant worldview of European-thought supremacism, continue to convey what is called a neo-Darwinian perspective, enhancing the aspect of Darwin you mention. The general view has its roots in Hobbes, promoted by Aldous Huxley, more recently by Richard Dawkins, to emphasize Hobbes' war of all against all, human selfishness, and genetic competition.[16] Darwin had conflicting views. Like many Indigenous people, Darwin was an observer of nature, believing much of it was mysterious. He was known to be unusually compassionate for a scientist.[17] He was trying to determine how species change and why (e.g., the beak size of finches) and discovered "natural selection"—offspring that fit the environment better than rivals survive better. He was unaware of genes, but even so, most genes and other characteristics stay the same generation after generation. (The real story is in epigenetics—if/when genes are expressed—through which the evolved nest helps shape human nature.) Darwin tried to correct Huxley's misuse of the term "struggle for existence" in a later edition of his *On the Origin of Species:*

> I should premise that I use the term Struggle of Existence in a large
> and metaphorical sense, including dependence of one being on
> another, and including (which is more important) not only the life of
> the individual but success in leaving progeny. . . . A plant on the edge
> of a desert is said to struggle for life against the drought, though more
> properly it should be said to be dependent on the moisture. . . . When
> we reach the Arctic regions, or snow-capped mountains, or abso-
> lute deserts, *the struggle for life is almost exclusively with the elements*
> [emphasis added].[18]

In his book *The Descent of Man,*[19] Darwin pointed out that human beings who survived (who were selected by natural selection) were the most sociable, the most cooperative. Darwin thought that more cooperative groups were more adaptive than groups of selfish individuals.

He thought human beings could only be understood as beings who share most of their traits, including social instincts, with other animals. This shocked European societies. Humans shared a history, a common ancestor (we know today it was likely a mollusk), with all animals through the tree of life. A prime constituent of humanity and its successful adaptation over generations is what Darwin called the "moral sense," a collection of traits other animals have that come together uniquely in human beings (e.g., pleasure being with others, concern with fitting into the social group, empathy, habit development), along with the intellect that allows for a comparison of one's behavior with what was planned or expected in terms of community values. I have written about how data suggest that industrialized people, such as those in the USA, may be losing Darwin's "moral sense" (because it appears to be mostly epigenetic, shaped after birth, and industrialized societies violate the evolved nest for raising children).[20] In fact, Darwin did not think his British compatriots exhibited the moral sense to the same degree at all as the Native peoples he encountered on his voyages to South America and various islands.

The work of decolonizing our minds of the industrialist-capitalist-supremacist worldview may have to emerge bottom up—among the populace, like our readers—because those with power tend to not want to risk their status.

Four Arrows: Darcia, your work about the loss of our moral sensibilities is crucial to understanding that we seem to have devolved into believing that nature is dog-eat-dog. Revisiting the work of Darwin and others can help with removing some misguided assumptions, and I am happy we got a bit academic in this chapter. However, for bottom-up transformation, metacognitive worldview reflection is vital and is the reason for our writing this book. CAT-FAWN Connection work, mentioned previously, must follow for change to truly occur. I offer here for our readers an overview of how CAT-FAWN works:[21]

1. Consider any attitude you have that creates discontentment or imbalance.

2. Try to identify the source of the assumption/belief/feeling. Then look for a way that some fear relates to your position. Identify the source of the fear.

3. When you identify it, ask next what authorizes or rationalizes the fear. This was often an occurrence in the first six years of life; you may have to go way back for the answer. Something your father said, or a teacher, might have caused it. It could be more recent also, especially if associated with a frightening or stressful event. During times of stress, we become hypersuggestible to authoritarian mandates and are literally hypnotized into adopting belief systems that go uninvestigated.

4. Now you have a sense of what you fear and the authority for having it. Ask yourself what words you use when you talk about it to yourself or others. Words are hypnotic and can maintain and strengthen misguided beliefs.

5. With these discoveries about the source of your hurtful belief in mind, go back and attach Indigenous worldview to fear by turning it into an opportunity for practicing a virtue such as patience, fortitude, courage, honesty, humility, or generosity. Use honest reflection on your lived experience to challenge the authority that caused the fear. Find words that are more accurate to describe it.

6. Now with these cognitive realizations in mind, do self-hypnosis by putting yourself into a slower brain-wave frequency and deeply imagining the more honest, healthful understandings that you now have that is founded on Indigenous worldview precepts.

7. Finally, seek out an other-than-human being, whether a colony of ants, a tree, the stars, or your pet animal, and consider what possible teachings they offer you that confirm your new understandings.

THEY SPOKE VERY LOUDLY WHEN THEY SAID
THEIR LAWS WERE MADE FOR EVERYBODY,
BUT WE SOON LEARNED THAT ALTHOUGH
THEY EXPECTED US TO KEEP THEM, THEY
THOUGHT NOTHING
OF BREAKING THEM
THEMSELVES.
THEY TOLD US
NOT TO DRINK
WHISKEY,
YET THEY
MADE IT
THEMSELVES
AND TRADED
IT TO US FOR
FURS AND
ROBES UNTIL
BOTH WERE
NEARLY
GONE.
THEIR
WISE ONES
SAID WE
MIGHT
HAVE THEIR
RELIGION
BUT WHEN
WE TRIED TO
UNDERSTAND
IT WE FOUND
THAT THERE
WERE TOO
MANY KINDS
OF RELIGION
AMONG WHITE
MEN FOR US TO
UNDERSTAND,
AND THAT
SCARCELY
ANY TWO WHITE MEN
AGREED WHICH WAS
THE RIGHT ONE TO LEARN

THIS
BOTHERED
US A GOOD DEAL
UNTIL WE SAW
THAT THE WHITE
MAN DID NOT TAKE
HIS RELIGION ANY
MORE SERIOUSLY THAN
HE DID HIS LAWS, AND
THAT HE KEPT BOTH OF THEM
JUST BEHIND HIM, LIKE HELPERS,
TO USE WHEN THEY MIGHT DO HIM
GOOD IN HIS DEALINGS WITH STRANGERS.
THESE WERE NOT OUR WAYS. WE KEPT THE
LAWS WE MADE AND LIVED OUR RELIGION.

Plenty Coups
marble stonecut

Harriet Greene
Taos, N.M.

22

Responsibility Emphasis

Xiuhtezcatl Martinez (Aztec)

[After introducing himself in his Indigenous language:]

Good morning, everybody. I think it is amazing to look around the room and see that there are almost two hundred countries represented here today. Because it is really going to take united action from all of us in order to make a difference. I'm fifteen years old and I am the youth director of an organization called Earth Guardians, and I'm working with young people around the planet to protect our earth, our air, our water, and our atmosphere, for my generation, and those to follow. . . . I was raised in the ceremonies of my people, learning the dances, the songs, and the language, and what I learned from my culture, my heritage, is that this life is a gift, and it is our responsibility to respect and protect that which gives us life. So I began to look at the world around me, and I saw that we were facing a crisis that was beginning to affect every living system on our planet. . . . Seeing my world collapsing around me pushed me into action. . . . Youth like myself across the United States are suing our state and federal governments, demanding that they take action. . . . Our generation is at the front of this movement and we need you to help us. We are approaching twenty-one years of United Nations climate talks, and almost no agreements have been made on a bonding climate recovery plan. . . . We need to end this mindset that we have, that we can take whatever we want without ever giving back or understanding the harm that we are doing to the planet. It's this mindset of destruction, of greed, that is tearing apart our planet. We need to change the fundamental beliefs of our entire society. We have to remember that we are all Indigenous to this earth, and that we are all connected. . . . We are being called upon to use our courage, our innovation, our creativity, and our passion to bring forth a new world. . . . It is time now to set aside everything that divides us. Who will stand with me now? It is our responsibility. We owe it to future generations. These are all very connected issues and therefore all the industries that play a part in these need to take responsibility. And this is not just about government responsibility and writing policy. It is about corporate responsibility. Our corporations hold a lot of power in the world. Young people are ready to use their art, their culture, their passion, their music, to engage with the world. Sure, we're a future generation, but we're here now and we are taking on the responsibility for making life suitable for more future generations.

Source

Office of the Secretary-General's Envoy on Youth. "Xiuhtezcatl, Indigenous Climate Activist at the High-level Event on Climate Change." June 29, 2015. Video, 9:31. www.youtube.com/watch?v=27gtZ1oV4kw.

Contextualized Biosketch

Xiuhtezcatl Martinez is, as of this writing, a nineteen-year-old advocate, leader, activist, and hip-hop artist. He was born in Colorado but moved to Mexico in his infancy, then back to Colorado. His Aztec father, Martinez, raised him in the tradition of the Mexica. He and his group, the Earth Guardians, believe that today's youth will play an important role in shaping our future. Earth Guardians is an environmental activist organization and school founded by his mother, Tamara Roske, in 1992. He serves as its youth director. He has spoken multiple times at the United Nations and has been a guest on the *Daily Show* with Trevor Noah and *Real Time* with Bill Maher. He has also been featured multiple times in *Rolling Stone* and on PBS, Showtime, National Geographic, and HBO. He has been a plaintiff in several class action lawsuits against polluting agencies, including the US government, showing how serious his activism is.

Indigenous Worldview Precept Dialogue

Four Arrows: Martinez has taken on a lot of responsibility at a very young age, and a number of interviewers have asked him if he has missed out on being a normal teenager. His answers convey a sincere sense of responsibility and a willingness to sacrifice as much as he can to prevent or minimize the suffering children will face in the future from climate change and other violences against nature. His priority is on responsible action more than on policy. It seems the Indigenous worldview precept here is saying that the dominant worldview has overemphasized rights and underemphasized responsibility. I was just talking with a friend about this, and he said that when talking about rights and responsibilities we should emphasize that the two are mutually constitutive and that the "complementary twins must begin and end as one." He gave land as an example, saying: "We have a right to a place to live, but that right bestows upon us responsibilities to care for the land and the other inhabitants of the land. To have a right to the land is to also have a responsibility to the land, and to renege upon our responsibilities to the land is to lose our right to the land."[1] Sherri Mitchell, author of *Sacred Instructions: Indigenous Wisdom for Living Spirit-Based Change,* articulates this partnership between rights and responsibilities as well. She writes:[2]

- Demanding rights without taking responsibility creates a warped sense of entitlement that often leads to violence, lawlessness and chaos.

- We cannot claim a right to peace without taking responsibility for cultivating peace within ourselves and in our relationships with others—even those we oppose.

- When we balance our demand for rights with our acceptance of our responsibility toward one another and all other living beings, we take back our power.

- We cannot claim a right to clean water without taking responsibility for actively protecting the water from contamination and overuse.

- We cannot claim a right to life without first taking responsibility for the lives that have already been created.

- The responsibility that we took on to balance that right [to life] was to live in harmony with the natural world.

Darcia, a number of young people are passionately speaking out about greed and what adults are doing that threatens future generations. They are sincere in their goals. However, I get a different feeling from the speeches of Martinez, who focuses on earth-based, nonanthropocentric interconnectedness. With this approach, I feel transformations can be more effective. I mean, we can talk all day about stopping COVID-19, but until our relationship with other-than-human sentience emerges, our actions are incomplete. This said, having young activists addressing climate change for future generations at any level is still wonderful. What can you say about early childhood development that can inspire even this?

Darcia: Research suggests that there were two childhood characteristics that were common among rescuers of Jews during World War II.[3] First, they were more likely to have an affectionate (secure) attachment to parents, which corresponds to a supportive early nest and is associated with well-functioning socioemotional intelligence. Also, the rescuers had a sense of connection to all of humanity, which would be encouraged by the stories and discourse of the family as well as adult role modeling. Rescuers were people who took responsibility to operationalize the truth about human oneness. But the focus was on human well-being. Such an anthropocentric focus seems also to be primary for many climate activists (though not all). Greta Thunberg, a teen activist, learned of the climate emergency when she was eight (in 2011) and went into depression for several years.[4] She was diagnosed with obsessive-compulsive disorder and Asperger's Syndrome (high-functioning autism), which she now calls her "superpower." At age eleven, she stopped eating most foods for a period of time and eventually was able to convince her parents to lower their carbon footprint with veganism, upcycling, and no longer flying (impeding her mother's career as an opera singer, but which her mother was happy to do for her daughter's health). According to her story, Greta convinced her parents not with logic and graphs but with concern for "stealing her future." At age fifteen, she went on a three-week climate strike in front of the Swedish parliament, which drew international attention. She has continued to be a spokesperson for children's futures.

In contrast, Martinez demonstrates the effects of the broader, earth-inclusive stories and modeling he received. Indigenous worldview and practices include concern for the well-being of the other-than-human world, for its own sake. He also demonstrates a heart openness and receptive intelligence toward the earth that comes from a nature-infused life. In this case, being responsible is not an intellectual endeavor ("what a good idea"), nor is it done only to keep one's family member happy. Instead, responsibility is deeply rooted in heart-minded intelligence and spiritual connection to the web of life. These are characteristics many Westernized peoples have neglected in themselves and their children. But we are at a turning point where Indigenous wisdom is awakening the world through activists like Martinez.

Four Arrows: Your remarkable scholarly background in moral development, the evolved nest, and Indigenous orientations that lead to moral cultures continues to show why our worldview precepts can and must be taught to children early on. I see this as essential for cultivating responsibility. I remember long ago, when I was director of education at Oglala Lakota College, I was studying Lawrence Kohlberg's stages of development. When I learned that research indicated that relatively few people make it to his sixth stage, where one makes self-chosen moral decisions regardless of laws or social pressures, I laughed. I knew if someone used the Kohlberg tests on Lakota youth under twelve years old, the results would show most would be in this sixth level. I was thinking of the many children on the Pine Ridge Reservation who took responsibility for the care of their siblings or parents, or who practiced remarkable generosity and a willingness to sacrifice for others despite many opposing pressures.

As you have stated several times in other chapters, children whose parents are authoritarian or neglectful do not learn how to take responsibility for their actions. As adults they cannot manage their lives well. In traditional Indigenous learning processes, the right balance comes from children continually observing and participating in family and community tasks. From being exposed to fluid and changing leadership, diverse ideas, positive work attitudes, and nonconfrontational ways, children quickly become intrinsically motivated to become a valued member of the community. Such motivation is reinforced by storytelling and spiritual practices. This contrasts with an approach that "involves adults attempting to control children's attention, motivation, and learning in *Assembly-Line Instruction,* which is a widespread way of organizing Western schooling."[5]

All of this seems to bring us back to Martin Brokenleg's Circle of Courage medicine wheel (discussed in chapter 15), where responsibility comes from the balance between (1) *independence,* where children have many chances to make choices without coercion; (2) *belonging,* where children feel related to everyone and everything; (3) *mastery,* where children have many opportunities to become competent in solving problems; and (4) *generosity,* where children prove their own worthiness by making positive contributions to another's well-being.[6] Perhaps if COVID-19 stays with us for a long time, children and parents will enter into this circle again as a matter of survival.

Darcia: You are reminding me that government and church leaders perceived American Indians to be neglectful of their children, justifying their kidnapping them, because parents were not training them to be orderly and obedient in that "assembly line" manner. Such treatment of children indicates ignorance about how to raise a flourishing, intelligent, moral human being. The Indigenous child raising that was disapproved by authorities represents a "harmonious" style that contrasts with the more prevalent authoritarian, permissive, and authoritative styles of parenting identified by Diana Baumrind.[7]

Kohlberg's focus on moral judgment reflected the Western philosophical view that emotionally detached, "objective" reasoning was the cause of moral action. This is a misunderstanding of the relation between thinking and feeling. Going into one's head undermines moral action because the heart is left out, one is decontextualized from relationships of responsibility. Even the ancient Greek philosophers, who inspired Western Enlightenment philosophy, accounted for well-functioning emotion systems; e.g., Aristotle noted the importance of shaping sensibilities well.[8]

My late husband, James Rest, identified the set of psychological processes that must occur for a moral/ethical behavior to take place.[9] They include moral sensitivity (e.g., empathy, relational awareness), moral judgment (prioritizing values and rationalizing choices), moral motivation (focus, identity), and moral action (ego strength and skill). Most writing about this four-component model of moral behavior focused on the human world only. My students and I spelled out skills that could be addressed in academic instruction.[10] Later, I expanded it to include the other-than-human world (Indigenous wisdom skills).[11] Thus, ethical sensitivity includes, for example, receptivity to the communications of the other-than-human, respecting diversity, and controlling bias towards human superiority. Ethical judgment includes honoring the laws of nature and aiming for the flourishing of all. Ethical motivation includes following the principles of the honorable harvest and cultivating a Commonself consciousness (oneness). Ethical action skills include cultivating fearlessness and working hard at self-development. All the skills require meta-wisdom (phronesis) of knowing when and how to apply them. All are learned through observation and practice that Indigenous peoples traditionally supplied to children.

Indigenous communities traditionally provided for everyone's basic needs (e.g., food, shelter, compassionate support, belonging, autonomy, play, self-actualization).[12] The evolved nest in early life is part of the support that prepares the grounding for compassionate moral development (rather than self-protective morality). Basic need provision along with the wisdom of the elders provided through stories and ceremony foster the ability to live one's life with the full-blown sense of responsibility that Martinez demonstrates.

23

Connection to the Land

Enrique Salmón (Rarámuri-Tarahumara)

he Rarámuri view themselves as an integral part of the life and place within which they live. There is among the Rarámuri a concept called iwígara, which encompasses many ideas and ways of thinking unique to the place with which the Rarámuri live. Rituals and ceremonies, the language, and, therefore, Rarámuri thoughts are influenced by the lands, animals, and winds with which they live. Iwígara is the total interconnectedness and integration of all life in the Sierra Madres, physical and spiritual. To say iwígara *to a Rarámuri calls on that person to realize life in all its forms. The person recalls the beginning of Rarámuri life, origins, and relationships to animals, plants, the place of nurturing, and the entities to which the Rarámuri look for guidance. . . .*

The natural world, therefore, is not one of wonder, but of familiarity. The human niche is only one of a myriad of united niches that work together to continue the process of iwígara. *If one aspect of the lasso is removed, the integrity of the circle is threatened and all other aspects are weakened. A certain attachment results from knowing that some of your relatives are the life-forms that share your place with you. This belief influences one's sense of identity and thought/language. . . .*

Indigenous people believe that they live interdependently with all forms of life. Their spiritual, physical, social, and mental health depends on the ability to live harmoniously with the natural world. Indigenous identity, language, land base, beliefs, and history are personifications of culture that regulate and manifest the health of the human as well as the natural world. It is understood that a person who harms the natural world also harms himself. . . .

The land base is often a central subject in nearly all Indigenous stories of historical origins. They often mention how they emerged in one way or another from the land. The land base, however, is the land to which they claim a relationship. It may be the land on which they now live, or a historical, or even mythical place to which they claim relationship. Nevertheless, the life-forms that occupy the cultural land base are direct relatives to the culture.

To all cultures, beliefs form and explain the human–nature relationship. Beliefs help a person recognize his/her link to the natural world and his/her responsibility to ensure its survival. No person is truly connected to the natural world or to his/her culture if he/she does not maintain physical, social, spiritual, and mental health; together, they form the breath of life. Breath is the matter and energy, which Indigenous people believe moves in all living things. Maintaining a balanced and pure human breath also ensures the purity and health of the breath of the natural world.

With the awareness that one's breath is shared by all surrounding life, that one's emergence into this world was possibly caused by some of the life-forms around one's environment, and that one is responsible for its mutual survival, it becomes apparent that it is related to you; that it shares a kinship with you and with all humans, as does a family or tribe. A reciprocal relationship has been fostered with the realization that humans affect nature and nature affects humans. This awareness influences Indigenous interactions with the environment. It is these interactions, these cultural practices of living with a place, that are manifestations of kincentric ecology.

Source

Enrique Salmón. "Kincentric Ecology: Indigenous Perceptions of the Human–Nature Relationship." *Ecological Applications* 10, no. 5 (2000): 1327–32. Excerpts from pp. 1328, 1329, 1331, 1332. www.researchgate.net/publication/242186767_Kincentric _Ecology_Indigenous_Perceptions_of_the_HumanNature_Relationship.

Contextualized Biosketch

Dr. Enrique Salmón is from the Rarámuri (Tarahumara) tribe of northwestern Mexico. He teaches American Indian studies in the Department of Ethnic Studies at California State University East Bay. As ethnobotanist and educator, his work explores traditional ecological knowledge as part of a complex and sophisticated environmental stewardship of landscapes and biocultural diversity. Enrique has been a scholar-in-residence at the Heard Museum and sat on the board of directors of the Society of Ethnobiology, and he has published several articles and chapters on Indigenous ethnobotany, agriculture, nutrition, and traditional ecological knowledge. His book *Eating the Landscape* describes small-scale Native farmers of the greater Southwest and their role in maintaining biocultural diversity. He suggests that foodways are connected to every element and process of sustainable bioculture, including cultural expressions and landscapes.

Indigenous Worldview Precept Dialogue

Four Arrows: Darcia, I love that you found this eloquent quote because, as you know, the Rarámuri are near and dear to me. It was a young Rarámuri who saved my life after my accident on the Rio Urique in Copper Canyon. Augustine Ramos, the 102-year-old Rarámuri spiritual leader, was my teacher fifteen years later in a remote place with little influence from Western culture.[1] Moreover, I do not know a better way to start talking about this worldview precept than by looking at the traditional Rarámuri beliefs. They represent what I consider an ideal model for addressing what a growing number of geologists are calling the Anthropocene—a new human epoch. Instead of looking at the problem of humanity's harmful influence on climate and life systems as an environmental, social, political, moral, or economic issue for resolution, Enrique Salmón's words reveal what I believe to be our only salvation—a focus on interspecies "kincentrism."

Rarámuri kincentric understanding is complex, but I would describe it as seeing relationality as being fundamental. The people see everything as a kinship network, with trees, mountains, rivers, and animals all possessing souls and living in a constant tension, with no divisions between humans and other-than-humans. They are constantly discussing and evaluating how well they are living on the land and with one another. Similar to the Lakota spiritual path that we call *chaŋkú lúta* (the red road), the Rarámuri refer to the path they walk as *anayáguari boé* (the path of the ancestors). These paths involve mental, physical, spiritual, and emotional states of being, both in terms of individual and collective ways of living in flowing balance.

The Rarámuri also refer to "the other path," the one that is destructive, as the *si'nú boé*. The two paths "contradict each other as they express contrary moral and political positions, while at the same time being inextricably linked."[2] This link is a constant reminder that we must sustain—and therefore create—the world we inhabit or we will contribute to its destruction. Until we deeply understand that we are intricately connected with *everything that surrounds us* we will not learn how to respect and live with our interconnected beingness with the land.

Darcia: This is so powerful. My research has revealed that children learn early on in life which of the two pathways they will continue on as adults. Without some degree of feeling interdependent with and respectful of natural surroundings, such as the Rarámuri children have, alienation and distrust of the land in the dominant culture occurs. The Indigenous philosopher Dr. Viola Cordova, whose father was Jicarilla Apache, described this contrast:

My daughter and a non-Native American school friend both gave birth to their first child in the early fall. On a sunny spring day, the two young women came together to give their infants their first outing. My daughter's friend has the backseat of their car loaded with the paraphernalia she thinks necessary for the outing. My daughter has only her son. At a nearby park my daughter places her son on a grassy area and he begins to crawl and inspect the strange territory. The friend, on the other hand, leaves her son in a car seat while she spreads out a blanket for the child and then proceeds to dump onto the blanket an assortment of familiar toys. Once the child is on the blanket, he is admonished about touching the ground—the grass is "yucky," he will get "dirty"—and the mother distracts the infant from exploring by handing him various toys. Occasionally the mother takes the infant's hands and walks him about on the blanket. My daughter follows her infant as he crawls on the ground, introduces him to trees, flowers, clouds, the wind on his face.

The non-Native American mother introduces her child into a potentially hazardous and alien environment; she offers him "safe" alternatives through the presence of the blanket and the toys. Everything else is "dirty." My grandson, on the other hand, is encouraged to touch, taste, and explore a new and delightful place. The non-Native American infant is taught to confront his environment; our child is shown what the world contains. This is the stuff of which a worldview is built. Without language, without explanation, each of the young women is saying to their infant: this is where you live. Each child is introduced into the "real" world: one carries with him a man-made environment that proclaims safety amid a potentially hostile earth; the other into a strange but interesting place that he is expected to "know" intimately.[3]

If you have been raised in the "nature is dangerous" atmosphere, it takes some effort to move away from the corresponding ignorance and fear. I grew up in a household mostly afraid of nature. We had no pets or intentional nature adventures. When I was a young adult, I luckily had friends who liked camping, and eventually I camped alone to help myself learn to be fearless in however small a way. After a sad but amicable divorce from years of marriage, I took a bus trip across the country to visit friends in different places. One of my mini-adventures was to camp alone overnight in the Rocky Mountains. When I was hiking in the forest, I had to duck from a shadow flying toward me—a snowy white owl. After the startle, I felt calm and at peace, ready for the night. There is nothing like seeing the Milky Way and experiencing the sacredness of the unimpeded outdoors.

Four Arrows: So what can we do to change such child-rearing practices, besides your historical scholarship and evolved nest work and people like us writing about the problem? Children living in cities cannot physically see the Milky Way even if they wanted to see it. A snowy white owl in the wild is also a rare possibility for most young children. You say that you took it upon yourself to overcome such an upbringing when you became a young adult. What intrinsic or extrinsic motivations prompted this and your decision to camp alone in the mountains?

Yesterday I took my four-year-old granddaughter and seven-year-old grandson on my paddleboard out to an island half a mile from my beach house here in Mexico. They reveled in crawling on the rocks and discovering the red, dried skeletons of crabs and watching the hermit crabs crawling around. Although I pointed out the potential danger of a maverick wave pulling them off the rocks into the ocean, I did so in such a way as to give them responsibility for watching for such waves, as opposed to yelling at them to get away from the edge. Of course, I remained vigilant, just in case. However, they learned that nature *could* be dangerous, but that with proper awareness, a partnership with that danger offers bountiful rewards.

They spent an hour sitting next to a tide pool looking at creatures while watching the wave patterns. They learned that the seventh wave was the biggest. When it came, they joyfully climbed safely up the rocks just in case. Doing so required their physical fitness. Both are little athletes, agile and strong. They needed such fitness to negotiate climbing quickly above the tide pool on the rugged rocks. This vitality also served when I helped them don snorkeling masks, and I took them into the ocean to see marine life.

Such engagement with nature may start with wonder, but eventually, it is the relationship that is important. Salmón says the Tarahumara understand the natural world not as a place "of wonder, but of familiarity," and it is this that leads to "the health of the human as well as the natural world." I would guess that your experience with the owl and the Milky Way represents, even today, more wonderment than familiarity. Subsequently, I would think the physical fitness you maintain is less derived from the interaction with nature (as happened with my grandchildren yesterday) than from more commonplace motivations for being fit?

So the question for all of us engaging this material—you, me, and the readers—is what can we do with and for children to create the kinds of experiences that introduce and nurture familiarity with nature early on and continually throughout life? Is it impossible? Can cities be built in ways that have waterways for swimming, land for running, trees and rocks for climbing, weather for adapting, star visibility for wonderment, animals and insects for teachings, and environments demanding enough to require physical vitality and fearless engagement?

Darcia: I agree that wonderment and familiarity are related but different. What a wonderful mentor of the outdoors you are for your grandchildren, building not only wonder and familiarity but also skill. The wild natural world is the true school for all ages, but it requires some guidance from family and community to develop and maintain (although, see David Abram's book *The Spell of the Sensuous*, where he tells the reader he got sick of human beings and found his community in other-than-human nature).

Richard Louv noted "nature deficit disorder" in children from industrialized nations like the USA and has made all sorts of recommendations for outdoor play in multiple books ever since.[4] His recommended practices increase wonderment, familiarity, and some skills (e.g., growing a native plant garden). One of the best approaches I've seen for building all three among children in industrialized nations is the forest kindergarten.[5] In these schools, children spend most of their time outside, exploring and learning about the world around them. In one video of a forest kindergarten in Denmark, children are climbing trees, and one is swaying back and forth high up in a birch tree, maybe three stories high, with the teacher on the ground. The interviewer nervously asked if the school has had injuries in its seventeen years of existence. The director replied calmly that yes, it happened once, when a parent drove over the foot of a child. The calmness of both the swaying child and the school director are remarkable to see from the eyes of a society (the USA) whose parents would be fearful in such a situation.

There are so many ordinances now across locales in the United States where children cannot play in a park without supervision. Famously, some years ago a parent named Lenore Skenazy agreed to let her ten-year-old son find his way home from the middle of New York City after she dropped him off. He did so safely, and was so proud of his accomplishment. She wrote about it in a column and was lambasted for putting her child in danger. Then she wrote a book about the need for children to have freedom to roam, titled *Free-Range Kids,* and hosted a television show to help parents learn how to let their children out to play.[6] In the one episode I watched, she finally convinced the featured mother to let her children have a lemonade stand in the driveway, in a suburb, while the mother watched anxiously from the window. How are children going to learn to feel connected to the land if they cannot even leave their homes? So we have an intergenerational challenge that has developed over the last few decades. For even getting to wonderment, the adults need to feel safe in the landscape and convey a safe feeling to the children so they can get outside to explore and start the path to connection.

The other challenge that has developed acutely over recent decades is the disappearance of undeveloped land for people to explore. It is also stressing ecosystems generally. For example, farms used to have fallow areas, but now everything is plowed up and planted with hybrid seeds that are resistant to the "weed" killer Roundup, which kills everything else.[7] Hence, the milkweed plants that monarch butterflies feed on during their thousands-of-miles migrations between Canada and Mexico have largely disappeared, putting them on the brink of extinction. The whole approach to the "green revolution" is contrary to kincentric ecology.

Kincentric ecology requires experience relating to the land and other-than-humans as partners. It seems that we need a concerted educational effort aimed at both adults and children about how "humans affect nature and nature affects humans," as Salmón says. Most industrialized people seem to have forgotten their interdependency, despite the fact that "their spiritual, physical, social, and mental health depends on the ability to live harmoniously with the natural world." The dominant culture makes us into numb and dumb robopaths[8] instead of full, kincentric human beings coexisting connected and respectfully with a living earth. We can restore our true, connected nature by using the practices discussed in the references in this book.

24

Centrality of Gratitude

Audrey Shenandoah (Onondaga; 1926–2012)

I would first give thanks for another day of life here on this earth. It is another day extended that we may enjoy the compassionate goodness of our Creator. Among my people we could not come together in this way—a conference—without first offering words of acknowledgment, respect, and thanksgiving for our fellow human beings. Now our words we direct to our Mother Earth, who supports all life. We look to the shortest grasses, close to the bosom of our Mother Earth, as we put our minds together as one mind. We include all the plant life, the woodlands, all the waters of Earth, the fishes, the animal life, the bird life, and the four Winds. As one mind, our acknowledgement, respect, and thanksgiving move upward to the Sky World: the Grandmother Moon, who has a direct relationship to the females of the species of all living things; the sun and the stars; and our Spiritual Beings of the Sky World. They will carry on the original Instructions in this great Cycle of Life. With one mind we address our acknowledgment, respect, and gratefulness to all the sacred Cycle of Life. We, as humans, must remember to be humble and acknowledge the gifts we use so freely in our lives.

Source

Audrey Shenandoah. Keynote address delivered at the Global Forum on Environment and Development for Survival, Moscow, Soviet Union, January 1990. Quoted in Steve Wall and Harvey Arden, eds. *Wisdomkeepers: Meeting with Native American Spiritual Elders*, 24. New York: Atria, 1990.

Contextualized Biosketch

Audrey Shenandoah was a member of the Eel Clan of the Onondaga Nation, and she was borrowed by the Deer Clan as a clan mother. Among the Haudenosaunee (i.e., the Iroquois Confederacy, which includes the Onondaga), clan mothers select chiefs. She was known as a peacemaker who oversaw the use of natural resources for her tribe, mediated the return of Iroquois artifacts, and confronted the United Nations about problems plaguing Haudenosaunee communities. An internationally known writer, teacher, and advisor to the United Nations, she was interviewed in the film *Hidden Medicine and Sacred Earth: Makoce Wakan*.

Indigenous Worldview Precept Dialogue

Four Arrows: As Shenandoah so beautifully expresses, Indigenous cultures are continually expressing gratitude for the many gifts of life. Note how in her words gifts come from outside ourselves. Plant life, water, winds, and much more are the givers. It is not just the internal thankfulness for some benefit one experiences. Gratitude expresses deep interconnectedness as a responsibility of authentic caring and reciprocity. In Lakota, we say *wopila tanka* to express our appreciation for the many beautiful blessings all around us. These include that which may cause suffering and challenge us to do better. People sometimes look at me strangely when I say that I interpreted my non-Hodgkin's lymphoma diagnosis as a reminder of the importance of rebalancing my life. Truly seeing it as a gift was why I did not do chemotherapy to attack it. That I have lasted years beyond survival statistics without ever losing vitality may be related, if not causal. Research on gratitude reveals that people who regularly feel and express gratitude authentically have better health, less depression, and fewer visits to physicians.[1]

Under the Indigenous worldview, the idea of continual flowing balance is a paramount requirement for living according to the laws of nature. The well-known Lakota phrase *mitakuye oyasin* expresses gratitude for the kinds of benefits described in our opening quotes. So does the Cherokee word *otsaliheliga,* which more directly translates as "we are grateful." Both recognize that being grateful and seeing the beauty all around is vital. You know how I often end my presentations by playing the Cherokee lullaby that Carlos Nakai told me the mothers sang to their children on the Trail of Tears.[2] Despite the horror of what was happening all around them, the lullaby reminded the children of the shapes of the clouds, the colors of the fish and flowers, the dancing of the prairie grasses, the music of the birds. As mentioned previously, one of the most famous of the gratitude prayers for the natural world is the Haudenosaunee Thanksgiving Address. I love it when different members of the community all choose something in the natural world to identify, express gratitude and the reason for it, and then all members say, "Now our minds are one."[3]

Darcia: I love this too. Ceremonies transcend the boundaries of the individual and resonate beyond the human realm. They magnify life. Starting every gathering with a ceremony acknowledging relationship and expressing gratitude toward the other-than-human sets the mind in the right space—for humility instead of arrogance, communal imagination instead of self-oriented imagination, emotional presence instead of mindlessness. Ceremony focuses attention where it becomes intention. When you stand together and profess a thing before your community, it holds you accountable. These acts of reverence are powerfully pragmatic. Robin Wall Kimmerer describes the giveaway ceremony:

> The berries are always present at our ceremonies. They join us in a wooden bowl. One beige bowl and one big spoon, which are passed around the circle, so that each person can taste the sweetness, remember the gifts, and say thank you. They carry the lesson, passed to us by our ancestors, that the generosity of the land comes to us as one bowl, one spoon, we are all fed from the same bowl that Mother Earth has filled for us. It's not just about the berries, but also about

the bowl. The gifts of the earth are to be shared, but gifts are not limitless. The generosity of the earth is not an invitation to take it all. Every bowl has a bottom. When it's empty, it's empty. And there is but one spoon, the same size for everyone.[4]

Regular ceremonies like this can keep one in an orientation of gratitude most of the time. It can become a habit. Everywhere you go there is a relation right there, whether the sun, the ant, the wind, the soil. You learn to recognize, respect, and cherish every diverse life and give thanks for its presence.

I love the following list, Cooper's[5] summary of Bopp, Lane, Brown, and Bopp's[6] assembly of Indigenous ethics. Gratitude is central to several of the ethical principles and sets the tone for the rest.

1. Daily sanctification (expression of gratitude)

2. Respect for all life through honoring and esteeming others, including nonhumans

3. Respect the tribal council

4. Truthfulness at all times

5. Extraordinary hospitality to guests

6. Empathize with others and understand the spirit of the whole

7. Receive strangers with a loving heart

8. Understand that all races are family members, beautiful creations of the Creator

9. Serving others is the meaning of life

10. Moderation and balance in all affairs

11. Understand what leads to destruction or to well-being

12. Follow the guidance given to the heart by dreams, prayer, solitude, and wise others

Four Arrows, do you see gratitude woven throughout this list of ethical guidance? How have you experienced gratitude in Lakota ceremonies?

Four Arrows: What a useful exercise your question offers for people wanting to understand the role of gratitude in Indigenous cultures. To see gratitude in each of the twelve ethical guidelines listed above is to understand the importance of appreciating the flowing balance of the medicine wheel. In the wheel, each stage of life, direction, or season must be understood with gratitude. The authors of the book from which this list comes refer to the "sacred tree" as being symbolic of the medicine wheel's cycle of protection, nurturing, growth, and wholeness. One can see how all twelve relate to one of these four aspects of life. Thus, if we are grateful for each of these four concepts, we should be grateful for how each goal on the list contributes to them. Shenandoah's reference to "gratefulness to all the sacred Cycle of Life" refers directly to this conclusion.

As far as your question about gratitude in ceremony, "the act of gratitude is at the heart of our key ceremony that connects us to our Earth as it dissipates this violent culture."[7] The authors of this quote are referring to our dominant culture, of course. In their piece, "Gratitude as Ceremony: A Practical Guide to Decolonization," they refer to the large international gathering at Standing Rock in North Dakota to protest the oil pipeline as a revelation of the power of continual gratitude in the face of such violence against Mother Earth and its life forms. They explain how ceremony "interrupts the cult of the disconnected individual" and talk about how capitalism violates natural law with its greedy, extractive practices that totally forget to express gratitude for the natural systems of energy Mother Earth provides to keep life in flowing balance. They refer to offerings of gratitude for maintaining this connection. During my own four "tours of duty" at Standing Rock, as a medic and as a trainer of people to go on the front lines, I noted how prayers of gratitude were continual during the protest, even in the worst of situations.

Our mutual friend David Abram refers to this awareness of our connection to the land in his book *The Spell of the Sensuous.* He writes,

"We are human only in contact, and conviviality, with what is not human."[8] This gets us back to the essence of Indigenous worldview as being about our intimate relationship with Nature in its totality. Such intimacy is guided by gratitude for everything in it that keeps us flourishing. I remember how after I helped guide David through his first Sun Dance experience, he and I went to my summer home on the west coast of Vancouver Island. We spent hours paddling around an island with the agreement that we would not speak words. When we saw beautiful sights, and there were many, we gestured or grunted our appreciation. We felt like children who were truly part of the spirituality that calls for gratitude that we experienced in the Sun Dance ceremony.

I close with a reference to gratitude from my book that was published recently called *Sitting Bull's Words: For a World in Crisis*.[9] I think it well expresses this connection between intimacy with nature and constant gratitude. I talk about how Sitting Bull would sing quietly to an animal before taking its life, expressing gratitude for its potential nourishment. I then refer to a time when his band came upon the skeletons of bison and he stopped, despite the need to escape from their enemies. He then told his people that they must honor these bones, reminding everyone that they were from those who gave their flesh to keep them alive the previous winter. "Showing gratitude to the non-human creatures for their gift of life, while acknowledging that humans can sometimes also be part of the food chain when in the wilderness, he recognized the interrelatedness of other-than-human energies and humanity. He and the other Lakota saw sentience in other creatures, including the animals and plants they used or consumed for survival. This sentience demanded respect."[10]

Darcia: These are very moving stories. I think that although the dominant worldview allows for gratitude, I'm not sure it often reflects the kind of gratitude we are discussing. It's more like "thanks for giving me the toy I asked for," or the Jewish male prayer—"thanks for not making me a woman." In positive psychology education, keeping a gratitude diary or writing a gratitude letter is very popular for its ability to make the doer feel happier.[11]

I think Indigenous gratitude always assumes a reciprocal relationship. It's about not only appreciating gifts you've received, but giving back with mindful respect. A friend who took up Indigeneity as an adult visited us for a few days, and at each meal he took some of his food and set it aside as a gift to his guiding spirits. Much like Indigenous ceremony involved in taking a life, animal or plant, he was offering something in return for the lives taken for his meal. Psychologically, this reciprocal type of gratitude does much more than make you feel happy. It keeps you aware of the price of life, of the responsibility to "all our relations," and keeps greed at bay. Because humans have more ability to make choices, we have more responsibility to make good choices and pay attention to what we are doing, keeping the welfare of all our kin in mind.

I remind myself to apply a gratitude principle in daily life, not only through gratitude over a meal or for gifts from family and work colleagues, but in minute ways for kin relations—the Indigenous way. For example, when I step on asphalt, I remember I walk on our fossil ancestors; on the sidewalk, I step on rock and sand kin. When I breathe, I benefit from the exhalations of plant kin. All around me are descendants of our common ancestors—trees, grasses, deer, flies—all are part of a web of a living earth that makes human life possible, a community of sisters, brothers, and elders. To give back, I sing to them, with gratitude and love, encouraging them to continue their being, their flourishing. My desire for finalizing my body's grateful return to the earth, rather than being buried isolated in a box of some sort, is to be buried in a mushroom suit, immediately feeding and rejoining the cosmos again.

ALL MEN WERE MADE BY THE SAME GREAT
SPIRIT CHIEF. THEY ARE ALL BROTHERS. THE
EARTH IS THE MOTHER OF ALL PEOPLE AND ALL
PEOPLE SHOULD HAVE EQUAL RIGHTS UPON IT
YOU MIGHT AS WELL EXPECT THE RIVERS TO
RUN BACKWARD AS THAT ANY MAN WHO
WAS BORN A FREE MAN SHOULD BE
CONTENTED WHEN PENNED UP AND DENIED
LIBERTY TO GO WHERE HE PLEASES.
HEAR ME MY CHIEFS! MY HEART IS
SICK AND TIRED. FROM WHERE THE SUN
NOW STANDS I WILL FIGHT NO MORE
FOREVER.

HINMAHTOO-YAHLATKEKHT
1840 1904
NEZ PERCE

Chief Joseph
marble stonecut

Harriet Greene
Taos, N.M.

25

Noninterference

Clare Brant (Mohawk, Wolf Clan; 1941–1995)

*T*he ethic of noninterference is a behavioural norm of North American Native tribes that promotes positive inter-personal relations by
discouraging coercion of any kind, be it physical, verbal, or psychological. Manifestations of it have been observed and described by Rosalie
Wax and Robert Thomas, among others. A high degree of respect for every
human being's independence leads the Native to view instructing, coercing or attempting to persuade another person as undesirable behaviour.
Accordingly, group goals are arrived at by consensus and achieved by reliance on voluntary cooperation. . . .

The white man who can out-advise another is "one up" and the individual over whom he has exerted influence is expected to take it all with
good grace. In Native society by contrast, such an attempt to exert pressure by advising, instructing, coercing or persuading is always considered
bad form or bad behaviour. The advisor is perceived to be "an interferer."
His attempt to show that he knows more about a particular subject than
the advisee would be seen as an attempt to establish dominance, however
trivial, and he would be fastidiously avoided in future. The ethic of noninterference, then, is an important social principle. . . .

The ethic of noninterference is one of the most widely accepted principles of behaviour among Native people. It even extends to adult relationships with children and manifests itself as permissiveness. A Native
child may be allowed at the age of six, for example, to make the decision
on whether or not he goes to school even though he is required to do so

by law. The child may be allowed to decide whether or not he will do his homework, have his assignments done on time, and even visit the dentist. Native parents will be reluctant to force the child into doing anything he does not choose to do.

Source

Clare Brant. "Native Ethics and Rules of Behaviour." *Canadian Journal of Psychiatry* 35, no. 6 (1990): 535–39.

Contextualized Biosketch

Clare Clifton Brant was a member of the Wolf Clan, Mohawks of the Bay of Quinte, Ontario. He first became a physician, and then a psychiatrist. He tried to create a bridge between the medical community and Native health. He educated non-Natives about First Nation cultures and the best ways to heal Native peoples—treating the causes (e.g., of addictions) rather than only the symptoms. He was chair of the Canadian Native Mental Health section of the Canadian Psychiatric Association, and he was the founding chair of the Native Mental Health Association of Canada. He advised the government on Aboriginal health policy at both the provincial and federal levels, and he directed psychiatric services for Health Canada's Medical Services Branch.

Indigenous Worldview Precept Dialogue

Four Arrows: Most mainstream teachers and parents have trouble with this precept, especially when it comes to children. Overprotection is generally the norm, whereas traditional Indigenous parents give their children much more free range. I remember once seeing some German tourists visiting a Lakota family on Pine Ridge. While talking to a spiritual leader, they watched his seven-year-old son crawl into a corral with a horse, trying to maneuver it to the fence so he could mount it. The horse was spirited, and to the Germans it seemed a dangerous, irresponsible act on the part of the father to let the process continue. I knew the father was watching out of the corner of his eye and that the child had observed him with the horse often enough for him to allow the daring effort.

Perhaps overprotection in dominant cultures can be understood as a loss of trusting people in a community to safeguard and teach children. In contrast, the more comprehensive range of support helps develop a sense of belonging and confidence while at the same time encouraging a sense of independence. Of course, ideas about responsibility and care for others are always modeled as well in traditional Indigenous communities. Unfortunately, we no longer live in such communities. Not only are cities and strangers less "safe" for children; in addition, most organizations are guided by restrictive rules and regulations that prohibit such independence.

As for adults, it seems as if "advising, instructing, coercing or persuading," which Brant says are considered inappropriate practices under the Indigenous worldview, are the norm rather than the exception in the dominant culture. I must admit that I have been guilty of these practices for most of my life, despite knowing that when my enthusiasm for and commitment to helping someone enhance their life is more significant than their own, I lose them. This problem seems to emerge whether or not someone solicits my help. For example, if I think that learning to play a musical instrument would significantly enhance someone's life, I am inclined to try to advise, instruct, coerce, or persuade them accordingly. Now, the dilemma is that over the years, my efforts have been successful here and there. It is a dilemma because I know if they don't play, they will lose out on a life-enhancing experience. However, if I manage to get them playing, they risk losing a degree of autonomy and reliance on self-motivation in other ways.

So the question is, my dear friend, without your evolved nest, are we creating vicious circles with all our efforts to motivate and instruct people to keep moving toward their highest positive potentiality? Without role modeling sufficing as the primary motivator, do we stifle intrinsic motivation? Are all of us "change agents" actually helping to maintain the dominant worldview's authoritarianism, loss of self-initiative, and increasing fear-based behaviors? In the Indigenous worldview, you cannot coerce people to accept or share knowledge. Even if you want knowledge from someone who has it, people won't give it to you unless they think you are ready for it. How do we get back to this?

Darcia: I think the answer to all your questions is affirmative. It's really hard for those of us who grew up coerced to step back from treating others that way—for their own good! There is a basic distrust of children to find their way without coercion. Dennis McPherson and Douglas Rabb provide some insight when they contrast the Indigenous approach to raising children with the Western (dominant) orientation,[1] as spelled out by the philosopher Immanuel Kant. According to the dominant view, to be moral means to choose to act on self-chosen principles—to act "rationally" as only humans can do—rather than acting on what you would like (desire). Children can only learn to be morally responsible adults *after they have been coerced* into obeying adults. Kant was expressing the common belief in eighteenth-century Europe (still prevalent today in the dominant culture). In other words, a child has to learn *not* to develop or follow their intuitions about what is right, obeying adult authorities instead. This is supposed to prepare the child to follow laws or principles later, allowing the child to develop freedom from personal desires and find freedom in the common good. *From an Indigenous perspective, this approach is all backward.* Breaking trust in one's own spirit, one's own intuitions, undermines development of the unique spirit the child holds.

In Indigenous communities around the world, children are not expected to subordinate their wills to those of others, but to align them over time, learning from a young age to coordinate preverbal, tactile impulses to enhance relational connection and rapport. Children are not expected to endure a period of heteronomy (subjection to adult authority) in order to gain autonomy and learn respect for others. Indigenous societies typically honor children, displaying as a primary principle noninterference in the self-growth of the child. The child is assumed to be guided by an inner spirit; coercion can interfere with this health-oriented guidance. Children are presumed autonomous agents from the time they are mobile. They can make their own decisions, are presumed independent, and not subject to rigid times for eating or sleeping. McPherson and Rabb note that instead of having laws and rules that others tell you to follow, Native elders speak indirectly, using stories.[2] This is what McPherson and Rabb call "interventive-noninterference,"[3] which they claim is the opposite of a Kantian approach. Noninterference is a sign of respect for personhood and a method that fosters self-reliance and independent thinking. Bossing someone, ordering them, criticizing someone—all are rude and inappropriate.

But we have to remember that besides noninterference over the course of childhood, adolescence, and adulthood, individuals are immersed in a community filled with respectful role models, stories, and ceremony, as well as one or more vision quests. McPherson and Rabb note that the vision quest is essential for reinforcing traditional values, including discovering how one is not apart from others or the earth, but a part of everything that is: "With this comes the knowledge that willing the good of others is not in any sense a form of self-sacrifice given the enlarged sense of self acquired in the journey into non-ordinary reality."[4]

What do you think of their analysis, Four Arrows? I bet you had some experiences of noninterference as you took up the red road in adulthood. How did that go?

Four Arrows: I would agree that noninterference is a form of respect for another's personhood. It is also true that a vision quest can lead toward a fearless sense of oneness with all. However, I believe both outcomes are contingent on some degree of preparation. Without it, an insight from a vision quest can disappear in the shadows of previous habits and beliefs. Without some practice in cultivating courage or a sense of oneness, a person left on their own may never come close to reaching their positive potential. Granted, the old saying that a teacher emerges when the student is ready still may apply. Noninter-vention in a culture without traditional Indigenous community values and role models could be unfortunate. I submit that even in precontact or minimal-contact cultures, noninterference is not a rigid concept. Keep in mind that Brant says, "Native parents will be reluctant to force a child to do what he does not want to do." In other words, noninter-ference is not as absolute as the literature, and even our quote, may imply.

Keep in mind that most of our Indigenous worldview precepts come from alignment with the goal of survival in the natural world. Egalitarian cultures emerged to maximize surviving and thriving in small groups. Although attempting to persuade, advise, or coerce can create tensions that can get in the way of the kind of cooperation needed for survival, there are always situations where respectful efforts to persuade, advise, or coerce are also needed for survival, especially when inexperience with a dangerous situation is involved.

I have been trying to reflect on my time with the Rarámuri people to see if I could remember exceptions to the noninterference mindset. I recall Augustine Ramos, a highly respected, 102-year-old medicine man, used humor, third parties, stories, and even some severe teasing to "persuade" people. Once, he stridently attempted to persuade some people to take action against *narcotraficantes* who had murdered some Indians nearby. My point is that as important as the precept of non-interference is on many levels, it is complex and dependent on many variables.

One of the best articles about noninterference as an Indigenous worldview precept that I have ever read reveals the complexities, exceptions, and deeper understandings about this topic. It concludes: "In contrast to the dominant discourse of non-interference as a rigid, overriding Indigenous value, a review of the literature reveals a cul-tural concept that is complex, fluid and influenced by context."[5]

Such a conclusion supports my earlier statements about my efforts to "encourage" others to do such things as a vision quest to overcome life problems. Caring, respect, generosity, empathy, and compassion must come first when we decide to offer advice or attempt to persuade anyone, as should respect for the person's autonomy. Wisdom about safety also plays a role in certain situations. The trick is in balancing all of these things in ways that maintain respectful egalitarian relationships.

Darcia: I agree with your discussion of nuance, though maybe it lets me off the hook telling my husband how to eat in a healthy manner (he was a bachelor for forty-five years). I used to sneak vegetables into his favorite foods without his knowledge but decided that was controlling, so I used "marketing" techniques—e.g., talking up broccoli ("yum, yum!"). After twenty-one years, he is a happy vegetable eater.

I am reminded of an experience that Jean Liedloff related in her book *The Continuum Concept*. She was living among the Yequana people of the Amazon. Tududu, the father of Canasinyuthen, a baby who had just started to walk, thought he would help his young one stay safe by building an enclosure, much like a playpen, that took a great deal of effort. When Tududu put the toddler into it, "Canasinyuthen stood uncomprehending for a few seconds at the center, then made a move to one side, turned about, and realized that he was trapped. In an instant he was screaming a message of utter horror, a sound rarely heard from children of his society. It was unequivocal. The playpen was wrong, unsuitable for human babies."[6]

Tududu immediately realized he had done wrong and quickly pulled Canasinyuthen out and let him toddle to find his mother. After admiring it briefly, Tududu dismantled the playpen, realizing that it was interfering with the child's independence. We can say that he showed responsive care, honoring the child's spirit and humbly changing course. Liedloff noted that if Westerners had not gotten caught up so much in their intellects and instead had maintained their own sense of the continuum of life, they too would have smashed the proverbial enclosures of their children.

Just to be clear, noninterference does not mean leaving a baby alone. Babies (under the age of three) are different from children. Babies need their needs to be met immediately (e.g., breast milk, nearly constant moving touch, companionship), just as in the womb, because they are so immature in the first years of life that every experience affects a rapidly growing brain (thousands of brain connections are growing every second). Noninterference for babies means keeping them calm during this rapid formation, provisioning support quickly so their growth is not impeded. For example, forcing babies into physical isolation (not being touched), which they protest, interferes with growth (e.g., it slows DNA synthesis and can enhance self-protective systems).[7] Unfortunately, in the USA there is a lot of bad parenting advice that counters the evolved nest,[8] resulting from a misunderstanding of child development and a detachment from nurturing generally. In fact, Liedloff admitted that she could not tell the Yequana mothers that American mothers listened to experts or read books to learn how to nurture their children—they had not developed, or lost confidence in, their maternal instincts and awareness of their child's internal compass.

Instead of following advice given to Western parents by experts, Jane Goodall followed the parenting instincts of the chimpanzees she was studying. For example, she did not let her son cry himself to sleep in a crib (which today is still advised by some "experts"!) but kept him with her wherever she went. Though her American friends predicted bad outcomes, she reported that at age four her son was independent, "obedient, extremely alert and lively, mixes well with other children and adults alike, is relatively fearless and is thoughtful of others."[9] Indigenous mothers of the world, upon hearing this, would think "of course." Traditional Indigenous communities have known, without scientific experiments, that early nested care is vital.[10] Otherwise, children can start life imbalanced—in body, psyche, spirit—causing illness and impaired cooperation, interfering with the development of their gifts to the community. Tududu followed the instincts and internal compass of his baby, Canasinyuthen, whose needs at that age were more important than his own.

In Indigenous communities, noninterference for older children and adults also assumes a foundational provision of basic needs by the community (e.g., food, shelter, welcoming climate and acceptance, participation in decision making).[11] A communal grounding like this gives individuals the freedom to grow in body, mind, and spirit in ways that make for a thriving community. With nestedness throughout life, they develop and maintain the self-control and flexible responsive cooperation that are fundamental for a democratic society.

26

Circular Time and Knowledge

Tyson Yunkaporta (Apalech Clan in far north Queensland)

*E*xplaining Aboriginal notions of time is an exercise in futility as you can only describe it as "nonlinear" in English, which immediately slams a big line right across your synapses. You don't register the "non"—only the "linear": that is the way you process that word. . . . We don't have a word for nonlinear in our languages because nobody would consider traveling, thinking, or talking in a straight line in the first place. The winding path is just how a path is, and therefore it needs no name. . . . Kinship moves in cycles, the sky moves in stellar cycles, and time is so bound up in those things that it is not even a separate concept from space. We experience time in a very different way from people immersed in flat schedules and story-less surfaces. In our spheres of existence, time does not go in a straight line, and it is as tangible as the ground we stand on. . . . A focus on linear, abstract, declarative knowledge alone not only fails to create complex connectivity but damages the mind. We are biologically punished for this destructive behavior with a neurochemical rush of lethargy and discomfort that most people call boredom. Extended periods of this affect a person's mental health, resulting in bouts of rage, depression and worse. . . . Without the spark of creation in your neural system, the mind-body system stagnates and falls apart, affecting not only your ability to learn but your health and relationships as well, leading to increasingly destructive behaviors.

It all comes back to notions of time, and the existential acrobatics required for Second Peoples* to make time run in a straight line, to create *a beginning, middle and end of things. First Peoples' law says that nothing is created or destroyed because of the infinite and regenerative connections between systems. Therefore time is nonlinear and regenerates creation in endless cycles. Second People's law says that systems must be isolated and exist in a vacuum of individual creation, beginning in complexity but simplifying and breaking down until they meet their end. Therefore time is linear, because all things must have a beginning, middle and end.*

*Second Peoples refers to persons within the European-derived dominant culture.

Sources

Tyson Yunkaporta. "A Rainbow Serpent Theory of Time." *Garland Magazine,* May 29, 2019. https://garlandmag.com/article/a-rainbow-serpent-theory-of-time/.
Tyson Yunkaporta. *Sand Talk: How Indigenous Thinking Can Save the World,* 18, 41, 100. New York: HarperCollins, 2020.

Contextualized Biosketch

Tyson Yunkaporta is a senior lecturer on Indigenous knowledges, a wood carver, and a poet at Deakin University's Geelong Waurn Ponds Campus. He is from the Apalech clan of Australia's west cape. He has worked with Aboriginal languages, and his research includes a focus on oral histories of natural disasters. He prefers to minimize his own narrative. Rather than "building a brand," he says in an interview that he is "trying to build a collective base of knowledge and relationships and conversations that might help try to stop the world from dying in the next few decades." His book *Sand Talk* won the Small Publishers' Adult Book of the Year Award.

Indigenous Worldview Precept Dialogue

Four Arrows: The circle is emphasized in Indigenous cultures, metaphorically and actually. The Lakota speak of the sacred hoop and the importance of keeping it unbroken. In the center of the circle is a metaphorical tree of life. This is represented by the Sun Dance (Wiwanke Wachipi) tree in the center of the circular arbor. Nature is full of representations of the circle's power, from the nest of a bird to how the round planets and stars travel. When Yunkaporta tells us that, when we conceive the world differently from this, it can lead to "bouts of rage, depression and worse," it is best we pay attention and recognize how our forgetting is why our world is so out of balance.

Kim Hudson directs the 2 Ways of Knowing project, which focuses on how to move from linear to circular thinking. She confirms what Yunkaporta says about how difficult or impossible it is for linear thinkers to understand circular thinking. In her workshops she asks participants which of the following two columns feels like the best way to proceed when facing a challenge:[1]

COLUMN 1	COLUMN 2
Define the goal	Gather and welcome everyone affected
Develop a strategy	Ask each person to express their feelings
Make a plan	Interactively share information
Set timelines, costs, tasks	Recognize a pattern, follow an idea
Activate the plan	Give language to what is meaningful
Measure progress	Respond to the information and redesign

The first column describes linear thinking. Hudson writes that "fear-activated emotions lead to a linear style of thinking. Here logic, focus, objectivity, and discipline push back against the danger fear has identified for us. Circular thinking focuses on pulling in more of what you want. It is rooted in a drive to be inclusive and transparent—a belief that the answer will come when everyone is included and a diverse array of thoughts are considered."[2]

I was not surprised to learn that Hudson, who is headquartered in the Yukon, has worked closely with Indigenous peoples for twenty-five years as a geological consultant and treaty negotiator for First Nations. If only more consultants could respect and learn from the dwindling Indigenous wisdom to address our world problems instead of ignoring, dismissing, or attacking it. I pray that future generations will rebuild life systems on Earth, avoiding the faulty narratives that evolved since our point of departure from our nature-based ways of being. Now, during the COVID-19 pandemic, linear thinking is not allowing for original ideas and solutions to be explored sufficiently. We could use circular time, thinking, and wisdom to respect and honor multiple perspectives, discuss their merits, and with authentic circularity, find ourselves working together toward solutions instead of putting up walls or worse.

Darcia: Oh, I like your idea. What comes to mind is the work of Sir Frederic C. Bartlett,[3] an early psychologist who studied how conceptual structures affect what people perceive and remember (something I studied for years). He collected stories from Indigenous peoples, famously using a story called "War of the Ghosts" in experiments with British participants.[4] They were very bad at retelling the stories and over time increasingly made them linear, conforming their memories to familiar linear story frames.

Barbara Alice Mann also contrasts linearity with the circular understandings of Native peoples. She describes Turtle Islanders (original Natives of North America) having clusters of knowledge that integrate twinship and fractals:

> As I see it, the root of the difficulty is that, whereas Westerners are linear thinkers, Turtle Islanders are cluster thinkers, who grasp reality in terms of natural, self-selecting bunches, handfuls of this or that, in halves aligned with the ultimate clusters of the Cosmic Twinship. Each half of the cosmos, be it Blood or Breath, endlessly replicates its essence by spinning out fractals, large and small, with those of each cluster in necessary coordination with their twin fractals in the other half, in the infinite process of balancing. This only looks confusing to those weaned on linearity, as the singularized "point" races

inexorably to lonely-only conclusion, hence the Western enthusiasm for a "Grand Unified Theory." For Indians, to whom linearity looks inadequate to describe reality, endlessly repeating pairs of fractals, sparkling out through the cosmos, look just about right.[5]

How beautiful the world looks from an Indigenous worldview! Cycles, fractals, circularity everywhere.

Marimba Ani (Dona Richards), in her book *Yurugu: An African-Centered Critique of European Cultural Thought and Behavior,* goes into great detail about how Europeans conquered not only the land of preexisting cultures in the rest of the world, but also their minds, planting the metaphor of linear progress. Interestingly, fitting with our chapter on complementarity, in *Yurugu* Ani refers to a Dogon tale of Mali where Amma, the Creator, mandated that all beings should manifest complementarity or twinness. But one of the male souls, Yurugu, did not wait for his full gestation. He wanted to compete with Amma and used his broken placenta to create the earth, resulting in imperfection, like himself. He requested his female soulmate from Amma, but she had been given away. Thus, Yurugu was doomed to search for but never reach completeness, much like the "single-souled, impure, incomplete beings" on the earth he had created.[6]

Perhaps Marimba Ani's book can help people understand the destructive dominating mindset and move to restore the holistic knowledge of the Indigenous worldview. Perhaps this process of cyclical return is underway as we face the current pandemic. Greg Cajete reminds us that traditional Indigenous cultures have always understood such cycles:

Native people have been good observers. They understood that things were always in process, that things were always being created and then destroyed and then created once again in new forms. These basic ideas of science, of evolution, of ways of understanding ecological processes are deeply embedded in symbols like Kokopelli that represent the creative process in nature, human beings, and even the

evolution of thought. . . . According to some philosophers, Indigenous and otherwise . . . knowledge is never really lost; it comes into
being when it is needed, and leaves when it is no longer needed or
properly used.[7]

As we open ourselves to Spirit, we receive needed insights: "Each
person is important and therefore each person's vision is important and
blends itself into either the construction or destruction of the world."[8]
To transform our minds, to shift out of the analytical, judgmental, linear
mode of being, Cajete tells us we must learn the creative process, learn
to trust intuition, and build confidence in our own creativity. When we
use symbols and images through art, music, poetry, we open up our
minds. We creatively participate with beautiful nonlinear nature.

Four Arrows: Indeed, it is no coincidence that our opening quote
on nonlinearity is from a person who is an established poet and artist.
In his book *Sand Talk,* Yunkaporta also refers to the current destruction as relating to a loss of creative complexity. He writes that our
current narcissistic ways of being in the world "break down creation
systems like a virus, infecting complex patterns with artificial simplicity, exercising a civilizing control over what some see as chaos.
The Sumerians started it. The Romans perfected it. The Anglosphere
inherited it. The world is now mired in it."[9] I think this reflects our
dominant worldview's fear-based separation from the drama of nature
and its destructive-re-creative cycles of life and death. Linearity came
into our thinking and caused us to forget how in nature nothing is ultimately destroyed, but rather it is regenerated. Sometimes the regen-
eration requires annihilation of systems that no longer work. If we
keep on our current trajectory and do not return to our Indigenous
worldview precepts, the human race may be such a system. Indeed,
our guest author also writes: "If you don't move with the land, the
land will move you. There is nothing permanent about settlements and
the civilizations that spawn them. Maybe the reason all the powerful
instruments pointed at the sky have not yet been able to detect high-
tech alien civilizations is that these unsustainable societies don't last

long enough to leave a cosmic trace. . . . Perhaps we need to revisit the brilliant thought-paths of our Paleolithic Ancestors and recover enough cognitive function to correct the impossible messes civilization has created."[10]

Darcia, if fear of nature's destructive cycles and fear of death are indeed major barriers in the dominant worldview to circular thinking and creativity, then it would seem your work with the evolved nest might offer ways for us to teach about life-death cycles early on. I have my seven-year-old grandson with me, and we talk about death and dying as a natural cycle often. Is there any research on how to go about embracing circularity early on by addressing death as an ally to the creative process?

Darcia: Ah, you are asking an Indigenous worldview question of Western science. The focus of most research is on children's *conceptions* of death—what it means biologically. There is little focus on the big picture, the life-death cycle. There are anecdotes, however. In *The Spiritual Child*, researcher Lisa Miller describes children who describe conversing with deceased friends or family members—in the context of families who welcome "spirit-deep relationships."[11] She provides several reports, such as this one:

> Mariah was three when she mentioned to her mother, Ellie, that when she played in the playpen she wasn't alone—that a woman often came and kept her company. Ellie was always near the playpen working, so she knew Mariah was alone—no one was sneaking into the house—and she assumed this was her daughter's version of the classic "imaginary friend" of very young children. Then one day as they sorted through some attic boxes of photos, Mariah went to a picture she had never seen before and said, "That's the woman, Mommy—that's the woman who comes to play with me." It was Mariah's great grandmother.[12]

Ellie was not afraid or worried but told her daughter how wonderful it was that she had that relationship with Great-Grandma, who loved her so. Miller discusses the importance of helping children grow a spiritual compass, a heart knowing that can guide decision-making in the future, link them to kindred spirits, help them develop spiritual multilingualism, empower them to create a culture of love, and gain knowledge through dreams and mystical experiences.

Miller illustrates how children desire to know that all relatives, alive or not, can play a role in healing family relations through their insatiable interest in estranged relations: "The natural sense of family bond with relatives who are no longer alive is culturally supported in most countries around the globe, often as some form of ancestor honoring, prayer, offering, or appreciation." The animated film *Coco* shows the ongoing interrelations of multiple generations through the Mexican Day of the Dead celebrations. This kind of "sanctification of family" (holding one's family sacred) is correlated with greater loyalty and effort at maintaining good relationships, forgiveness and appreciation of family members, and perceiving relational work as an opportunity for spiritual growth.[13]

I know of no Western researchers or filmmakers who examine the view that a life is regenerated—e.g., that this baby may be a reincarnation of Great-Grandfather or that these rocks, trees, or mountains are relatives.[14] In the Indigenous worldview, this broader circularity sanctifies the whole world. In every moment, there are relations all around. One is never alone but is rather cycling through the flow of life. There is no need for church or priests if everything about life is considered sacred—whether fishing for a salmon relative, growing a corn relative, hunting an animal relative; all happens under the guidance of ancestors and other holy spirits. It makes me think of B. Traven, a pseudonymous fiction writer who lived in Mexico at the turn of the twentieth century and who wrote about the colliding worldviews between Western missionaries and the Native peoples. In Traven's story "Conversion of Some Indians," a monk is trying to convert a chief and his followers to Christianity, explaining the death of Jesus and telling them about their future in hell if they do not convert. After lengthy conversations back and forth that reflect different worldviews, this scene takes place:

> The chieftain remained very calm and serene. With a quiet, soft voice he said: "Here, my holy white father, is what our god had put into our hearts and souls, and it will be the last word I have to say to you before we return to our beautiful and tranquil *tierra:* Our god dies every evening for us who are his children. He dies every evening to bring us cool winds and freshness of nature, to bring us peace and quiet for the night so that we may rest well, man and animal. Our god dies every evening in a deep golden glory, not insulted, not spat upon, not spattered with stinking mud. He dies beautifully and gloriously, as every real god will die. Yet he does not die forever. In the morning he returns to life, refreshed and more beautiful than ever, his body still trailing the veils and wrappings of the dead. But soon his golden spears dart across the blue firmament as a sign that he is ready to fight the gods of darkness who threaten the peoples on earth. And before you have time to realize what happens, there he stands before wondering human eyes, and there he stays, great, mighty, powerful, golden, and in ever-growing beauty, dominating the universe.
>
> "He, our god, is a spendthrift in light, warmth, beauty, and fertility, enriching the flowers with perfumes and colors, teaching the birds to sing, filling the corn with strength and health, playing with the clouds in an ocean of gold and blue. As my beloved mother does, so does he give and give and never ceases giving; never does he ask for prayers, not expecting adoration or worship, not commanding obedience or faith, and never, ever condemning anybody or thing on earth. And when evening comes, again he passes away in beauty and glory, a smile all over his face, and with his last glimmer blesses his Indian children. Again the next morning he is the eternal giver; he is the eternally young, the eternally beautiful, the eternally new-born, the ever and ever returning great and golden god of the Indians.

"And this is what our god has put into our hearts and souls and what I am bound to tell you, holy white father: 'Do not, not ever, beloved Indian sons of these your beautiful lands, give away your own great god for any other god.'"[15]

This is the sacred circularity of a living world.

27

Self-Initiated Relational Healing

Gloria Lee (Cree—Pelican Lake)

*D*isease or bodily ailment is traditionally viewed as the physical manifestation of a weakness—a symptom of something deeper that comes
from the spiritual, emotional or psychological aspects of a person. When
a person is afflicted with a disease, the traditional view is that the disease
exists to offer the individual a teaching. The teaching will ultimately be
about oneself, but the person may choose to deal only with the physical
manifestation of the weakness—the symptom—and not address its root. If
the person chooses to treat only the symptom and ignores the teaching that
is being offered, then the disease will return. Physical manifestations may
continue to appear until the individual accepts the teaching.

The weakness is caused by our being out of balance or out of center,
and there can be many reasons for being out of balance. These reasons
may involve, for example, working too much in one area, overworking
on the job, being too greedy, or wanting too much—in other words, not
attending to the many parts of ourselves, our lives, and our families in a
balanced way. If we do not pay attention to all these aspects, then we will
become unbalanced. That is when an illness may appear to remind us that
we are overlooking some area. . . .

Because traditional healing is within each of us, we are all capable of
healing ourselves, sometimes with the assistance or support of others, such
as Elders, Healers, and Helpers. Healing begins at one's own centre; this is
the ultimate responsibility for one's own well being. We can find the right

healing for an illness, and an explanation for why it happened in the first place. If we ignore this explanation and continue with the same behavior or activity that is said to have caused the illness, then the illness will return because we continue to be out of balance. Being out of balance happens whenever we have not lived a "careful" life.

Source

Gloria Lee. "Defining Traditional Healing." In *Justice as Healing: Indigenous Ways*, edited by Wanda D. McCaslin, 98–99. St. Paul: Living Justice Press, 2005.

Contextualized Biosketch

Gloria Lee is the Prince Albert Grand Council justice director and past research and curriculum developer for the Saskatchewan Indian Institute of Technologies. She is of Cree ancestry from the Pelican Lake area and has a bachelor of law degree. Lee is also an artist, and some of her work hangs in the College of Law at the University of Saskatchewan. Lee collected the information in this quote through the oral tradition from elders Mary Lee, Danny Musqua, and Henry Ross, and from publications cited, including Linda C. Garro's article "Ways of Talking About Illness in a Manitoba Anishinable (Ojibwa) Community" (in *Circumpolar Health*, 1990, p. 226). Lee's chapter in *Justice as Healing* was originally a research paper for a native studies research course at the University of Saskatchewan, under the advisement of the late Patricia Monture-Angus, a Mohawk educator, activist, and author.

Indigenous Worldview Precept Dialogue

Four Arrows: In Western-oriented dominant cultures, we generally conceive of disease, medicine, and healing as dependent on objective, scientific, technological interventions by highly skilled physicians. Understanding recovery as "within us" or illness caused by not "living a careful life" and "being out of balance" are not usually a primary focus. Thus, Lee's claim that "healing is within us" is rarely contained in a physician's advice. I shared my personal story about my Indigenous approach to healing my lymphoma in our chapter on ceremony, noting that ceremony is a form of self-hypnosis, trance-based healing and learning. However, this goes deeper and wider. I believe the plight of our world ahead will include a continuation of pandemics, climate change, rising extinction rates, authoritarian governments, and interpersonal violence that require an understanding of Indigenous worldview approaches to healing. I believe one of the most important things to understand is hidden in two of Lee's claims in the quote above:

- Because traditional healing is within each of us, we are all capable of healing ourselves, sometimes with the assistance or support of others, such as Elders, Healers, and Helpers.

- Healing begins at one's own centre; this is the ultimate responsibility for one's own well being.

What even Lee may not have realized when she wrote these insightful assertions is that the phenomenon of trance-based learning is fundamental in Indigenous healing and health maintenance.[1] It focuses on what Indigenous spiritual leaders and medicine persons do. "Shamanic trance is a volitional, self-induced state of consciousness that historically served the purposes of social cohesion and healing interventions in diverse tribal settings."[2] Such healing, as I describe in the first chapter of my book *Point of Departure,* has been used for thousands of years. And "the key to shamanic healing is trance."[3] One will find multiple distinct yet related definitions of "trance" on the internet. I personally define it as a state of consciousness resulting from a concentrated focus on an image that results in a shift into a lower brain wave frequency that ultimately influences brain synapses in ways to create transformed behaviors, abilities, and/or dispositions, even those that can have epigenetic influences. Ultimately all hypnotic inductions into trance are self-imposed, but they can also result from giving authority, intentionally or unintentionally, to someone else.

What does shamanic traditional healing and its utilization of trance have to do with a relational worldview? Everything. Indigenous worldview is all about one's relationship with the universe, seen and unseen, as all of our quotes have expressed. Personal and communal transformations are about harmony, not control. Many living creatures utilize trance phenomena for survival, and the nonhuman teachers are largely the source of healing rituals. Such rituals stem from purposeful ambitions for walking the path in balance and becoming truly human, in harmony with all. Such an approach is very different from our dominant worldview assumptions about health. Indeed, Indigenous and dominant worldviews are "diametric trajectories in the realm of knowledge,"[4] according to Willie Ermine, a member of the Sturgeon Lake First Nation and professor at First Nations University of Canada. In my humble opinion, the continued rejection of trance-based, community-based, Spirit-based healing by the dominant medical professions are what will prevent us from rebalancing our world.

Darcia, I may have engaged in too much enthusiasm in relation to this important precept and my interpretations about Indigenous trance-based healing ways. What more can we share with the reader about how healing relates to "starting with one's center," as Lee states?

Darcia: I've been reading about *ho'oponopono,* the Hawaiian and South Pacific form of creating balance and goodness. Illness is assumed to come from imbalance, manifested in bodily, psychic, or relational illness. It is a group healing process of confession, forgiveness, and reconciliation that focuses on repair of one's center, one's spirit, and one's connections. Morrnah Simeona,[5] a kahuna (shamanic healer), noted: "Western man has gone to the extremes with his intellectualism, it divides and keeps people separate. Man then becomes a destroyer because he manages and copes, rather than letting the perpetuating force of the Divinity flow through him for right action." Simeona modernized the practice of *ho'oponopono.* Popularized approaches refer to her work for individual self-healing, largely through repeating a set of statements throughout the day or targeted at particular relational issues to "clean" one's spirit through forgiving and loving.

With deeper investigation, I discovered that these methods are different from Simeona's more complex approach. Her recommended group-healing *ho'oponopono* practice was changed into an individual do-it-yourself method to take care of personal obstacles. So it is making me wonder, how can we appropriately apply helpful healing practices when we are out of the cultural context and when we are lacking a supportive community? Most people in industrialized-technologized nations do not have the earth-rooted cultural history or intimate community of our ancestors. Can we still achieve the deeper healing that needs to take place?

Western religions had both a community and a personal practice approach for centuries. As humans are generally highly social animals, both seem needed for self-transformation and support of individual transformation. But when a millennia or so ago Western Christianity shifted to seeing beliefs as central to faith, abandoning self-transformation practices in the process, they lost the individual aspect, apart from rote ritual. In recent decades, that has become of greater interest, at least on the West Coast of North America. So I am wondering whether the individualized *ho'oponopono* may be part of this shift. What do you think? If not, we may need to discuss how people can find their ancestral healing practices and a supportive community.

My other thought is that the dominant culture is blind to most of its relationships—with other-than-humans—and so typically has no thoughts about healing them. So maybe readers without a human community can find community and mutual healing with the other-than-humans where they live. And maybe that community can guide them in healing ceremony. Many years ago, the land on which we live gave me a song to sing to/with it. I sing it as a greeting and prayer of support when I am outside. But of course it also makes me feel connected and cared for.

Four Arrows, can you say more about your healing practices and how you deal with the issues I raised?

Four Arrows: I agree with you that the popularization of *ho'opono-pono* has morphed from its original relational process into a more self-centered healing concept. I do not, however, think Simeona's more complex version, grounded in Christianity and Eastern karma, escapes from this either. The Wikipedia entry about her talks about how some Hawaiian purists criticized her for using it for "self-help rather than the traditional Hawaiian group process."[6] I have always understood the idea as the Indigenous way of resolving conflict resulting from a violation of spiritual laws in order to return someone back into community, a topic we discussed in chapter 18. And since spiritual laws in the Indigenous perspective define community to include both humans and nonhumans, this would tend to support what you are saying. A respected source book about Hawaiian traditional beliefs defines it as a way to "set right" in order "to restore and maintain good relationships among family and supernatural powers."[7]

As for how my own healing practices relate to *ho'oponopono*, I start with offering Dr. Manulani Aluli Meyer's description of it as a healing modality that is "a form of wisdom that you express because of your intentionality and your commitment to be of service." She continues: "*Ho'oponopono* is when you use *pono* to return to *pono*. *Pono* is the Hawaiian ideal of Truth, of healing, of rightness, of doing the right thing, of doing what is meant to be done because of the needs of that moment.... *Ho'ponopono* is when that practice takes you into a ritualized way of communication that helps families and others heal."[8]

What Manulani says here is exactly the foundation behind my spontaneous remissions of terminal cancer, since I have managed a second one during the writing of this book. I see the process as simply trying to do the right thing with the goal of doing service to others. For example, when I focus on my healing in the first round of the *inipi* ceremony in the sweat house, I do that so I can have the strength and will to help others. I am thinking to myself that if I can no longer do some service to others in the world, then it is probably time for me to move on from this life. Remember the four rounds of the *inipi* as practiced by the Medicine Horse (the extended family in which I am a member). The first round is to pray for ourselves so we can help others. The second round is praying for all our relations; the third is about praying for flowing balance in the world, with an emphasis on women regaining their power; and the last is about expressing gratitude.

Another reason for my choice to ignore the medical prescriptions for chemotherapy and surgery was to express another truth in which I believe. In addition to wanting to be around for my work of promoting Indigeneity as a healing solution for the world, I want to do my best to take responsibility for my healing, perhaps as a model for us all to get back into balance. I was successful the first time. Then I got out of balance again, and the lymphoma returned. Then—against advice saying a second time would be impossible—I did it again. I'm not saying everyone should reject conventional medicine; I'm saying that making our best choice to be responsible for our healing is crucial, whatever choices we make. For me, both my motivations are about *pono*—practicing what I believe to be truth.

Darcia: What you say makes sense to me. Indigenous traditions understand health to require balance in every realm—body functioning, psychic functioning, relational functioning (human and other-than-human), and spiritual functioning. When any is out of balance, we can become ill in some fashion. In my previous work,[9] I described how easy it is to get out of balance in our relationships throughout the day by taking defensive positions: either a position of inferiority where I won't be my authentic self out of fear, refusing my agency; or a position of superiority where I dominate or exploit the other out of anger, refusing communion with them. One must experience some pain to move out of these defensive modes, letting go of self-delusions. In the first case, instead of distancing, we accept self and responsibility, finding our courage, strength, and voice. In the second case, we let go of the inflated ego, of grandiosity, and realize our need for others, becoming receptive to the beauty in the other. We move into the flowing interpersonal dance of co-creation, self-transcending in a mutual trance of relating. "We then can again take up the dance of communication with the Other, an initially frightening but ultimately exhilarating experience because it puts us at the very heart of being, knowing and being known."[10]

Now if we expand the rebalancing beyond human relations, there is a lot to pay attention to across realms if we want to be a responsive, responsible member of the community. Physical: am I attending to the critical needs of my body in the moment? Psychic: is my psyche free of self-recriminations, other-recriminations, worries about the future, and so on, so that I am free to *be* fully present emotionally and mentally in this moment? Relational: am I maintaining a balanced, centered self with others in this moment—including all the other-than-human entities here, aware of their sentience? Am I being a responsible member of my community? Spiritual: am I respectful of the spiritual realm in this moment—of my ancestors, divine spirits and the unmanifest universe? Each area requires some understanding of health needs and how to meet them so we grow our best selves.

Physical: Each of us is a community of beings, with a host of microorganisms keeping us alive—e.g., in what probiotic foods and activities do we engage? Our bodies are full of delicate but resilient processes—how do we maintain their optimal functioning?

Psychic: Our psyches are affected by the feelings or ideas we host for more than fifteen seconds. What we immerse our minds in, then, becomes our truth. When we immerse ourselves in the Indigenous wisdom precepts—through contemplation, journaling, or reading more deeply, for example—over time they become our reality.

Relational: Everything we think, do, or say has an effect on our relationships with entities in all realms. We can practice a set of virtues that encompass not only human beings but other-than-humans. The path will be painful as we realize and slowly revamp all the ways we have not acted according to our virtuous ideals.

Spiritual: Western wisdom tradition practices for self-transformation typically emphasize personal openness to the divine, and one must clear away impediments.[11] The Indigenous orientation is less a soloist affair. Instead, we are accompanied by helpers, on this or other planes, so we never feel alone as we take the healing journey. We make an intentional commitment to seek health on every level. We ask for guidance from our helpers and it is forthcoming. Four Arrows, I hope you feel accompanied on your journey to healing, every step of the way.

28

An Emphasis on Heart Wisdom

Ilarion "Larry" Merculieff (Unangan)

*S*ince the age of six, I've known how to get "out of my head." As one of the last Unangan (Aleut) to experience a true traditional upbringing, I was allowed to walk the six miles from the village out to the bird cliffs, even as a very young child. In my six-year-old mind, I decided that the only difference between those birds and myself was that they drew upon a vast field of awareness rather than an intellectual thought process (although I did not use such words at the time). I wanted to be like a bird, so, after months of effort, I developed the capacity to maintain this state of "awareness without thinking" for several hours at a time. That was when the magic happened: I could sense many things I'd never experienced before, and my world expanded enormously.

From then on, I understood how Unangan people received their spiritual instructions for living, principles that had helped them sustain their communities for thousands of years: reciprocity with all living things, humility, respect for all life, honoring Elder wisdom, giving without expectation of a return to self, thinking of others first, and many more.

Such spiritual principles for living did not come from logic or thought but from a much deeper source of wisdom, which our Unangan culture referred to as the "heart." When Unangan Elders speak of the "heart," they do not mean mere feelings, even positive and compassionate ones. "Heart" refers to a deeper portal of profound interconnectedness and awareness that exists between humans and all living things. Centering oneself there *results in humble, wise, connected ways of being and acting in the world. Indigenous peoples have cultivated access to this source as part of a deep experience and awareness of the profound interdependency between the natural and human worlds. To access it, you must drop out of the relentless thinking that typically occupies the Western mind.*

When accessed, this portal provides the inner wisdom that keeps us in right relationship with all of life, thus ensuring our long-term survival and well-being, individually and collectively. Our fallible thought processes regularly deceive us. Yet, when guidance or information comes from the heart, it can be relied upon and has impeccable integrity. . . .

And the most dire reversal is that now the mind tells the heart what to do instead of the mind following the heart.

Still, when you access this heart center, you must have great courage to follow what it is telling you. Sometimes that feels like jumping from a cliff. But when you do, you will never regret it. Once you have accessed the heart, you enter into the vast field of awareness in the company of birds and connect in a deep and profound way with all living things.

Source

Ilarion Merculieff. "Out of the Head, into the Heart: The Way of the Human Being."
Center for Humans & Nature, June 16, 2017. www.humansandnature.org
/out-of-the-head-into-the-heart.

Contextualized Biosketch

Ilarion "Larry" Merculieff, also known as Larry "Kuuyux" Merculieff, is one of the last generation of Aleuts of the Alaskan Pribilof Islands to be fully raised in the traditional way. Recipient of the 2017 Wisdom Treasure Award, he continues to facilitate the use of traditional ways of dialogue, decision-making, and consensus building, sharing traditional wisdom with Indigenous people around the world. Larry is currently an independent consultant and president of the Global Center for Indigenous Leadership and Lifeways, and he serves as a senior advisor to the World Wilderness Congress and advisor to the Native Lands Wilderness Council.[1]

Indigenous Worldview Precept Dialogue

Darcia: We end our quotes about Indigenous worldview precepts with this one because we feel it describes the central source fueling all the precepts—heart wisdom. As it turns out, virtually all traditional societies and major religions emphasize heart wisdom, an expansive sense of being, as Merculieff describes. The heart is the aspect of personhood able to perceive and synchronize to the life force in the cosmos. Sufi master Kabir Helminski described what is missing when intellect is the focus:

> We have subtle subconscious faculties we are not using. In addition to the limited analytic intellect is a vast realm of mind that includes psychic and extrasensory abilities; intuition; wisdom; a sense of unity; aesthetic, qualitative and creative capacities; and image forming and symbolic capacities. Though these faculties are many, we give them a single name with some justification because they are operating best when they are in concert. They comprise a mind, moreover, in spontaneous connection to the cosmic mind. This total mind we call "heart."[2]

Science has shown us that "heart" involves a well-functioning right hemisphere. In a healthy brain, the right hemisphere (RH) collects experiences and passes them to the left hemisphere (LH), which unpacks and analyzes them to identify algorithms and generalize for predictions, and then sends those analyses back to the RH for intuitive assessment and integration into an experiential wholeness.[3] An underperforming RH doesn't pick up very well the signals in the environment. The hubris of the LH (ego) still assumes it knows what's going on, even making things up.[4] When the RH is not working properly, the final gestalt unification with LH detail is impaired too. The individual's mind/brain gets caught up in the illusions of an LH communicating with itself, the madness referred to by David Bohm, discussed in chapter 7.[5] The common condition among those living within societies governed by the dominant worldview—feeling fragmented, devitalized, depersonalized, depressed, or dissociated, along with lost emotional depth and empathy—corresponds to an overbearing LH and underactive, often underdeveloped, RH.[6]

This presents yet another reason to adopt the Indigenous kincentric worldview and practices. In many of our chapters, I have noted how important child raising is, especially in the first months and years, for establishing the foundations for human capacities. In evolved nested care, responsive nurturers co-construct the rapidly developing brain with right-brain-to-right-brain resonance through soothing caregiver touch and vocalization, eye contact and facial expressions, and stimulating exchanges. But in societies embedded in the dominant worldview, child raising practices often neglect right-brain development—which is fostered by immersed, embodied early experience of being on caregiver bodies, kept calm and even joyous. The absence of these experiences undermines the development of critical capacities seen among Indigenous peoples. To restore whole-brain functioning, it often takes purposeful effort to enhance right-brain function—including the free-flowing trancelike state Merculieff describes. Four Arrows, I think your CAT-FAWN is one of those practices.

Four Arrows: What an interesting connection you are making between "heart wisdom" and brain laterality, or more accurately, what one of your references refers to as "total mind." From an Indigenous perspective, as we discussed in chapter 14 on complementarity, difference does not always imply dichotomy, which some have applied to left- and right-brain functioning—e.g., reasoning versus emotional or analytical versus creative.[7] It is more helpful to understand their complementary functions, as you describe them, and to understand that when their complementarity is compromised, it affects heart wisdom. In the article "No Word for Art in Tewa Language—Only Meaning," the San Ildefonso ceramicist Lorenzo Gonzales says, "In non-Indian terms, I'm an artist. In the Tewa world, they say of me, 'He's a very skilled person. He knows many things.'"[8]

I am pleased we continue to refer to CAT-FAWN work as a way to truly live the wisdom of our quoted guests. Concentration-Activated Transformation (CAT), which is essentially self-hypnosis or trance-based learning that Indigenous people have long used via ceremony, is crucial for transformations and healings. Fear, Authority, Words, and Nature (FAWN) reveal how dominant worldview attitudes about these four forces are very different from Indigenous worldview attitudes. How CAT-FAWN relates to heart wisdom is illustrated in an article by Bickel and Fisher. The first lines of their abstract hint at the connection: "The arts-based co-inquiry engages the intersection of the Western-medical based world/reality and the Natural world/reality. To bridge these worlds the co-authors utilize a spiritual-based trance-formative practice using trance and arts-based inquiry."[9] Fisher is well-versed in CAT-FAWN "technology" (as he refers to it) because he is the author of an intellectual biography about my work.[10] He and his scholar-wife, who is the lead author of the article, fully understand how the concept of heart wisdom aligns with embracing Indigenous worldview and using natural trance-based learning to do so. David Larson Levine, a former student of mine, has also created trainings for people to use CAT-FAWN work as a way to bring trance-based learning and metacognitive worldview reflection into the world.[11]

The question I have for you as we close our dialogue is: What can we do to bring CAT-FAWN evolved nest work forward to bring this book's messages into hearts and minds in ways that are transformational?

Darcia: If you have not been raised in a community that is heart-centered and heart-guided, you will have to learn the alternative mode to that of the intellect—the judging, analyzing, narrowly focused, categorizing mode—which is so well learned and practiced in schooling. I worked with my college students to help them develop and practice the alternative mode—the receptive, open, holistic, intuitive mode described by Merculieff. Most students have the "heart" mode very underdeveloped. This is what I tell the students (from my syllabus):

> The course is intended to develop both left-hemisphere directed (FOCUSED; beta brain wave) and right-hemisphere directed (RECEPTIVE, OPEN, CREATIVE; alpha brain wave) styles of attention (mostly the latter since you spend most of your education in the former). Both are needed for living wisely and sustainably. Schooling generally focuses on focused thinking. The goal is to develop all capacities and use them wisely. Focused attention is more verbal so it tends to dominate but it is also narrower and more limited in awareness. We will do activities to increase receptive intelligence.[12]

Importantly, each mode reflects a different way of being in the world. The two modes are asymmetrical.[13]

It turns out that at the beginning of each situation, we can choose which mode we will employ. Warning: once we have chosen the intellect mode, it is very difficult to shift to the heart mode. We have all probably noticed this, such as when brainstorming ideas in a group. If someone starts to edit or criticize, the creative juices stop flowing, and it is hard to get back to the free-flowing mode. The intellect mode comes to a social situation by categorizing the other person (e.g., fatter than me, weaker than me, more important than me), selecting a script or set of rules for the encounter (e.g., they should show subservience to my superior intellect), and critiquing anything that doesn't follow the script. In fact, this mode is unaware of the whole. The goal by and large is domination and control of what is perceived, governed by some abstracted ideal.

In contrast, the heart mode comes to a situation with an openness to the beauty and uniqueness of the other, ready to co-create a new interpersonal dance in the moment, aware of shared living energy, dissolving separation, "connecting us with our ground of being."[14] Sorenson describes this holistic approach in heart-centered (Indigenous) communities: "People freely spread their interests, feelings and delights out for all to see and grasp as they lurched toward whatever delightful patterns of response they found attractive."[15] It is not about control, planned outcomes, or rules, but about creative interaction. In contrast, the dominant worldview has taught us to be afraid of this mode as scary and dangerous or childish (that is the intellect's analysis!). Iain McGilchrist, who reviewed a host of experimental studies examining brain hemisphere differences (e.g., by numbing one side of the brain and examining the responses and orientations of the other) wrote about their different forms of attention:

> I believe the essential difference between the right hemisphere and the left hemisphere is that the right hemisphere pays attention to the Other: to whatever it is that exists apart from ourselves, with which it sees itself in profound relation. It is deeply attracted to, and given life by, the relationship, the betweenness, that exists with this Other. By contrast, the left hemisphere pays attention to the virtual world that it has created, which is self-consistent but self-contained, ultimately disconnected from the Other, making it powerful—but also curiously impotent, because it is ultimately only able to operate on, and to know, itself.[16]

To be able to practice the heart mode, individuals may need to first practice self-calming, which I briefly described in chapter 18, "Conflict Resolution as Return to Community." If you feel anxious around people generally, you likely automatically go into the intellect mode or withdraw yourself into numbness (indicative of undercare or trauma in early life—you learned these ways to survive). There are various approaches to learn self-calming. With my students, we practiced deep belly breathing and vagus nerve stimulation (you can find You-Tube videos on these).

When Westerners discuss openness to the Other, they typically mean other human beings. The Indigenous worldview embraces much more—*all* the Others. The fullest heart mode, as Merculieff shows us, includes the other-than-human. In the full heart mode, everything around us is alive, unique, energetically resonating as part of the whole.

The dominator mode treats all non-ego-self as other-to-be-controlled. Unfortunately, it is fairly easy to shift into this mode when we treat the other-than-human as commodities. As described in chapter 6, in a decades-long study of Nayaka hunter-gatherers in India, at the outset they were observed to treat local animals as partners, but when pushed into raising animals for sale, they depersonified those animals, treating them more like objects.[17] So we must learn to be aware of the dangers of our human manipulative powers and instead stay in an all-inclusive heart mode. All our kin are partners in the story of life, from the bacteria in our yogurt to the breeze that touches us, the flies that want to share our food, and the tomatoes we grow, pick, and put in our salads. They can be powerful allies when we are respectful and attuned.[18] In every moment, we can take up Lame Deer's aim: "I wanted to see with the eye of the heart. . . . All nature is within us and all of us in is nature."[19] *Sensing* with the heart is the first step toward *acting with* heart, according to our deepest, awakened intuitions. When we act with heart, we will not be destructive but instead will follow the courageous red road path of sustainable parnership with all our kin.

Four Arrows: Darcia, with you having a doctorate in educational psychology and me with one in health psychology—despite my skepticsm of it, as illustrated in my previously referenced coauthored text *Critical Neurophilosophy and Indigenous Wisdom*—I think we both see some useful merit in the neurosciences. As relates to our "heart wisdom" topic for this final chapter, I offer that there are studies that show that cardiac vagal tone correlates with Indigenous oneness and complementarity precepts. Cardiac vagal tone represents the contribution of the parasympathetic nervous system to cardiac regulation and "is acknowledged to be linked with many phenomena relevant for psychophysiological research, including self-regulation at the cognitive, emotional, social, and health levels."[20] For example, a 2016 study concluded that wisdom-related judgment is neither an exclusive function of the mind nor of the body. "Rather, both greater heart-rate-variability and an ego-decentered mind are required for a wiser, less biased judgment."[21] The study suggests that increasing the psychological distance from our own self-centered perspective when assessing events that we experience allows for a wiser perspective on reality. I think we can use studies like this to support what you say about becoming aware of our human manipulative powers and about leading with an all-inclusive heart mode. It can also support what Larry Merculieff says about the problem of allowing our ego-based thoughts to deceive us about the nature of reality.

Certainly, the current situation in our world reflects such self-deception. As we end this book, it is important to note that noninclusive thinking and being has brought us all into existential crises that can only be solved by the kind of heart wisdom that most humans attained via living according to the nature-based kinship worldview. I say this knowing how academic scholarship, schooling, and popular media have falsely stereotyped Indigeneity and Indigenous histories. When not being dangerously romanticized, precontact Indigenous cultures and facts about them have been misrepresented as relates to their ecological sustainability and peacefulness.[22,23] By noting this continuing "anti-Indianism,"[24] especially in the Americas, our Indigenous quotes and analysis of them in this book offer a proven way to reconcile and transform life systems. If we are unable turn things around in our lifetime, which is likely, those who rebuild can do so effectively if they have learned from whomever has re-embraced our kinship worldview from those who role model it or have taught it via CAT-FAWN work that uses metacognitive worldview reflection and self-hypnosis for the transformation.

Notes

Epigraph

1 S. Díaz et al., Summary for Policymakers of the Global Assessment Report on Biodiversity and Ecosystem Services of the Intergovernmental Science-Policy Platform on Biodiversity and Ecosystem Services (Bonn, Germany: IPBES, 2019), https://ipbes.net/sites/default/files/2020-02/ipbes_global_assessment _report_summary_for_policymakers_en.pdf.

2 Monica Dean, "Key Findings to Know from the IPBES Report On Biodiversity," United Nations Foundation, May 6, 2019, https://unfoundation.org/blog/post /key-findings-to-know-from-the-ipbes-report-on-biodiversity/.

3 Kai M. A. Chan et al., "Unedited Draft Chapter 31" (Bonn, Germany: IPBES, 2019), 74, https://ipbes.net/sites/default/files/ipbes_global_assessment _chapter_5_unedited_31may.pdf.

4 Chan et al., "Unedited Draft," 67.

5 Chan et al., "Unedited Draft," 81–82.

6 Chan et al., "Unedited Draft," 93.

Introduction

1 Paul Shepard, *Coming Home to the Pleistocene,* ed. Florence R. Shepard (Washington, DC: Island Press, 1998).

2 A. H. de Witt, "Worldviews and the Transformation to Sustainable Societies: An Exploration of the Cultural and Psychological Dimensions of Our Global Environmental Challenges" (PhD diss., Vrije Universiteit Amsterdam, 2013), https:// dare.ubvu.vu.nl/bitstream/handle/1871/48104/dissertation.pdf?sequence.

3 David K. Naugle, *Worldview: The History of a Concept* (Grand Rapids, MI: William Eerdmans, 2002).

4 Martin Heidegger, *The Basic Problems of Phenomenology,* trans. Albert Hofstadter (Bloomington: Indiana University Press, 1982), 4.

5 Mark E. Koltko-Rivera, "The Psychology of Worldviews," *Review of General Psychology* 8, no. 1 (2004): 3–58.

6 Koltko-Rivera, 15.

7 Lisa Reagan, "Seeking Wellness and Wisdom with Worldview Literacy (Part 2 of 2)," *Pathways for Family Wellness* 31, 2011, 2, https://pathwaystofamilywellness.org /The-Conscious-Path/seeking-wellness-and-wisdom-with-worldview-literacy -part-2-of-2/Page-2.html.

8 Edgar Mitchell, quoted in John Perkins, Shapeshifting: Shamanic Techniques for Global and Personal Transformation (Rochester, VT: Destiny Books,1997), back cover.

9 Walter Ong, "World as View and World as Event," *American Anthropologist* 71 (1969): 634–47.

10 Steve Draper, "How Many Senses Do Humans Have?" December 8, 2019, www.psy.gla.ac.uk/~steve/best/senses.html.

11 Robert Wolff, *Original Wisdom* (Rochester, VT: Inner Traditions, 2001).

12 Steve J. Langdon. "Spiritual Relations, Moral Obligations and Existential Continuity: The Structure and Transmission of Tlingit Principles and Practices of Sustainable Wisdom," in *Indigenous Sustainable Wisdom: First Nation Know-how for Global Flourishing*, eds. Darcia Narvaez, Four Arrows, Eugene Halton, Brian Collier, and Georges Enderle (New York: Peter Lang, 2019), 153–82. See also: Steve J. Langdon, "Tlingit Engagement with Salmon: The Philosophy and Practice of Real Sustainability," in Thomas F. Thornton and Shonil A. Bhagwat, eds., *The Handbook of Indigenous Environmental Knowledge* (London: Routledge, 2020), 169–85.

13 Dennis Martinez, "Native Perspectives on Sustainability: Dennis Martinez (O'odham/Chicano/Anglo)," interview by David E. Hall, Native Perspectives on Sustainability, January 3, 2008, www.nativeperspectives.net/Transcripts/Dennis _Martinez_interview.pdf.

14 Rhett A. Butler, "Colombia, Ethnobotany and America's Decline: An Interview with Wade Davis," *Mongabay,* October 21, 2020, https://news.mongabay.com/2020/10 /colombia-ethnobotany-and-americas-decline-an-interview-with-wade-davis.

15 Worldview Chart and introduction by Wahinkpe Topa (Four Arrows), a.k.a. Don Trent Jacobs. Originally published in *The Red Road (chanku luta): Linking Diversity and Inclusion Initiatives to Indigenous Worldview* (Charlotte, North Carolina: Information Age Publishing, 2020).

16 Eduardo S. Brondizio, Josef Settele, Sandra Díaz, and Hien T. Ngo, eds., *Global Assessment Report on Biodiversity and Ecosystem Services of the Intergovernmental Science-Policy Platform on Biodiversity and Ecosystem Services* (Bonn, Germany: IPBES, 2019), https://ipbes.net/global-assessment.

17 Robert Redfield, *The Primitive Worldview and Its Transformations* (Ithaca, NY: Cornell University Press, 1953).

18 Darcia Narvaez, "Ecocentrism: Resetting Baselines for Virtue Development," *Ethical Theory and Moral Practice* 23, no. 2 (2020): 391–406, https://doi.org /10.1007/s10677-020-10091-2.

19 Denise Marsden, "Indigenous Principles for Single Mothering in a Fragmented World," in D. Memee Lavell-Harvard and Kim Anderson, eds., *Mothers of the Nations: Indigenous Mothering as Global Resistance, Reclaiming and Recovery* (Bradford, ON: Demeter Press, 2014) 267–90; Stephen M. Sachs, Bruce E. Johansen, Ain Haas, Betty Booth Donohue, Donald A. Grinde Jr., and Jonathon York, *Honoring the Circle: Ongoing Learning of the West from American Indians on Politics and Society, Volume I: The Impact of American Indians on Western Politics and Society to 1800* (Cardiff, CA: Waterside Productions, 2020).

20 Sachs et al., xvii.

21 Medicine Story, *Return to Creation* (Spokane, WA: Bear Tribe Publishing, 1991), 45.

22 Thomas Mails and Dallas Chief Eagle, *Fools Crow* (Lincoln: University of Nebraska Press, 1990), 52.

1. Recognition of Spiritual Energies in Nature

1 Marvin Bram, *The Recovery of the West: An Essay in Symbolic History* (self-pub., Xlibris Corporation, May 6, 2002).

2 Graham Harvey, *Animism: Respecting the Living World,* 2nd ed. (London: C. Hurst & Co., 2017).

3 Morgan Brigg and Mary Graham, "The Relevance of Aboriginal Political Concepts: Autonomous Selfhood," ABC Religion & Ethics, July 2020, www.abc.net .au/religion/aboriginal-political-concepts-autonomous-selfhood/12472310.

4 Jon Young, "Connection Modeling Metrics for Deep Nature-Connection, Mentoring and Culture Repair," in *Indigenous Sustainable Wisdom: First Nation Know-How for Global Flourishing,* eds. Darcia Narvaez, Four Arrows, Eugene Halton, Brian Collier, and Georges Enderle (New York: Peter Lang, 2019), 219–43.

5 Angel M. Kurth, Darcia Narvaez, Reilly Kohn, and Andrea Bae, "Nature Connection: A 3-Week Intervention Increased Ecological Attachment," *Ecopsychology* 12, no. 2 (2020): 1–17.

6 See https://EcoAttachment.dance.

2. Nonhierarchical Society

1 Wenona Victor Hall, "Indigenous Justice: Clearing Space and Place for Indigenous Epistemologies," Indigenous Governance Database, December 2007, 5-6, www.fngovernance.org/ncfng_research/wenona_victor.pdf.

2 Dennis M. McIneerney and Junnat Ali, "Indigenous Motivational Profiles: Do They Reflect Collectivism?" in R. G. Craven, G. H. Bodkin-Andrews, and J. Mooney, eds., *International Advances in Education: Global Initiatives for Equity and Social Justice* (Charlotte, NC: Information Age Publishing, 2012), 209–30.

3 Marlies Glasius, "What Authoritarianism Is . . . and Is Not: A Practice Perspective," *International Affairs* 94, no. 3 (2018): 515–33, https://academic.oup.com/ia/article/94/3/515/4992409.

4 David Graeber and David Wengrow, "How to Change the Course of Human History (at Least, the Part That's Already Happened)," *Eurozine,* March 2, 2018, www.eurozine.com/change-course-human-history/; David Graeber and David Wengrow, *The Dawn of Everything: A New History of Humanity* (New York: Mac-Millan, 2021).

5 Douglas P. Fry, *The Human Potential for Peace: An Anthropological Challenge to Assumptions about War and Violence* (New York: Oxford University Press, 2006); Christopher Boehm, *Hierarchy in the Forest: The Evolution of Egalitarian Behavior* (Cambridge, MA: Harvard University Press, 1999).

6 Darcia Narvaez, *Neurobiology and the Development of Human Morality: Evolution, Culture, and Wisdom* (New York: W. W. Norton, 2014).

7 Alice Miller, *For Your Own Good: Hidden Cruelty in Child-Rearing and the Roots of Violence* (New York: Noonday Press, 1990).

8 Tim Ingold, "On the Social Relations of the Hunter-Gatherer Band," in Richard B. Lee and Richard Daly, eds., *The Cambridge Encyclopedia of Hunters and Gatherers* (New York: Cambridge University Press, 2005), 399–410.

9 Richard B. Lee, *The !Kung San: Men, Women, and Work in a Foraging Community* (Cambridge: Cambridge University Press, 1979).

10 Lee, *The !Kung San.*

11 E. Richard Sorenson, "Preconquest Consciousness," in Helmut Wautischer, ed., *Tribal Epistemologies* (Aldershot, UK: Ashgate, 1998), 80.

12 Sylvan S. Tomkins, "Affect and the Psychology of Knowledge," In Sylvan S. Tomkins and Carol E. Izard, eds., *Affect, Cognition, and Personality* (New York: Springer, 1965).

13 Sorenson, "Preconquest," 82, 84.

14 Narvaez, *Neurobiology;* Riane Eisler and Douglas P. Fry, *Nurturing Our Humanity* (New York: Oxford University Press, 2019).

15 Lesley Evans Ogden, "What Animals Tell Us about Female Leadership," BBC Worklife, accessed August 29, 2021, www.bbc.com/worklife/article/20180925-with-females-in-charge-bonobo-society-is-more-chilled-out.

16 Robert M. Sapolsky, *A Primate's Memoir* (New York: Scribner, 2001).

17 Frans de Waal and Frans Lanting, *Bonobo: The Forgotten Ape* (Berkeley: University of California Press, 1998).

18 Indigenous Corporate Training, "What Is the Relationship Between Indigenous Peoples and Animals?" April 4, 2016, www.ictinc.ca/blog/what-is-the-relationship-between-Indigenous-peoples-and-animals.

19 Boehm, *Hierarchy*.

20 Frans de Waal, *Good Natured: The Origins of Right and Wrong in Humans and Other Animals* (Cambridge, MA: Harvard University Press, 1996); de Waal and Lanting, *Bonobo*.

21 Judith M. Burkart, Sarah B. Hrdy, and Carel P. van Schaik, "Cooperative Breeding and Human Cognitive Evolution," *Evolutionary Anthropology* 18 (2009): 175–86.

22 Camilla Power, "The Role of Egalitarianism and Gender Ritual in the Evolution of Symbolic Cognition," in Tracy Henley, Matthew Rossano, and Edward Kardas, eds., *Handbook of Cognitive Archaeology: A Psychological Framework* (London: Routledge, 2019), 354–74.

23 Miller, *Own Good*.

24 Michael J. Meaney, "Epigenetics and the Biological Definition of Gene X Environment Interactions," *Child Development* 81, no. 1 (2010): 41–79.

25 Peter D. Gluckman and Mark Hanson, *Fetal Matrix: Evolution, Development and Disease* (New York: Cambridge University Press, 2005).

26 Pedro Carrera-Bastos et al., "The Western Diet and Lifestyle and Diseases of Civilization," *Research Reports in Clinical Cardiology* 2, no. 2 (2011): 15–35, www .dovepress.com/the-western-diet-and-lifestyle-and-diseases-of-civilization-peer -reviewed-fulltext-article-RRCC.

27 See https://EvolvedNest.org.

28 "Navajo Roles and Responsibilities of a Leader: Navajo Nation Supreme Court 2010," accessed August 29, 2021, www.nahmus.org/navajonationsurpremecourt .pdf.

29 Joe Sheridan and Roronhiakewen "He Clears the Sky" Dan Longboat, "Walking Back into Creation: Environmental Apartheid and the Eternal—Initiating an Indigenous Mind Claim," *Space and Culture* 17, no. 3 (2014): 308.

3. Courage and Fearless Trust in the Universe

1 "Berta Cáceres's Daughter Speaks Out After Surviving Assassination Attempt in Honduras," *Democracy Now!*, July 7, 2017, video, 10:26, www.youtube.com /watch?v=4JHFDzxkFWw.

2 R. Michael Fisher, *Fearless Engagement of Four Arrows: The True Story of an Indigenous-Based Social Transformer* (New York: Peter Lang, 2018), 281.

3 Iain McGilchrist, *The Master and His Emissary: The Divided Brain and the Making of the Western World* (New Haven, CT: Yale University Press, 2009); Allan N. Schore, *The Development of the Unconscious Mind* (New York: W. W. Norton, 2019).

4 Darcia Narvaez, *Neurobiology and the Development of Human Morality: Evolution, Culture, and Wisdom* (New York: W. W. Norton, 2014).

5 Allan N. Schore, "Effects of a Secure Attachment Relationship on Right Brain Development, Affect Regulation, and Infant Mental Health," *Infant Mental Health Journal* 22 (2001): 7–66; *The Development of the Unconscious Mind* (New York: W. W. Norton, 2019).

6 Richard Louv, *Last Child in the Woods: Saving our Children from Nature Deficit Disorder* (New York: Workman, 2005); Lenore Skenazy, *Free-Range Kids: How to Raise Safe, Self-Reliant Children (without Going Nuts with Worry)* (San Francisco: Jossey-Bass, 2010).

7 Narvaez, *Neurobiology.*

8 David James Duncan, "The Unbreakable Thread," *The Sun,* November 2014, 45.

9 Joo-yeon Christina Ri, "The Last Leaf: A Triangulated Study of a 'Sights and Sounds of Nature' Film Motivator for Ecologically Sustainable Practices" (PhD diss., Fielding Graduate University, 2008).

10 Kristen R. Monroe, *The Hand of Compassion: Portraits of Moral Choice During the Holocaust* (Princeton, NJ: Princeton University Press, 2004).

11 Darcia Narvaez and Tonia Bock, "Developing Ethical Expertise and Moral Personalities," in Larry Nucci and Darcia Narvaez, eds., *Handbook of Moral and Character Education,* 2nd ed. (New York: Routledge, 2014), 140–58.

12 Angela Kurth, Reilly Kohn, Andrea Bae, and Darcia Narvaez, "Nature Connection: A 3-Week Intervention Increased Ecological Attachment," *Ecopsychology* 12, no. 2 (2020): 1–17, https://doi.org/10.1089/eco.2019.0038.

4. Understanding/Embracing Death and Dying

1 Dianne M. Longboat, "Indigenous Perspectives on Death and Dying," in *Ian Anderson Continuing Education Program in End-of-Life Care,* module 10, University of Toronto, 2002, www.cpd.utoronto.ca/endoflife/Modules/Indigenous %20Perspectives%20on%20Death%20and%20Dying.pdf.

2 Larry Dossey, "Is the Soul Obsolete?" Science and Nonduality, March 16, 2017, video, 37:01, www.youtube.com/watch?v=DSUfQH2MhFM.

3 Gregory Shushan, "Near-Death Experience in Indigenous Religions," *Oxford Scholarship Online,* August 2018, https://oxford.universitypressscholarship.com /view/10.1093/oso/9780190872472.001.0001/oso-9780190872472.

4 Barbara G. Walker, *The Crone: Woman of Age, Wisdom and Power* (New York: HarperOne, 1985).

5 Iain McGilchrist, *The Master and His Emissary: The Divided Brain and the Making of the Western World* (New Haven, CT: Yale University Press, 2009).

6 Alexander R. Luria, *Cognitive Development: Its Cultural and Social Foundations,* trans. M. Lopez Morillas and L. Solataroff (Cambridge, MA: Harvard University Press, 1976).

7 Cynthia Bourgeault, *The Wisdom Way of Knowing: Reclaiming an Ancient Tradition to Awaken the Heart* (San Francisco: Jossey-Bass, 2003).

8 Christian De Quincey, *Radical Knowing: Understanding Consciousness through Relationship* (Rochester, VT: Park Street Press, 2005), 32.

5. Emphasis on Community Welfare

1 Wikipedia, s.v. "Enriqueta Contreras," last modified March 11, 2020, 12:46, https://es.wikipedia.org/wiki/Enriqueta_Contreras.

2 Chet A. Bowers, *Mindful Conservatism: Rethinking the Ideological and Educational Basis of an Ecologically Sustainable Future* (Lanham, MA: Rowman & Littlefield, 2003).

3 Darcia Narvaez, Four Arrows, Eugene Halton, Brian Collier, and Georges Enderle, eds., *Indigenous Sustainable Wisdom: First Nation Know-How for Global Flourishing* (New York: Peter Lang, 2019).

4 "La Ciudad Perdida (The Lost City)," Ciudad Perdida, December 15, 2011, video, 1:26:53, www.youtube.com/watch?v=Tq0kWs1q3hI&t.

5 Thomas W. Cooper, *A Time before Deception: Truth in Communication, Culture, and Ethics* (Santa Fe: Clear Light Publications, 1998), 98.

6 "Aluna," accessed August 30, 2021, https://web.archive.org/web/20120531035111 /http://www.alunathemovie.com/en.

7 The Coguí are also known as Kogi or Kágaba, meaning "jaguar."

8 Jon Young, "Connection Modeling Metrics for Deep Nature-Connection, Mentoring and Culture Repair," in Darcia Narvaez, Four Arrows, Eugene Halton, Brian Collier, and Georges Enderle, eds., *Indigenous Sustainable Wisdom: First Nation Know-How for Global Flourishing* (New York: Peter Lang, 2019), 219–43.

9 James Clark Moloney, *Fear: Contagion and Conquest* (New York: Philosophical Library, 1957), 53.

10 To see images of Pino Gordo, go to: www.youtube.com/watch?v=siI8vxZZK5w.

11 Claire Revol, "Henri Lefebvre's Rhythm Analysis as a Form of Urban Poetics," in Michael E. Leary-Owhin and John P. McCarthy, eds., *The Routledge Handbook of Henri Lefebvre, the City and Urban Society* (New York: Routledge, 2019), https:// halshs.archives-ouvertes.fr/halshs-02010529/document.

6. High Respect for the Sacred Feminine

1 Four Arrows, ed., *Unlearning the Language of Conquest* (Austin: University of Texas Press, 2008); Douglas P. Fry, *The Human Potential for Peace: An Anthropological Challenge to Assumptions about War and Violence* (New York: Oxford University Press, 2006).

2 Four Arrows, "The Media Missed a Crucial Message in the UN's Biodiversity Report," *The Nation,* May 26, 2019, www.thenation.com/article/archive /biodiversity-un-report-Indigenous-worldview.

3 Barbara Mann, "Where Are Your Women? Missing in Action," in Four Arrows, ed., *Unlearning the Language of Conquest* (Austin: University of Texas Press, 2008), 129.

4 Heide Goettner-Abendroth, *Matriarchal Societies: Studies on Indigenous Cultures across the Globe* (New York: Peter Lang, 2013).

5 Online Etymology Dictionary, s.v. "archetype," accessed August 30, 2021, www.etymonline.com/word/archetype.

6 Heide Goettner-Abendroth, "Re-thinking 'Matriarchy' in Modern Matriarchal Studies Using Two Examples: The Khasi and the Mosuo," *Asian Journal of Women's Studies* 24, no. 1 (2018): 3–27, doi.org/10.1080/12259276.2017.1421293.

7 Goettner-Abendroth, "Re-thinking 'Matriarchy,'" 25.

8 Marvin Bram, *A History of Humanity* (Delhi: Primus Books, 2018).

9 Carolyn Merchant, *The Death of Nature: Women, Ecology and the Scientific Revolution* (New York: Harper & Row, 1983), 2.

10 David Naveh and Nurit Bird-David, "How Persons Become Things: Economic and Epistemological Changes among Nayaka Hunter-Gatherers," *Journal of the Royal Anthropological Institute* 20 (2014): 74–92.

11 Dacher Keltner, *The Paradox of Power* (New York: Penguin, 2017).

12 Christopher Boehm, *Hierarchy in the Forest: The Evolution of Egalitarian Behavior* (Cambridge, MA: Harvard University Press, 1999).

13 "The Relationship between Nature and Culture," *Britannica,* accessed August 30, 2021, www.britannica.com/topic/history-of-Europe/The-relationship-between -nature-and-culture.

14 Howard Teich, *Solar Light, Lunar Light: Perspectives in Human Consciousness* (Sheridan, WY: Genoa House, 2021).

15 Charlotte Black Elk, "The Homelands of Religion: The Clash of Worldviews over Prayer, Place, and Ceremony," in Phil Cousineau, ed., *A Seat at the Table: Huston Smith in Conversation with Native Americans on Religious Freedom* (Berkeley: University of California Press, 2006), 58–74.

16 Lee T. Gettler, "Applying Socioendocrinology to Evolutionary Models: Fatherhood and Physiology," *Evolutionary Anthropology* 23, no. 4 (2014): 146–60.

17 Sarah Hrdy, *Mothers and Others: The Evolutionary Origins of Mutual Understanding* (Cambridge, MA: Belknap Press, 2009.)

18 See the work of Genevieve Vaughan at http://gift-economy.com/gift-giving-as -the-female-principle-vs-patriarchal-capitalism.

19 Allan N. Schore, "All Our Sons: The Developmental Neurobiology and Neuroendocrinology of Boys at Risk," *Infant Mental Health Journal* 38, no. 1 (2017): 15–52.

20 James W. Prescott, "The Origins of Human Love and Violence," *Pre- and Perinatal Psychology Journal* 10, no. 3 (1996): 143–88.

21 Robin L. Fox, *Augustine: Conversions to Confessions* (New York: Basic Books, 2015).

22 Philip Greven, *The Protestant Temperament: Patterns of Child-Rearing, Religious Experience and the Self in Early America* (New York: Knopf, 1977); Philip Greven, *Spare the Child: The Religious Roots of Punishment and the Psychological Impact of Physical Abuse* (New York: Knopf, 1991).

23 Darcia Narvaez, *Neurobiology and the Development of Human Morality: Evolution, Culture, and Wisdom* (New York: W. W. Norton, 2014).

24 Elizabeth T. Gershoff, "Spanking and Child Development: We Know Enough Now to Stop Hitting Our Children," *Child Development Perspectives* 7, no. 3 (2013): 133–37.

25 Rosemary Radford Ruether, *Sexism and God-Talk: Toward a Feminist Theology* (Boston: Beacon Press, 1983), 143–44.

26 Christian De Quincey, *Radical Knowing: Understanding Consciousness through Relationship* (Rochester, VT: Park Street Press, 2005), 38.

27 Alex White Plume, "As Pandemic Rips Through Indian Country, Indigenous Communities Work to Save Elders and Languages," *Democracy Now!*, January 21, 2021, www.democracynow.org/2021/1/22/native_elders_Indigenous _language_preservation_covid.

7. Respect for Gender Role Fluidity

1 Navajo Nation Human Rights Commission, *The Status of Navajo Women and Gender Violence: Conversations with Diné Traditional Medicine People and a Dialogue with the People,* July 26, 2016, www.nnhrc.navajo-nsn.gov/docs/NewsRpt Resolution/PublicHearingReports/The%20Status%20of%20Navajo%20Women %20and%20Gender%20Violence%20Report%20-%20Copy.pdf.

2 Navajo Nation, *Status,* 18.

3 Navajo Nation, 116.

4 Darcia Narvaez, *Neurobiology and the Development of Human Morality: Evolution, Culture, and Wisdom* (New York: W. W. Norton, 2014).

5 David Bohm, *Thought as a System* (London: Routledge, 1994).

6 Barry Commoner, *The Closing Circle: Nature, Man & Technology* (New York: Alfred A. Knopf, 1972), 41. The second law of ecology is that nothing is destroyed, only recycled. The third law is that nature knows best. Also see: Holmes Rolston III, *Philosophy Gone Wild* (Buffalo, NY: Prometheus Books, 1989).

7 Cynthia Bourgeault, *The Wisdom Way of Knowing: Reclaiming an Ancient Tradition to Awaken the Heart* (San Francisco: Jossey-Bass, 2013).

8 Joseph Chilton Pearce, *The Bond of Power* (New York: Elsevier-Dutton, 1981), 38–39.

9 Pearce, *Bond*, 39.

10 Tim Ingold, "On the Social Relations of the Hunter-Gatherer Band," in Richard B. Lee and Richard Daly, eds., *The Cambridge Encyclopedia of Hunters and Gatherers* (New York: Cambridge University Press, 2005), 399–410.

11 Interaction Design Foundation, "Affordances," accessed August 30, 2021, www.interaction-design.org/literature/topics/affordances.

12 "Online Variorum of Darwin's *Origin of Species*: First British Edition (1859), Page 490," Darwin Online, accessed August 30, 2021, http://darwin-online.org.uk/Variorum/1859/1859-490-c-1860.html. See also: Sean Carroll, *Endless Forms Most Beautiful: The New Science of Evo Devo* (New York: W. W. Norton, 2005).

13 Barry Lopez, *Horizon* (New York: Alfred A. Knopf, 2019).

14 Marvin Bram, *A History of Humanity* (Delhi: Primus Books, 2018).

15 Roy J. Eidelson and Judy I. Eidelson, "Dangerous Ideas: Five Beliefs That Propel Groups Toward Conflict," *American Psychologist* 58 (2003): 182–92.

16 Jack D. Forbes, *Columbus and Other Cannibals: The Wétiko Disease of Exploitation, Imperialism, and Terrorism*, rev. ed. (New York: Seven Stories Press, 2008).

17 https://evolvednest.org.

18 Lewis Yablonsky, *Robopaths: People as Machines* (New York: Pelican, 1972).

19 Charles Derber, *Sociopathic Society: A People's Sociology of the United States* (Boulder, CO: Paradigm Press, 2013).

20 Iris Murdoch, "Metaphysics and Ethics," in Maria Antonaccio and William Schweiker, eds., *Iris Murdoch and the Search for Human Goodness* (Chicago: University of Chicago Press, 1996), 236–52.

21 Murdoch, "Metaphysics," 250.

8. Nonmaterialistic Barter, Gift, and Kinship Economics

1 Lewis Hyde, *The Gift: Imagination and the Erotic Life of Property* (New York: Vintage, 1983).

2 Daniel Quinn, *Ishmael* (New York: Bantam, 1992).

3 Timothy Kasser, *The High Price of Materialism* (Cambridge, MA: MIT Press, 2002).

4 "Enoughness: Restoring Balace to the Economy in the Most Awesome Way Ever," Films for Action, accessed August 30, 2021, www.filmsforaction.org/watch/enoughness-restoring-balance-to-the-economy.

5 Ella Deloria, "Yankton Dakota," in Judith Fitzgerald and Michael Oren, eds., *The Spirit of Indian Women* (Bloomington, IN: World Wisdom, 2005), 114.

6 Genevieve Vaughan, "Introduction: A Radically Different Worldview Is Possible," in G. Vaughan, ed., *Women and the Gift Economy* (Toronto, ON: Inanna Publications, 2007), 1–40.

7 Vaughan, "Introduction," 8.

8 Donald Worster, *Nature's Economy: A History of Ecological Ideas,* 2nd ed. (Cambridge, UK: Cambridge University Press, 1994).

9 Elliot W. Eisner, *The Educational Imagination* (New York: Macmillan, 1979).

10 Benjamin Franklin, "Remarks Concerning the Savages of North America," Wampum Chronicles, accessed August 30, 2021, www.wampumchronicles.com /benfranklin.html.

9. All Earth Entities Are Sentient

1 Robin Wall Kimmerer, *Braiding Sweetgrass: Indigenous Wisdom, Scientific Knowledge, and the Teachings of Plants* (Minneapolis: Milkweed Editions, 2013), 34.

2 Kimmerer, *Braiding,* 39.

3 Kimmerer, 37.

4 James Yeh, "Robin Wall Kimmerer: People Can't Understand the World as a Gift Unless Someone Shows Them How," *The Guardian,* May 23, 2020, www .theguardian.com/books/2020/may/23/robin-wall-kimmerer-people-cant -understand-the-world-as-a-gift-unless-someone-shows-them-how.

5 Four Arrows, *The Red Road: Connecting Diversity and Inclusions Initiatives to Indigenous Worldview* (Charlotte, NC: Information Age Publishing, 2020).

6 The songs and lyrics are available at https://evolvednest.org.

7 Jane Goodall with Phillip Berman, *Reason for Hope: A Spiritual Journey* (New York: Grand Central Publishing, 1999), 82.

8 Goodall, *Reason,* 74.

10. The Sacred Nature of Competition and Games

1 Tabitha Maarshal, "Shirley and Sharon Firth," *Canadian Encyclopedia,* September 24, 2013, www.thecanadianencyclopedia.ca/en/article/shirley-and-sharon-firth.

2 Joseph Oxendine, *American Indian Sports Heritage* (Champaign, IL: HumanKinetics, 1988), 5.

3 Peter Nabokov, *Indian Running: Native American Running and Tradition* (Santa Fe, NM: Ancient City Press, 1987).

4 John Watson, "The Relation of Philosophy to Science," in James D. Rabb, ed., *Religion and Science in Early Canada* (Kingston, ON: Ronald P. Frye, 1988), 37–38.

5 Peter Gray, "Play Theory of Hunter-Gatherer Egalitarianism," in Darcia Narvaez, Kristin Valentino, Agustin Fuentes, James J. McKenna, and Peter Gray, eds., *Ancestral Landscapes in Human Evolution: Culture, Childrearing and Social Wellbeing* (New York: Oxford University Press, 2014), 192–215.

6 Gray, "Play Theory," 193.

7 Greg Cajete, *Look to the Mountain: An Ecology of Indigenous Education* (Santa Fe, NM: Clear Light, 1994), 170–80.

8 Valery Pavlovich Krasilnikov, "Traditional Games and Competitions in Original Physical Training of Siberian Indigenous Population," *efdeportes.com* 11, no. 2 (November 2006), www.efdeportes.com/efd102/siberia.htm.

9 Colin M. Turnbull, *The Human Cycle* (New York: Simon and Schuster, 1984).

10 Quoted in Gray, "Play Theory," 201.

11. Nonanthropocentrism

1 Your Dictionary, accessed August 30, 2021, https://quotes.yourdictionary.com /author/quote/574482.

2 Robert Lanza with Bob Berman, *Beyond Biocentrism: Rethinking Time* (Dallas: BenBella Books, 2016), 87.

3 Martin Drenthen, "Ecocentrism as Anthropocentrism in Ethics, Policy and Environment," *Ethics, Policy and Environment* 14, no. 2 (June 2011): 151–54.

4 William McDougall, "Animism in the Ancient World," in William McDougall, ed., *Body and Mind: A History and a Defense of Animism* (New York: Macmillan, 1913), 1–27, https://doi.org/10.1037/13043-001.

5 Jens Korff, "What Is Aboriginal Spirituality?" Creative Spirits, May 7, 2019, www .creativespirits.info/aboriginalculture/spirituality/what-is-aboriginal-spirituality.

6 https://indigenouspathways.com/resources/NAIITS-Journal/NAIITS-Volume-11.pdf.

7 Four Arrows, "'False Doctrine' and the Stifling of Indigenous Political Will," *Critical Education* 5, no. 13 (September 15, 2014), https://ices.library.ubc.ca/index .php/criticaled/article/view/184496.

8 Four Arrows, *Unlearning the Language of Conquest: Scholars Expose Anti-Indianism in America* (Austin: University of Texas Press, 2008).

9 Four Arrows, "Roy Rogers, Twin Heroes, and Exclusive Salvation," in Four Arrows, ed., *Unlearning the Language of Conquest: Scholars Expose Anti-Indianism in America* (Austin: University of Texas Press, 2008), 144–45.

10 Hyllus Maris, "Spiritual Song of the Aborigine," Worawa Aboriginal College, accessed August 30, 2021, www.worawa.vic.edu.au/our-school/aboriginal -culture/spiritual-song-of-the-aborigine.

11 Darcia Narvaez, *Neurobiology and the Development of Human Morality: Evolution, Culture, and Wisdom* (New York: W. W. Norton, 2014), 251.

12 Colin M. Turnbull, *The Human Cycle* (New York: Simon and Schuster, 1984), 76–77.

12. Words Are Sacred (Truthfulness)

1 Thomas W. Cooper, *A Time before Deception: Truth in Communication, Culture, and Ethics* (Santa Fe, NM: Clear Light Publications, 1998), 3.

2 Quoted in Steve Wall, *To Become a Human Being: The Message of Tadodaho Chief Leon Shenandoah* (Charlottesville, VA: Hampton Roads, 2001), 15.

3 Mary Tarsha and Darcia Narvaez, "The Evolved Nest: A Partnership System That Fosters Child Wellbeing," *International Journal of Partnership Studies* 6, no. 3 (2019), https://doi.org/10.24926/ijps.v6i3.2244.

4 E. Richard Sorenson, "Preconquest Consciousness," in Helmut Wautischer, ed., *Tribal Epistemologies* (Aldershot, UK: Ashgate, 1998), 97.

5 Jane Mayer, *Dark Money: The Hidden History of the Billionaires behind the Rise of the Radical Right* (New York: Anchor, 2017).

6 Quoted in Four Arrows, ed., *Teaching Truly: A Curriculum to Indigenize Mainstream Education* (New York: Peter Lang, 2013), 74–78.

7 David Livingston Smith, *Why We Lie: The Evolutionary Roots of Deception and the Unconscious Mind* (New York: St. Martin's Press, 2007), 146.

8 Four Arrows, Greg Cajete, and Jonmin Lee, eds., *Critical Neurophilosophy and Indigenous Wisdom* (Rotterdam, Netherlands: Sense Publishers, 2010), 35.

9 Jiddu Krishnamurti, "This Matter of Culture-1964," in Michael Mendizza, ed., *Unconditionally Free: The Life and Insights of J. Krishnamurti* (Ojai, CA: Krishnamurti Foundation of America, 2020), 165–66.

10 Robert M. Fisher, "Teaching as a Fear Vaccine: Response-Ability in Pandemics," In Search of Fearlessness Research Institute, technical paper no. 116., October 26, 2020, https://prism.ucalgary.ca/bitstream/handle/1880/112708/Tech%20Paper%20116.pdf?sequence=1.

13. Mutual Dependence

1 Abraham H. Maslow, *The Farther Reaches of Human Nature* (New York: Viking, 1971).

2 Kirkpatrick Sale, *After Eden: The Evolution of Human Domination* (Durham, NC: Duke University Press, 2006).

3 Lucien Lévy-Bruhl, *How Natives Think*, trans. Lilian A. Clare (Eastford, CT: Martino Fine Books, 2015).

4 Marvin Bram, *A History of Humanity* (Delhi: Primus Books, 2018).

5 Rob Dunn, *The Wild Life of Our Bodies: Predators, Parasites, and Partners That Shape Who We Are Today* (New York: Harper, 2011).

6 "Oil & Gas Pollution's Impacts on North Dakota Families," Dakota Resource Council, 2017, http://drcinfo.org/wp-content/uploads/2017/08/ND-Methane-Report-DRC.pdf.

7 Beth Gardiner, "Why Covid-19 Will End Up Harming the Environment," *National Geographic,* June 18, 2020, www.nationalgeographic.com/science/2020/06/why-covid-19-will-end-up-harming-the-environment/.

8 Quoted in Jeff Tollefson, "Why Deforestation and Extinctions Make Pandemics More Likely," *Nature,* August 7, 2020, www.nature.com/articles/d41586 -020-02341-1.

14. Complementary Duality

1 Paula Allen Gunn, *The Sacred Hoop: Recovering the Feminine in American Indian Traditions* (Boston: Beacon Press, 1986), 3.

2 Barbara Ehrenreich and Deirdre English, *Witches, Midwives & Nurses: A History of Women Healers,* 2nd ed. (New York: Feminist Press, 2010).

3 Maureen Murdock, *The Heroine's Journey* (Boulder, CO: Shambala, 1980).

4 Darcia Narvaez, Angela M. Kurth, and Mary S. Tarsha, "The Centrality of Mothering for Human Flourishing," in Kaarina Kailo and Erella Shadmi, eds., *Matriarchal Values, Free Maternal Gift-Giving and Child-Rearing: Essays in Honor of Genevieve Vaughan* (Finland: Kaarina Kailo, 2020), 161.

5 David Maybury-Lewis, "The Quest for Harmony," in David Maybury-Lewis and Uri Almagor, eds., *The Attraction of Opposites: Thought and Society in the Dualistic Mode* (Ann Arbor: University of Michigan Press, 1989), 1–17.

6 Howard Teich, "The Twins: An Archetypal Perspective," Solar Lunar, accessed August 30, 2021, https://solarlunar.com/articles/the-twins-archetype.

7 Carl Jung, *Mysterium Coniunctionis,* Collected Works, ed. and trans. Gerhard Adler and R. F. C. Hull, vol. 14, 2nd ed. (Princeton, NJ: Princeton University Press, 1970), 134.

8 Kenneth L. Golden, *Uses of Comparative Mythology: Essays on the Work of Joseph Campbell* (New York: Routledge, 2015), 88.

9 Four Arrows, *Point of Departure: Returning to Our More Authentic Worldview for Education and Survival* (Charlotte, NC: Information Age Publishing, 2018).

10 Teich, "The Twins."

11 Jack D. Forbes, *Columbus and Other Cannibals: The Wétiko Disease of Exploitation, Imperialism, and Terrorism,* rev ed. (New York: Seven Stories Press, 2008).

12 Iain McGilchrist, *The Master and His Emissary: The Divided Brain and the Making of the Western World* (New Haven, CT: Yale University Press, 2009).

13 Gunn, *Sacred Hoop.*

14 Daniel Pauly, "Anecdotes and the Shifting Baseline Syndrome of Fisheries," *Trends in Ecology and Evolution* 10, no. 10 (1995): 430.

15 Darcia Narvaez, David S. Moore, David C. Witherington, Timothy L. Vandiver, and Robert Lickliter, "Evolving Evolutionary Psychology," *American Psychologist,* in press.

16 Darcia Narvaez, *Neurobiology and the Development of Human Morality: Evolution, Culture, and Wisdom* (New York, NY: W. W. Norton, 2014).

17 Daniel J. Goldhagen, *Worse Than War: Genocide, Eliminationism, and the Ongoing Assault on Humanity* (New York: Public Affairs, 2009).

18 Hillary S. Webb, "The Splendid and the Savage: The Dance of Opposites in Indigenous Andean Thought," *Journal of Transpersonal Research* 4 (2012): 69–93, https://philpapers.org/archive/WEBTSA.

15. Generosity as Way of Life

1 Larry Brendtro, Martin Brokenleg, and Steve Van Bockern, *Reclaiming Youth at Risk: Our Hope for the Future*, 3rd ed. (Bloomington, IN: Solution Tree Press, 2019).

2 Martin Brokenleg, "Indigenous Perspectives on Mastery," *Reclaiming Children and Youth* 7, no. 4 (winter 1999): 194–96, http://martinbrokenleg.com/wp-content/uploads/2016/02/07_4_Brokenleg.pdf.

3 Christopher Columbus, "Letter to King Ferdinand of Spain, Describing the Results of the First Voyage," American Studies at the University of Virginia, accessed August 30, 2021, https://xroads.virginia.edu/~Hyper/HNS/Garden/columbus.html.

4 Greg Cajete, "Generosity," in Four Arrows, Greg Cajete, and Jongmin Lee, eds., *Critical Neurophilosophy and Indigenous Wisdom* (Rotterdam, Netherlands: Sense Publishers, 2010), 11.

5 Jennifer Mitchell and Shahzad Chaudhry, "Neuroscience Studies Overview," in Four Arrows, Greg Cajete, and Jongmin Lee, eds., *Critical Neurophilosophy and Indigenous Wisdom* (Rotterdam, Netherlands: Sense Publishers, 2010), 1.

6 Candice Gaukel Andrews, "Is Animal Altruism Real?" *Good Nature Travel* (blog), *Natural Habitat Adventures,* February 5, 2013, www.nathab.com/blog/is-animal-altruism-real.

7 Darcia Narvaez, "Humility in Four Forms: Intrapersonal, Interpersonal, Community, and Ecological," in Jennifer Wright, ed., *Humility* (New York: Oxford University Press, 2019), 117–45.

8 John L. Weil, *Early Deprivation of Empathic Care* (Madison, WI: International Universities Press, 1992).

9 James Woodburn, "Egalitarian Societies," *Man* 17 (1982): 431–51.

10 David Harvey, *A Brief History of Neoliberalism* (New York: Oxford University Press, 2005).

11 Gary Weiss, *Ayn Rand Nation: The Hidden Struggle for America's Soul* (New York: Macmillan, 2012).

12 Anand Giridharadas, *Winners Take All: The Elite Charade of Changing the World* (New York: Knopf, 2018).

13 Four Arrows, *Unlearning the Language of Conquest: Scholars Expose Anti-Indianism in America* (Austin: University of Texas Press, 2008).

14 "South Korea," Countries and Their Cultures, accessed August 30, 2021, www
.everyculture.com/Ja-Ma/South-Korea.html#ixzz6fHEM5tit.

15 Karen Armstrong, *The Great Transformation: The Beginnings of Our Religious Traditions* (New York: Knopf, 2006).

16 Father John Romanides, "What Is the Human Nous? Chapter 1 from *Patristic
Theology*," Orthodox Christian Information Center, April 29, 2008, http://
orthodoxinfo.com/phronema/patristic-theology-romanides-chapter-1-what
-is-the-human-nous.aspx.

17 Sotiris Mitralexis, "Person, Eros, Critical Ontology: An Attempt To Recapitulate
Christos Yannaras' Philosophy," July 9, 2012, www.academia.edu/3801424
/Person_Eros_Critical_Ontology_An_Attempt_to_Recapitulate_Christos
_Yannaras_Philosophy.

18 Darcia Narvaez, "Baselines for Virtue," in Julia Annas, Darcia Narvaez, and Nancy
Snow, eds., *Developing the Virtues: Integrating Perspectives* (New York: Oxford
University Press, 2016), 14–33.

19 "The Science of Generosity," John Templeton Foundation, accessed August 30,
2021, www.templeton.org/discoveries/the-science-of-generosity.

16. Ceremony as Life Sustaining

1 Linda Hogan, "The History of Red," in *The Book of Medicines* (Minneapolis:
Coffee House Press, 1993), 9.

2 Carole Kammen and Jodi Gold, *Call to Connection: Bringing Sacred Tribal Values
into Modern Life* (Salt Lake City: Commune-A-Key, 1998).

3 Cynthia Bourgeault, *The Heart of Centering Prayer: Nondual Christianity in Theory
and Practice* (Boulder, CO: Shambala, 2016).

4 Quoted in Steve Wall, *To Become a Human Being: The Message of Tadodaho Chief
Leon Shenandoah* (Charlottesville, VA: Hampton Roads, 2001), 27.

5 Wall, *To Become*, 29.

6 Dan Harris and Lauren Effron, "James Ray Found Guilty of Homicide in Arizona
Sweat Lodge Case," ABC News, June 22, 2011, https://abcnews.go.com/US
/james-ray-found-guilty-negligent-homicide-arizona-sweat/story?id=13908037.

7 War Against Exploiters of Lakota Spirituality, "Preventing the Exploitation of
Native American Cultures," 1998, www.digitalhistory.uh.edu/disp_textbook
.cfm?smtid=3&psid=730.

8 Frank Fools Crow and Thomas Mails, *Fools Crow* (Lincoln: University of
Nebraska Press, 1990), 51.

9 Daniel Wolpert, *Creation's Wisdom: Spiritual Practice and Climate Change* (Mary-
knoll, NY: Orbis, 2020).

17. Humor as Essential

1 Elizabeth Blair, "Native American Comic Living the 'Indigenous Dream,'" NPR, June 21, 2012, www.npr.org/2012/06/21/155116734/native-american-comic-living-the-Indigenous-dream.

2 Quoted in Drew Hayden Taylor, *Me Funny* (Madeira Park, BC: Douglas & McIntyre, 2006), 36.

3 Punyashree Panda, "The Back of the Turtle: An Ecocritical Perspective," *Studies in American Humor* 6, no. 2 (2020): 24.

4 Jaroslav Tucek, "Power through Humor: Thomas King's Strategies for Decolonizing Canada" (PhD diss., University of Sakatchewan, 2006), 22.

5 Lawrence J. Cohen, *Playful Parenting* (New York: Ballantine Books, 2002).

6 Cohen, *Playful*, 78.

7 Colwyn Trevarthen and Jon-Roar Bjørkvold, "Life for Learning: How a Young Child Seeks Joy with Companions in a Meaningful World," in Darcia Narvaez, Julia Braungart-Rieker, Laura Miller-Graff, Lee Gettler, and Paul Hastings, eds., *Contexts for Young Child Flourishing: Evolution, Family and Society* (New York: Oxford University Press, 2016), 45.

8 Trevarthen and Bjørkvold, "Life for Learning," 36.

9 Margot Sunderland, *The Science of Parenting* (New York: DK Press, 2006).

10 Peter Gray, "Play Theory of Hunter-Gatherer Egalitarianism," in Darcia Narvaez, Kristin Valentino, Agustin Fuentes, James J. McKenna, and Peter Gray, eds., *Ancestral Landscapes in Human Evolution: Culture, Childrearing and Social Wellbeing* (New York: Oxford University Press, 2014), 192–215.

11 Steve Allen, *Make 'Em Laugh* (Buffalo, NY: Prometheus, 1993).

12 Adam Blatner and Allee Blatner, *The Art of Play: Helping Adults Reclaim Imagination and Spontaneity* (New York: Brunner/Mazel, 1997).

13 Films for Action, "The War on Kids (2009)," accessed August 30, 2021, www.filmsforaction.org/watch/the-war-on-kids-2009/.

14 Aletha J. Solter, *Attachment Play: How to Solve Children's Behavior Problems with Play, Laughter, and Connection* (Goleta, CA: Shining Star Press, 2013).

18. Conflict Resolution as Return to Community

1 International Institute for Restorative Practices, "3. History," *Defining Restorative,* accessed August 30, 2021, www.iirp.edu/defining-restorative/history.

2 Denise C. Breton, "Decolonizing Restorative Justice," in Unsettling Minnesota Collective, eds., *Reflections and Resources for Deconstructing Colonial Mentality: A Sourcebook,* https://unsettlingminnesota.files.wordpress.com/2009/11/um_sourcebook_jan10_revision.pdf.

3 Rupert Ross, *Indigenous Healing: Exploring Traditional Paths* (Toronto, ON: Penguin Canada, 2014); *Dancing with a Ghost: Exploring Aboriginal Reality* (Toronto, ON: Penguin Canada, 2006); *Returning to the Teachings: Exploring Aboriginal Justice* (Toronto, ON: Penguin Canada, 2006).

4 Ross, *Indigenous*, 253, 252.

5 Ross, 252.

6 Ross, 261.

7 Ross, 260.

8 Edward O. Wilson, "Biodiversity, Prosperity, and Value," in F. Herbert Bormann and Stephen R. Kellert, eds., *Ecology, Economics, Ethics: The Broken Circle* (New Haven, CT: Yale University Press, 1991).

9 Chet A. Bowers, "Toward an Eco-Justice Pedagogy," *Environmental Education Research* 8, no. 1, (2002): 21–34, https://doi.org/10.1080/13504620120109628.

10 Marshall B. Rosenberg, *Nonviolent Communication: A Language of Life*, 2nd ed. (Encinitas, CA: PuddleDancer Press, 2003).

11 Marshall B. Rosenberg, *Speak Peace in a World of Conflict: What You Say Next Will Change Your World* (Encinitas, CA: PuddleDancer Press, 2005).

12 E. Richard Sorenson, "Preconquest Consciousness," in Helmut Wautischer, ed., *Tribal Epistemologies* (Aldershot, UK: Ashgate, 1998), 79–115.

13 Sorenson, "Preconquest," 7.

14 Albert Einstein Institution, "198 Methods of Nonviolent Action," accessed August 30, 2021, www.aeinstein.org/nonviolentaction/198-methods-of-nonviolent -action.

15 International Center on Nonviolent Conflict, accessed August 30, 2021, www .nonviolent-conflict.org.

19. Laws of Nature as Highest Rules for Living

1 Dennis Martinez, Enrique Salmón, and Melissa K. Nelson, "Restoring Indigenous History and Culture to Nature," in Melissa K. Nelson, ed., *Original Instructions* (Rochester, VT: Bear & Co, 2008), 101.

2 William Easterly, *The White Man's Burden: Why the West's Efforts to Aid the Rest Have Done So Much Ill and So Little Good* (London: Penguin, 2007).

3 Darcia Narvaez, "Species-Typical Phronesis for a Living Planet," in Mario De Caro and Maria S. Vaccarezza, eds., *Practical Wisdom: Philosophical and Psychological Perspectives* (London: Routledge, 2021), 160–80.

4 John Perkins, *The New Confessions of an Economic Hitman*, 2nd ed. (San Francisco: Berrett-Koehler Publishers, 2016).

5 David Korten, *Change the Story, Change the Future* (Oakland, CA: Berrett-Koehler Publishers, 2015).

6 Guy R. McPherson, "The Means by Which COVID-19 Could Cause Extinction of All Life on Earth," *Environmental Analysis & Ecology Studies* 7, no. 2 (2020): 711–13; Rajani Canth, "On Imminent Human Extinction," October 13, 2018, https://litvote.com.

7 Jean Liedloff, *The Continuum Concept* (Cambridge, MA: Perseus Books, 1977).

8 R. D. Laing, *The Divided Self* (London: Penguin, 1959/1990), 17.

9 Tiokasin Ghoshorse, "Living with Relativity: The Story of *Mni*," Center for Humans and Nature, August 26, 2016, www.humansandnature.org/living-with-relativity.

20. Becoming Fully Human

1 Abraham Maslow, *Motivation and Personality*, 2nd ed. (New York: Harper & Row, 1970).

2 Steve Taylor, "Original Influences: How the Ideals of America Were Shaped by Native Americans," *Psychology Today*, March 22, 2019, www.psychologytoday.com/intl/blog/out-the-darkness/201903/original-influences.

3 Edward Hoffman, "Abraham Maslow: A Biographical Sketch," in *Future Visions: The Unpublished Papers of Abraham Maslow* (Newbury Park, CA: Sage, 1996).

4 Karen Lincoln Michel, "Maslow's Hierarchy Connected to Blackfoot Beliefs," April 19, 2014, https://lincolnmichel.wordpress.com/2014/04/19/maslows-hierarchy-connected-to-blackfoot-beliefs/.

5 For documentation of Maslow's notes on this, see Sidney Brown's book *Transformation Beyond Greed: Native Self-Actualization* (The Book Patch, 2014).

6 Four Arrows, *Point of Departure: Returning to Our More Authentic Worldview for Education and Survival* (Charlotte, NC: Information Age Publishing, 2016), 119.

7 Robert F. Sayre, *Thoreau and the American Indians* (Princeton, NJ: Princeton University Press, 1977), 122.

8 Sayre, *Thoreau*, 24.

9 Tim Ingold, *The Perception of the Environment: Essay on Livelihood, Dwelling and Skill* (London: Routledge, 2011), 69.

10 Quoted in Steve Wall, *To Become a Human Being: The Message of Tadodaho Chief Leon Shenandoah* (Charlottesville, VA: Hampton Roads, 2001), xii.

11 Darcia Narvaez, "The Ontogenesis of Human Moral Becoming," in Agustin Fuentes and A. Visala, eds., *Verbs, Bones and Brains: Interdisciplinary Perspectives on Human Nature* (Notre Dame, IN: University of Notre Dame Press, 2016), 114–21.

12 Stephen H. Buhner, *Sacred Plant Medicine: The Wisdom in Native American Herbalism* (Rochester, VT: Bear & Co., 2006), xiii.

13 Melissa K. Nelson, "Mending the Split-Head Society with Trickster Consciousness," in Melissa K. Nelson, ed., *Original Instructions: Indigenous Teachings for a Sustainable Future* (Rochester, VT: Little Bear & Co, 2008), 291.

14 Chief Leon Shenandoah, "Speech to the United Nations," Manitou Foundation and Institute & Conservancy, accessed August 30, 2021, www.manitou .org/chief-leon-shenandoah-un-speech-1985.

15 See his speech on videos at: Toby McLeod, "Hopi Prophecy: A Timeless Warning," Sacred Land Film Project, April 4, 2020, https://sacredland.org/hopi-prophecy/.

21. Nature Seen as Benevolent

1 Kent Nerburn, ed., *The Wisdom of the Native Americans* (Novato, CA: New World Library, 1999), 5.

2 Clinton Ober, Stephen T. Sinatra, and Martin Zucker, *Earthing: The Most Important Health Discovery Ever!* (Laguna Beach, CA: Basic Health Publications, 2010).

3 Stephen H. Buhner, *Sacred Plant Medicine: The Wisdom in Native American Herbalism* (Rochester, VT: Bear & Co., 2006).

4 Suzanne Simard, *Finding the Mother Tree: Discovering How the Forest Is Wired for Intelligence and Healing* (New York: Knopf, 2021).

5 Monica Gagliano, *Thus Spoke the Plant: A Remarkable Journey of Groundbreaking Scientific Discoveries and Personal Encounters with Plants* (Berkeley: North Atlantic Books, 2014).

6 Simard, *Finding*, xiii, xxi.

7 George Nicholas, "When Scientists 'Discover' What Indigenous People Have Known for Centuries," *Smithsonian Magazine,* February 21, 2018, www .smithsonianmag.com/science-nature/why-science-takes-so-long-catch -up-traditional-knowledge-180968216.

8 Four Arrows and Walter Block, *Differing Worldviews in Higher Education: Two Scholars Argue Cooperatively about Justice Education* (Rotterdam: Sense Publishers, 2011), 62.

9 Peter Amato, "Hobbes, Darwinism and Conceptions of Human Nature," *Minerva—An Internet Journal of Philosophy,* 6 (2002), www.minerva.mic.ul.ie /vol6/hobbes.html.

10 Alvaro Giron-Sierra, "Kropotkin between Lamarck and Darwin: The Impossible Synthesis," *Asclepio* 55, no. 1 (2003), www.researchgate.net/publication/39392768 _Kropotkin_between_Lamarck_and_Darwin_The_impossible_synthesis.

11 Peter Kropotkin, *Mutual Aid: A Factor of Evolution* (London: Freedom Press, 1902/1992).

12 Let's not forget Aristotle's position in *Politics* that tame animals are better than wild ones and live better when ruled by humans, that men are by nature superior to women, etc.

13 Merlin Sheldrake, *Entangled Life: How Fungi Make Our Worlds, Change Our Minds and Shape Our Futures* (New York: Random House, 2021).

14 Lynn Margulis, *Symbiotic Planet: A New Look at Evolution* (Amherst, MA: Sciencewriters, 1998).

15 Rob Dunn, *The Wild Life of Our Bodies: Predators, Parasites, and Partners That Shape Who We Are Today* (New York: Harper, 2011).

16 Mary Midgely, *The Solitary Self: Darwin and the Selfish Gene* (Durham, UK: Acumen, 2010).

17 Algis Valiunas, "Darwin's World of Pain and Wonder," *The New Atlantis*, 26, fall 2009/winter 2010, www.thenewatlantis.com/publications/darwins-world-of -pain-and-wonder.

18 Charles Darwin, *On the Origin of Species* (Harmondsworth, UK: Penguin, 1859/1985), 116.

19 Charles Darwin, *The Descent of Man* (Princeton, NJ: Princeton University Press, 1871/1981).

20 Darcia Narvaez, "Are We Losing It? Darwin's Moral Sense and the Importance of Early Experience," in Richard Joyce, ed., *Routledge Handbook of Evolution and Philosophy* (London: Routledge, 2017), 322–32.

21 For more details, see Four Arrows, "The CAT-FAWN Connection: Using Metacognition and Indigenous Worldview for More Effective Character Education and Human Survival," *Journal of Moral Education* 45 (2016): 261–75. For trainings, visit www.catfawn.com.

22. Responsibility Emphasis

1 Luke Barnesmoore, personal communication, December 13, 2020. Luke was a doctoral student of Indigenous worldview and a prolific writer whose radical work was too much for his doctoral committee.

2 Sherri Mitchell, "Standing on Indigenous Rights," Maine Organic Farmers and Gardners Association, September 23, 2017, https://mofga.org/The-Fair/Keynote -Speaker-Index/Sherri-Mitchell-2017-Keynote-Speech.

3 Samuel P. Oliner and Pearl M. Oliner, *The Altruistic Personality: Rescuers of Jews in Nazi Europe* (New York: Free Press, 1988).

4 Malena Ernman, Beata Ernman, Svante Thunberg, and Greta Thunberg, *Our House Is on Fire: Scenes of a Family and a Planet in Crisis* (London: Penguin Books, 2020).

5 Barbara Rogoff, "Learning by Observing and Pitching in to Family and Community Endeavors: An Orientation," *Human Development* 57, no. 2–3 (2014): 69–81.

6 Larry Brendtro, Martin Brokenleg, and Steve Van Bockern, *Reclaiming Youth at Risk: Our Hope for the Future,* 3rd ed. (Bloomington, IN: Solution Tree Press, 2019). See also: www.edu.gov.mb.ca/k12/cur/cardev/gr9_found/courage _poster.pdf.

7 Diana Baumrind, "Harmonious Parents and Their Preschool Children," *Developmental Psychology* 4, no. 1 (1971): 99–102.

8 Darcia Narvaez, "Species-Typical Phronesis for a Living Planet," in Mario De Caro and Maria S. Vaccarezza, eds., *Practical Wisdom: Philosophical and Psychological Perspectives* (London: Routledge, 2021), 160–80.

9 James Rest, "Morality," in John Flavell and Ellen Markham, eds., *Cognitive Development,* Manual of Child Psychology, ed. Paul Mussen, vol. 3, 556–629 (New York: Wiley, 1983); Darcia Narvaez and James Rest, "The Four Components of Acting Morally," in William Kurtines and Jacob Gewirtz, eds., *Moral Behavior and Moral Development: An Introduction* (New York: McGraw-Hill), 385–400.

10 Darcia Narvaez, *Ethical Action,* Nurturing Character in the Classroom, EthEx series, book 4 (Notre Dame, IN: ACE Press, 2009); Darcia Narvaez and Tonia Bock, *Ethical Judgment,* Nurturing Character in the Classroom, EthEx series, book 2 (Notre Dame, IN: ACE Press, 2009); Darcia Narvaez and Leilani Endicott, *Ethical Sensitivity,* Nurturing Character in the Classroom, EthEx series, book 1 (Notre Dame, IN: ACE Press, 2009); Darcia Narvaez and James Lies, *Ethical Motivation,* Nurturing Character in the Classroom, EthEx series, book 3 (Notre Dame, IN: ACE Press, 2009).

11 Darcia Narvaez, *Neurobiology and the Development of Human Morality: Evolution, Culture, and Wisdom* (New York: W. W. Norton, 2014).

12 Darcia Narvaez, ed., *Basic Needs, Wellbeing and Morality: Fulfilling Human Potential* (New York: Palgrave-MacMillan, 2018); Darcia Narvaez and Mary S. Tarsha, "The Developmental Neurobiology of Moral Mindsets," in Martha Berg and Edward Chang, eds., *Motivation and Morality: A Biopsychosocial Approach* (Washington, DC: APA Books, in press).

23. Connection to the Land

1 Don Trent Jacobs, *Primal Awareness: A True Story of Survival, Transformation and Awakening with the Rarámuri Shamans of Mexico* (Rochester, VT: Inner Traditions International, 1998).

2 Alejandro Fujigaki Lares, "Rarámuri Pathways to Sustain or End the World: Ethnographic Theory, Climate Change and the Anthropocene," *Manna* 26, no. 1 (April 30, 2020): www.scielo.br/scielo.php?script=sci_abstract& pid=S0104-93132020000100202&lng=en&nrm=iso.

3 Quoted in Kathleen D. Moore, Kurt Peters, Ted Jojola, and Amber Lacy, eds. *How It Is: The Native American Philosophy of V. F. Cordova* (Tucson: University of Arizona Press, 2007), 82.

4 Richard Louv, *Last Child in the Woods: Saving Our Children from Nature Deficit Disorder* (New York: Workman, 2005); Richard Louv, *Vitamin N: The Essential Guide to a Nature-Rich Life* (Chapel Hill, NC: Algonquin Books, 2016).

5 David Sobel, ed., *Nature Preschools and Forest Kindergartens: The Handbook for Outdoor Learning* (St. Paul, MN: Redleaf Press, 2015).

6 Lenore Skenazy, *Free-Range Kids: How to Raise Safe, Self-Reliant Children (without Going Nuts with Worry)* (San Francisco: Jossey-Bass, 2010).

7 This is a problem all over the world where Monsanto moves in and forces farmers to use its seeds at yearly expense, instead of what is usually done: saving seeds from one's harvest to plant the following year. Farmers have to use Roundup (with glyphosate), another expense, and the soil and landscape are decimated. Vandana Shiva has been fighting the biopiracy of Monsanto and other corporations for decades in India. See: Vandana Shiva, *Biopiracy: The Plunder of Nature and Knowledge* (Berkeley: North Atlantic Books, 2016); Vandana Shiva, *Oneness vs. the 1%* (White River Junction, VT: Chelsea Green Publishing, 2020).

8 Lewis Yablonsky, *Robopaths: People as Machines* (New York: Pelican, 1972).

24. Centrality of Gratitude

1 Robert A. Emmons and Michael E. McCullough, "In Praise of Gratitude," *Harvard Medical School Newsletter*, June 16, 2019, www.health.harvard.edu/newsletter_article/in-praise-of-gratitude.

2 "American Crime: The Trail of Tears," Displaced Films, July 7, 2020, video, 6:25, https://vimeo.com/436245804.

3 "Haudenosaunee Thanksgiving Address Greetings to the Natural World," National Museum of the American Indian, https://americanindian.si.edu/environment/pdf/01_02_Thanksgiving_Address.pdf.

4 Robin Wall Kimmerer, *Braiding Sweetgrass: Indigenous Wisdom, Scientific Knowledge and the Teachings of Plants* (Minneapolis, MN: Milkweed Editions, 2013), 249, 382.

5 Tom Cooper, *A Time before Deception: Truth in Communication, Culture, and Ethics* (Santa Fe, NM: Clear Light Publications, 1998), 92–93.

6 Judie Bopp, Michael Lane, Lee Brown, and Patricia Bopp, *The Sacred Tree* (Wilmot, WI: Lotus Light, 1989).

7 Kahsto'sera'a Paulette Moore and Tehahentech Frank Miller, "Gratitude as Ceremony: A Practical Guide to Decolonization," *Journal of Sustainability Education*, July 15, 2018, www.susted.com/wordpress/content/gratitude-as-ceremony-a-practical-guide-to-decolonization_2018_07.

8 David Abram, *The Spell of the Sensuous: Perception and Language in a More Than Human World* (New York: Vintage Books, 1997), x.

9 Four Arrows, *Sitting Bull's Words: For A World in Crisis* (New York: DIO Press, 2020), 21.

10 Four Arrows, *Sitting Bull's Words*.

11 "Giving Thanks Can Make You Happier," Harvard Health Publishing, August 14, 2021, www.health.harvard.edu/healthbeat/giving-thanks-can-make-you-happier; Joshua Brown and Joel Wong, "How Gratitude Changes You and Your Brain," *Greater Good Magazine,* June 6, 2017, https://greatergood.berkeley.edu/article/item/how_gratitude_changes_you_and_your_brain.

25. Noninterference

1 Dennis H. McPherson and J. Douglas Rabb, *Indian from the Inside: Native American Philosophy and Cultural Renewal,* 2nd ed. (Jefferson, NC: MacFarland & Co., 2011).

2 Keith Basso, *Wisdom Sits in Places: Landscape and Language among the Western Apache* (Albuquerque: University of New Mexico Press, 1996).

3 McPherson and Rabb, *Indian,* 105.

4 McPherson and Rabb, 100.

5 Joe Wark, Raymond Neckoway, and Keith Brownlee, "Interpreting a Cultural Value: An Examination of the Indigenous Concept of Non-Interference in North America," *International Social Work* 62, no. 1 (2017): 419–32, https://journals.sagepub.com/doi/full/10.1177/0020872817731143.

6 Jean Liedloff, *The Continuum Concept* (Cambridge, MA: Perseus, 1975), 75.

7 Darcia Narvaez, *Neurobiology and the Development of Human Morality: Evolution, Culture, and Wisdom* (New York: W. W. Norton, 2014).

8 https://EvolvedNest.org.

9 Jane van Lawick-Goodall, *In the Shadow of Man* (Boston: Houghton Mifflin, 1971), 238.

10 Narvaez, *Neurobiology.*

11 Mary S. Tarsha and Darcia Narvaez, "The Developmental Neurobiology of Moral Mindsets: Basic Needs and Childhood Experience," in Martha Berg and Edward Chang, eds., *Motivation and Morality: A Biopsychosocial Approach* (Washington, DC: APA Books, in press).

26. Circular Time and Knowledge

1 Kim Hudson, "Are You a Circular or a Linear Thinker?" 2 Ways of Knowing, November 3, 2017, https://2wkblog.com/2017/11/03/are-you-a-circular-or-a-linear-thinker-2/.

2 Hudson, "Circular."

3 www.bartlett.psychol.cam.ac.uk/index.html.

4 http://penta.ufrgs.br/edu/telelab/2/war-of-t.htm.

5 Barbara Alice Mann, *Spirits of Blood, Spirits of Breath: The Twinned Cosmos of Indigenous America* (New York: Oxford University Press, 2016), 101.

6 Marimba Ani (Dona Richards), *Yurugu: An African-Centered Critique of European Cultural Thought and Behavior* (Washington, DC: Nkonimfo Publications, 1994), 11.

7 Greg Cajete, *Native Science: Natural Laws of Interdependence* (Santa Fe, NM: Clear Light, 2000), 36, 9.

8 Cajete, *Native Science*, 45.

9 Tyson Yunkaporta, *Sand Talk: How Indigenous Thinking Can Save the World* (New York: HarperCollins, 2020), 3.

10 Yunkaporta, *Sand Talk*, 3.

11 Lisa Miller, *The Spiritual Child: The New Science of Parenting for Health and Life-long Thriving* (New York: St. Martin's Press, 2015), 184.

12 Miller, *The Spiritual Child*, 204.

13 Annette Mahoney, "The Spirituality of Us: Relational Spirituality in the Context of Family Relationships," in Ken Pargamen, Julie Exline, and James Jones, eds., *APA Handbook of Psychology, Religion and Spirituality (1): Context, Theory and Research* (Washington, DC: APA Press, 2013), 365–89.

14 Marshall Sahlins, *The Western Illusion of Human Nature* (Chicago: Prickly Paradigm Press, 2008).

15 B. Traven, *The Night Visitor and Other Stories* (Chicago: Elephant Paperbacks, 1993), 191–92, https://anarchiststudies.org/re-evaluating-b-traven-by-john-z-komurki.

27. Self-Initiated Relational Healing

1 Stanley Krippner, "Indigenous Healing Practitioners and Their Use of Hypnotic-Like Procedures," *Activitas Nervosa Superios* 51 (2009): 51–63, https://doi.org/10.1007/BF03379923.

2 Pierre Flor-Henry et al., "Brain Changes during a Shamanic Trance: Altered Modes of Consciousness, Hemispheric Laterality and Systemic Psychobiology," *Cogent Psychology* 4, no. 1 (2017): 1313522, www.tandfonline.com/doi/full/10.1080/23311908.2017.1313522.

3 Soren Ventegodt and Pavlina Kordova, "The Thousand-Year-Old Shamanistic Tradition of Healing Touch in the Northeast Australian Rain Forrest," *International Journal Complementary Alternative Medicine* 8, no. 3 (2017): 00259, https://doi.org/10.15406/ijcam.2017.08.00259.

4 Willie Ermine, "Aboriginal Epistemology," In Marie Battiste and Jean Barman, eds., *First Nations Education in Canada: The Circle Unfolds* (Vancouver: University of British Columbia Press, 1995), 101–12.

5 "Morrnah Nalamaku Simeona, Hawaiian Healer," Amazing Women in History, accessed August 31, 2021, https://amazingwomeninhistory.com/morrnah-nalamaku-simeona-hawaiian-healer/?fbclid=IwAR2LLvfPCryCCULtyt4n FvKwocEznOlD-8Qc2cYdQgU5GSEmB_UcBJq9MFM.

6 Wikipedia, s.v. "Morrnah Simeona," last modified April 18, 2019, 18:08, https://en.wikipedia.org/wiki/Morrnah_Simeona.

7 Mary Kawena Pukui, E. W. Haertig, and Catherine A. Lee, *Nana I Ke Kumu (Look to the Source)* (Honolulu: Hui Hani, 1983), 61.

8 Manulani Aluli Meyer, "Awakin Call with Manulani Aluli Meyer," interview by Pavi Mehta and Kozo Hattori, Works & Conversations, December 15, 2017, www.conversations.org/story.php?sid=565.

9 Darcia Narvaez, *Neurobiology and the Development of Human Morality: Evolution, Culture, and Wisdom* (New York: W. W. Norton, 2014).

10 Narvaez, *Neurobiology,* 301.

11 Richard Rohr, *What the Mystics Know: Seven Pathways to Your Deeper Self* (New York: Crossroad Publishing, 2015).

28. An Emphasis on Heart Wisdom

1 "Larry Merculieff," Sacred Fire Foundation, accessed August 31, 2021, www.sacredfire.foundation/elder/larry-merculieff.

2 Kabir Helminski, *Living Presence: A Sufi Way to Mindfulness and the Essential Self* (New York: Tarcher/Putnam, 1992), 157.

3 Iain McGilchrist, *The Master and His Emissary: The Divided Brain and the Making of the Western World* (New Haven, CT: Yale University Press, 2009).

4 Michael S. Gazzaniga, *The Social Brain* (New York: Basic Books, 1985).

5 David Bohm, *Thought as a System* (London: Routledge, 1994).

6 Ron Tweedy, "Introduction," in Ron Tweedy, ed., *The Divided Therapist: Hemispheric Differences and Contemporary Psychotherapy* (London: Routledge, 2021), 1–69.

7 Lisa Learman, "Left vs. Right Brained: Why the Brain Laterality Myth Persists," *Biomedical Odyssey* (blog), Johns Hopkins Medicine, May 22, 2019, https://biomedicalodyssey.blogs.hopkinsmedicine.org/2019/05/left-vs-right-brained-why the-brain-laterality-myth-persists.

8 Gussie Fauntleroy, "No Word for Art—Only Meaning," Pasa-tiempo, *Santa Fe New Mexican,* October 9–15, 1992, 7.

9 Barbara A. Bickel and R. Michael Fisher, "Heart of the Mountain: A Nature, Arts and Trance-Based Intervention into a Medical Crisis," *Art Research International: A Transdisciplinary Journal* 5, no. 2 (2020), https://journals.library.ualberta.ca/ari/index.php/ari/article/view/29471.

10 R. Michael Fisher, *Fearless Engagement of Four Arrows: The True Story of an Indigenous-Based Social Transformer* (New York: Peter Lang, 2018).

11 www.catfawn.com.

12 Darcia Narvaez, "PSY 43242-01—Morality, Parenting, and Nature Connection in the Anthropocene" (syllabus, University of Notre Dame, Notre Dame, IN, 2020).

13 McGilchrist, *Master.*

14 Barbara Dowds, "Going Beyond Sucking Stones: Connection and Emergent Meaning in Life and in Therapy," in Ron Tweedy, ed., *The Divided Therapist: Hemispheric Differences and Contemporary Psychotherapy* (London: Routledge, 2021), 186.

15 E. Richard Sorenson, "Preconquest Consciousness," in Helmut Wautischer, ed., *Tribal Epistemologies* (Aldershot, UK: Ashgate, 1998), 82.

16 Iain McGilchrist, "Ways of Attending: How Our Divided Brain Constructs the World," in Ron Tweedy, ed., *The Divided Therapist: Hemispheric Differences and Contemporary Psychotherapy* (London: Routledge, 2021), 103.

17 David Naveh and Nurit Bird-David, "How Persons Become Things: Economic and Epistemological Changes among Nayaka Hunter-Gatherers," *Journal of the Royal Anthropological Institute* 20 (2014): 74–92.

18 Stephen H. Buhner, *Sacred Plant Medicine: The Wisdom in Native American Herbalism* (Rochester, VT: Bear & Co., 2006).

19 Richard Erdoes and Lame Deer (John Fire), *Lame Deer, Seeker of Visions* (New York: Washington Square Press, 1994), 29.

20 Sylvain Laborde, Emma Mosley, and Julian F. Thayer, "Heart Rate Variability and Cardiac Vagal Tone in Psychophysiological Research," *Frontiers in Psychology,* February 20, 2017, www.ncbi.nlm.nih.gov/pmc/articles/PMC5316555.

21 Igor Grossmann, Baljinder K. Sahdra, and Joseph Ciarrochi, "A Heart and a Mind: Self-Distancing Facilitates the Association between Heart Rate Variability and Wise Reasoning," *Frontiers in Behavioral Sciences,* April 8, 2016, www.frontiersin .org/articles/10.3389/fnbeh.2016.00068/full.

22 David H. Dye, "The Portrayal of Native American Violence and Warfare: Who Speaks for the Past?" in Richard J. Chacon and Ruben G. Mendoza, eds., *The Ethics of Anthropology and Amerindian Research: Reporting on Environmental Degradation and Warfare* (New York: Springer, 2012), 51–72.

23 Douglas P. Fry, *The Human Potential for Peace: An Anthropological Challenge to Assumptions about War and Violence* (New York: Oxford University Press, 2006).

24 Four Arrows, ed., *Unlearning the Language of Conquest: Scholars Expose Anti-Indianism in America* (Austin: University of Texas Press, 2008).

Index

About the Authors

Four Arrows Currently a professor of educational leadership at Fielding Graduate University, Four Arrows (a.k.a. Wahinkpe Topa), a.k.a. Donald Trent Jacobs, is a made relative of the Oglala Lakota and a member of the Medicine Horse Tiospaye. He is a pipe carrier, having fulfilled his Sun Dance vows while living on the Pine Ridge Reservation and serving as director of education at Oglala Lakota College. His great grandmother was adopted by a white family in Missouri after escaping from the Trail of Tears, according to family history and an old photo, but he had no exposure to that culture while growing up. After his experiences with the Rarámuri of Mexico, as described in his book *Primal Awareness*, he obtained a doctorate in education focusing on Indigenous worldview from Boise State University. The Alternative Education Resource Organization selected him as one of thirty-five visionaries in education who tell their stories in the book *Turning Points*. His many books, chapters, peer-reviewed papers, journal articles, and online presentations have made him an internationally recognized and respected authority on decolonizing, counterhegemonic democracy, and Indigeneity. His work has been endorsed by such notables as Vine Deloria Jr., Greg Cajete, Daniel Wildcat, Ed McGaw, Rebecca Adamson, Noam Chomsky, Vandana Shiva, Bill McKibben, Thom Hartmann, John Pilger, and many others. He is a recipient of a Martin-Springer Institute Moral Courage Award for his activism on behalf of American Indians, and he has continued such activism for Indigenous peoples in many countries. He lives with his wife, Beatrice Angela, in Mexico and British Columbia, where eco-activism, surfing, handball, horses, music, and grandchildren are important focuses.

Darcia Narvaez Professor emerita of psychology at the University of Notre Dame, Darcia Narvaez investigates moral development and human flourishing from an interdisciplinary perspective, integrating anthropology, neuroscience, and clinical, developmental, and educational sciences. Her earlier careers include professional musician, business owner, classroom music teacher, classroom Spanish teacher, and seminarian, among other things. She grew up, living half her childhood outside the US, as a bilingual/bicultural Puerto Rican but calls Earth her home. Dr. Narvaez's current research explores how early-life experience influences well-being and moral character in children and adults. She is a fellow of the American Psychological Association and the American Educational Research Association and former editor of the *Journal of Moral Education*. She is on the advisory boards of Attachment Parenting International, Your Whole Baby, and the Self Regulation Institute and is president of Kindred World. She has numerous publications, including more than twenty books, such as *Indigenous Sustainable Wisdom: First Nation Know-How for Global Flourishing; Basic Needs, Wellbeing and Morality: Fulfilling Human Potential;* and *Embodied Morality: Protectionism, Engagement and Imagination.* A recent book, *Neurobiology and the Development of Human Morality: Evolution, Culture, and Wisdom,* won the 2015 William James Book Award from the American Psychological Association and the 2017 Expanded Reason Award. She blogs for *Psychology Today* ("Moral Landscapes") and hosts the website https://EvolvedNest.org.

About the Illustrations

In 1985, while living in Jackson Hole, Wyoming, a sculptor named Harriet Greene desperately felt the need to carve the amazing speeches of eight American Indian chiefs and their images into 16″ × 30″ white marble slabs. It took her fifteen years. Harriet, now Harriet Goldman, lives on remote forested acreage in southern Oregon with her husband, Marty, also a highly respected artist, writer, and film director. You can watch Marty's short film of Harriet's creation, *Native American Oratory of Seven Great Chiefs,* online at www.youtube.com /watch?v=RHBtCbJxjVY. It won an honorable mention for the Ohio Film Festival's People's Choice Award. A set of 8½″ × 5½″ postcards made from inking the slabs and pulling hand-rubbed, stonecut prints is available for $15 (backroadspr@gmail.com).

About North Atlantic Books

North Atlantic Books (NAB) is a 501(c)(3) nonprofit publisher committed to a bold exploration of the relationships between mind, body, spirit, culture, and nature. Founded in 1974, NAB aims to nurture a holistic view of the arts, sciences, humanities, and healing. To make a donation or to learn more about our books, authors, events, and newsletter, please visit www.northatlanticbooks.com.